T0064818

GUNSMITHING
Made Easy

PROJECTS FOR THE HOME GUNSMITH

Bryce M. Towsley

Skyhorse Publishing

Skyhorse Publishing books may be purchased in bulk at special discounts
for sales promotion, corporate gifts, fund-raising, or educational purposes.
Special editions can also be created to specifications. For details, contact
the Special Sales Department, Skyhorse Publishing, 307 West 36th Street,
11th Floor, New York, NY 10018 or info@skyhorsepublishing.com.

www.skyhorsepublishing.com

14 13 12 11 10

Library of Congress Cataloging-in-Publication Data

Towsley, Bryce M.
    Gunsmithing made easy : projects for the home gunsmith / Bryce M. Towsley.
       p. cm.
    Includes index.
    ISBN 978-1-61608-077-8 (hardcover : alk. paper)
    1. Gunsmithing—Amateurs' manuals.   I. Title.
    TS535.T69 2010
    683.4--dc22

                              2010016076

Printed in China

Foreword

"Gunsmith." Just the word itself brings to mind images of the Hawken Brothers, in St. Louis, hand-building the rifles that would dominate the Great Plains, or the old-school gunsmiths, such as my friend the late *American Rifleman* field editor Russ Carpenter. Russ was one of those guys who could do or fix anything that involved a gun. From the time he made a new extractor from scratch for my well-worn L.C. Smith or the odd hammer spring he made for *Rifleman* editor Pete Dickey's Robin Hood revolver, he personified the old-school gunsmith. (Russ' time on that spring probably exceeded the gun's value by a factor of ten, by the way.) He could be cranky, he could be brusque, but he could also be jovial and share his incredible knowledge and skill gladly—and he always did the job right or he wouldn't do it. I can think of no higher praise for someone who makes their living with guns than another saying, "He's a really good gunsmith."

What about the "new school" of gunsmiths? There are dozens of excellent gunsmithing courses that turn out thousands of qualified gunsmiths every year, yet it seems harder to find a "really good" one. They're out there, and most do great work, but they never seem to be anywhere near me when something happens that I can't fix.

There has also been another evolution in gunsmithing that's on the rise. And that's the home gunsmith. It turns out that working on your own guns is, well, pretty fun. And more and more shooters are giving it a try. Just look at the pages of the Brownells or Midway catalogs and you will instantly realize that even if every professional gunsmith in the country was spending money like a drunken sailor, there's no way they could support such a wide range of items as presented in those catalogs. So, who's buying this stuff? Guys like you and me.

American Rifleman readers reflect the heart and soul of the American shooting and hunting community. It used to be that the average guy getting the *Rifleman* either had a lathe in his basement or a distinguished marksman's badge on the wall. Almost every issue in the 1950s had a story about sporterizing a military rifle or rechambering one to a different caliber. As time has gone by, NRA's role and membership have changed. Now NRA is nearly four million members strong, and while there are still a lot of guys with lathes in their basements, many others don't have them. That doesn't mean they are not interested in working on their own guns, just that the tools or skills of the traditional gunsmith are beyond their reach.

When it came to bringing that home-gunsmithing type of story back to *American Rifleman*, the guy I went to, without hesitation, was field editor Bryce M. Towsley. I've worked with Bryce for more than 10 years and I am pleased to count Bryce as a dear friend, good for a good two-hour conversation on just about any aspect of guns, shooting or hunting. The thing I enjoy most about Bryce, be it in his writing or tales of hunting camps from Alaska to Africa, is his enthusiasm for all aspects of firearms. From bullet performance to bedding a rifle stock, his energy and passion for the subject rings throughout his text. You'd have a hard time finding a guy who enjoys guns—and home gunsmithing—more than Bryce.

In addition, Bryce offers the reader his excellent photography. I can't count the times I've tried to figure out exactly how to do something in my well-worn copy of Walther J. Howe's *Modern Gunsmithing*, thinking that a photo or two might have helped me avoid ruining a piece of metal or wood. Bryce has done a superb job of describing the process—be it fixing an inexpensive injection-molded stock or chambering a bolt-action rifle—in a clear, step-by-step manner backed up with excellent photos that show you how to do it.

That's why I think this book is so important. In one place, you can find a host of projects that you can do yourself. Even if you are not interested in anything more than putting on a new scope, Bryce's insights and helpful tips make me wish he had done this book 15 years ago when I was trying to figure out a lot of this stuff for myself.

Bryce has learned gunsmithing by actually doing it and is not afraid to ask for help. He might try something for himself and realize it's not going well. Then he will go to the right guy for help. He asked Mark Bansner for help on chambering a rifle and, thanks to Mark's instructions, Bryce was able to chamber his rifle without having to recut the threads or start over.

Another thing you can count on with Bryce is that if says he did it, he really did. Whether it's shooting too many groups from the bench with a .458 Winchester Magnum rifle or botching a bedding job, he will tell you not only the truth, but what he learned from it. He might be opinionated about things—and you may not agree with him—but you never have to doubt his sincerity or veracity. Bryce Towsley is a "gun guy" through and through, and that's who this book is written to entertain and inform, other "gun guys."

Mark A. Keefe IV
Editor-in-Chief *American Rifleman*

Contents

Chapter 1
The Gunsmith's Shop *page 11*

Chapter 2
How We Learn *page 35*

Chapter 3
Cleaning & Maintenance *page 81*

Chapter 4
Enhancing Accuracy *page 97*

Chapter 5
"Pimp My Rifle" *page 125*

Chapter 6
An Excuse for a New Rifle *page 137*

Index *page 156*

Introduction

I knew it would be trouble when the music man called a meeting. The guy was from another town, one that was about twenty miles from us, but back then it might as well have been on Mars for all I knew. His meeting was to be held in the tiny cafeteria of our small-town elementary school on a Friday night. The teacher said that attendance was mandatory and I was mad. That was supposed to be my time, not theirs.

It turned out that the school was starting a band. (It was a convenient thing for the "music guy" who would act as music teacher and bandleader because he owned the store where we would all buy our instruments.) At that news, my buddies and I tried to make it to the back door unnoticed, but parents have a sixth sense about that sort of thing and we got ambushed.

When it came my turn to pick an instrument, the music guy was pushing too hard for the clarinet (my guess was he had an overstock), so partly out of stubbornness and partly because I thought playing the clarinet was too sissy, I insisted on the trumpet.

I tried, but I could never understand any of it. I love music, I listen to it constantly and I marvel at the magic it inspires, but how it is created is a vast mystery to me. My wife and daughter, who both have musical talent, talk about "sharp" or "flat" notes or which "key" something is in, but to my ear, it all sounds the same. I enjoy and recognize good music, but when it comes to the specifics, I honestly can't tell the difference. Apparently, in learning to play the trumpet it's important that you can.

It wasn't long before I wanted to quit and nothing could change my mind. I begged, I pleaded, I fought, I screamed, pouted and I even ran away. Then my dad offered me a deal. "Stick with this for a year and I'll give you a .22 rifle."

That's all it took. When it was daylight out and I wasn't corralled into playing that devil's instrument, I was shooting. My uncle Frank was overseas with the military and he had loaned me his .22 rifle. I was doing all I could to wear it out before he got home, but the most important mission in my young life was to get a rifle of my own. Clearly, my dad understood that.

I kept my end of the deal, more or less. I stayed with the band; I played in the concerts, marched in the parades and attended all my lessons. I even endured most of the assigned practice hours and made an honest effort to make it work. At the end of the year, I called the note due. Dad kept his end of the deal, too, and gave me his rifle. I realize now that with a factory worker's income and five kids to raise, it was probably because there was not enough money for a new gun, but that point was lost on me at the time. His rifle was better than any new gun. It was the one I had coveted for years, the one I begged to be allowed to shoot and the one I stared at through the glass doors of his tiny gun cabinet for hours.

I was delirious. Life was good. No, it was great. It was perfect. I had a rifle to call my own and I could finally quit the Sisyphus-like quest of trying to master the impossible. I put down the trumpet, picked up the rifle and never looked back.

The rifle was a Marlin Model 80E, bolt action. It fed from a clip, had a receiver mounted peep sight and it was the best .22 rifle ever made. Even today I'll fight any man who would dispute that claim. My life from that point on was consumed with finding ways to make enough money for ammo and then shooting the ammo I bought. The general store in town sold ammo back then, even to kids. It simply never occurred to anybody that there was any reason not to. I can't remember exactly how much it cost for a box of shells, but I do recall that longs were about a dime less than long rifles so that's what I used when I was paying the tab. My mother would always put a few boxes in my stocking at Christmas and one in my candy basket on Easter and she always sprung for the top-shelf Long Rifle ammo, which I horded to use only for "serious hunting."

My buddies and I were in the woods every afternoon as soon as the misery of school finally ended. On the weekends and during summer vacation we made "expeditions" where we hiked for miles on the back roads and woods trails. We explored old farms and abandoned buildings, sometimes spending the night in them or in the shelters along the Long Trail (part of the Appalachian Trail system). We always carried lots of canned beans and our .22 rifles.

I lived in town and so getting to any woods meant a

walk. I simply took my rifle and carried it to where I had to go. Nobody thought much about it, a kid walking down the sidewalk with a rifle was just part of small-town life back then. On the days when I planned to ride the school bus home with one of my buddies who lived in the country, I just brought the gun to school and had a teacher keep it until the bell rang. Then it went on the bus with me. Things have changed a bit since then.

We hunted woodchucks in the summer and squirrels and rabbits in the fall and winter. In the spring we would walk the banks of Otter Creek for miles hunting for muskrats. On the weekends we could sometimes talk my mother into getting up at dawn and driving the truck with Dad's old johnboat in the back to a spot miles upstream. Then we would spend the day floating home and hunting muskrats. We would skin them, stretch their hides, sell them for about a buck apiece and spend the money on more ammo.

When hunting season was closed, we just rambled the woods with our rifles, shooting at just about anything we could find. Pine cones, apples, rocks, old cans, sparrows and to be perfectly honest, far too many chipmunks. While I do regret the chipmunks, it truly was a great way to grow up.

That rifle taught me a lot about shooting, about the awesome power over life inherent to any gun, and about responsibility. It also inspired my hidden gunsmithing talents and probably set me on the path to writing this book. One of the first things I did was to refinish the stock with a complicated and time-consuming process that my grandfather explained to me and which even today I can recite by rote. It was a process better suited to an expensive rifle with fine walnut, not a kid's .22, but to me they were one and the same. It took the rifle out of commission for a couple of months, so I planned the project for when the snow was deep and the only hunting was for rabbits in front of the dogs. I was using Uncle Frank's bolt-action 16-gauge shotgun for that, so I could spare the rifle's downtime. The Marlin has a surprisingly good piece of walnut and I just assumed that it looked so good when I finished because of the process and, of course, my gunsmithing talents. I didn't know about wood quality back then and when my buddies tried the same thing on their cheap single-shot rifles, I ridiculed them for doing it wrong. It never occurred to any of us that the lesser wood on their rifles was the main culprit.

I can also remember a couple of crisis moments. The magazine is made from stamped sheet metal and as I was loading it one day, it flew apart in my hands. There was no fixing it and I was devastated. That Saturday morning my mother drove me the ten miles of narrow country roads to the only "big" sporting goods store for miles. It puzzles me today, but seemed quite sensible at the time that they actually had a magazine in stock to fit this rifle. Mom loaned me the money to buy it and I was back in business.

Some months later I was out squirrel hunting with my buddies when I discovered that the peep sight had broken. Most of it was missing and no amount of searching could turn it up. That night Dad took the rifle and me to my grandfather's and explained the problem. *Gunsmoke* was on the television and Gramp rarely missed an episode in that show's long run and would not tolerate an interruption. So we left the rifle and went home. Late the next day Gramp called and, as was his way on the telephone, said to me, "come get your rifle" and then hung up.

I walked to his house and found the gun standing in the living room corner with a brand-new Lyman receiver sight. I didn't have any money to pay for the sight and I guess he knew that. "I happened to have one in a drawer that was a perfect fit. Just help me with some firewood this winter and we'll call it even," was all he said when I asked how much it cost. But I knew he had probably driven to the sporting goods store that morning and bought the sight.

Today, I make my living writing about guns and hunting and while I live just up the road from the town where I grew up, I have traveled a long way. I have been lucky to live the life I dreamed about back then and looking back it's clear that this rifle was important in what I have become.

That .22 rifle set me out on the path that led to writing this book. It was the start of a life filled with guns, hunting, shooting and adventure. While it was a rocky road to get here, I am now earning my living doing what I love most in life. Not many men can claim that, and I can trace it all back to that Marlin .22 rifle. A lot of guns have come and gone over the years and my collection has expanded quite a bit from that first rifle. I haven't shot the Marlin much in recent times, but I keep it in the vault with the others as a reminder of the past and as a connection to my roots. I don't know what the future will bring, but often late at night when I am in a dark and brooding mood I think that it won't be good for people like me. But there is one solid truth I know. Nobody can ever take that .22 rifle away from me.

⌒ This one is for Dad ~ for giving me my first "real" gun. ⌒

The Gunsmith's Shop
Chapter 1

Exterior of the new workshop.

One of my whitetail hunting buddies has something he calls the "Jennifer Lopez Syndrome" that he brings up every time somebody talks about how they want to shoot a Boone and Crockett buck.

"I want to date J-Lo too," he says. "I am a man and she is a woman and we both live on planet Earth. All the elements are in place, so theoretically it could happen. But, it's got about the same chance of success as you do shooting a Boone and Crockett whitetail."

I feel the same way about my gunsmith shop. I would love a 5,000 square-foot shop that's fully equipped with a CNC mill, a big lathe, a surface grinder and all the other latest cutting-edge machinery. It could happen, but like Boone and Crockett whitetails and other fantasies, it's not likely. I am a hobby gunsmith, I spend money at this, not earn income. Justifying a shop like that, I would have to win the lottery or marry a rich movie star. Since I don't buy lottery tickets and I am quite satisfied with the wife I have, I guess I'll make do.

Actually, my new shop is a huge improvement. For many years I had a little corner of my basement to work in. I had one small bench with a path through the clutter to get to it. It was so crowded that some of my power tools were set up in an unheated storage shed out in back of the house. In the winter I had to wade through waist-deep snow to use them with frozen fingers. Other power tools had to take turns on my bench. When I was finished with one, I would remove it to make room for something else. It got pretty frustrating but, looking back, I did a lot of gun work under those conditions, so I guess I can't buy the argument that "I don't have enough room to work on guns." Anybody has who is not homeless has enough room, that's why they call it "kitchen table gunsmithing."

Back in my single days I lived for a few years in a mobile home. (Yes, it's true; I did a stint as "trailer park trash!") The spare bedroom was smaller than most walk-in closets, but I had a reloading and hobby gunsmithing shop set up in there. It wasn't ideal, but I managed to complete a lot of projects. I paid a lot of entry fees to shooting matches with trigger and tuning jobs on handguns, all done in that cramped and campy space with the puke green shag carpet. Compared to that room, my corner in the basement was a step up in the world. And from that perspective, my new shop is a glimpse of heaven.

My point is you can work on guns just about anyplace, just that "some's better than others." Don't let a lack of space keep you from tinkering on your guns, simply get creative. But, keep the florist's phone number on speed dial. You are going to need it if you get bedding compound on your wife's kitchen floor!

Don't bother asking why I know that.

Setting Up Shop

Interior of workshop, note the bank of fluorescent lights.

We all need a place to work and I certainly can't define where yours will be. But, I can speak to setting up a shop like the one I just built, which is just about right for a serious hobby gunsmith. Most people will be working in the basement or garage, which will be similar. But anybody, even the guy working on the kitchen table, can find something in here that will apply to the space they have. You can do as I once did and keep your tools and materials in toolboxes that can be stored off-site and brought out when you have a project going on. That works well for a kitchen table approach and it sure keeps things easy to find. The key is to adapt, improvise and make do.

Obviously, you can't buy everything at once so don't expect a complete shop right out of the gate. You will find that over time you will buy the tools you need for the specific job each time you start a new project and before you know it, you have a pretty well stocked shop.

This section covers the general use tools, the ones that should be in your shop because they are used often and will be needed for a wide range of projects. I think of these as "shop tools" because they belong in every well-equipped shop. Each project may have further specialty tools and they will be identified in those chapters dealing with the jobs they are used for.

My new place is actually a two-car garage that I had built in the back yard. It measures 24 feet by 28 feet and has two stories. The upstairs is shelving and storage for tools, ammunition and reloading components. The downstairs has a cement floor. It is insulated, finished with drywall and heated. It's fast becoming my favorite place and I love the time I spend out there working on guns. But, I have only been working in it for less than year as I write this. For decades I made do with something much smaller and more crowded. This is heaven, that was reality, and I understand them both.

LIGHTING • Ideally, any work area should be well lighted. I buy inexpensive four-foot florescent shop lights and hang them everywhere as supplemental lighting to the banks of incandescent lights on the ceiling. All my benches have these hanging over them, as do all the power tools.

I also keep a flashlight handy for peering into actions and looking for dropped parts.

BENCH • A bench can mean many things. Your wife might call yours "the dinner table," but if so, clearly she is not into gunsmithing. However, it's a good idea to have a bench to work on that doesn't include a centerpiece or place settings. It's a pain in the neck to pick up and move in the middle of glass bedding a stock, just because the in-laws are coming over for dinner, or some other equally frivolous reason.

The workbench should be the right height for working while standing up. For me that is 36 or 37 inches. If you wish to sit, you can use an adjustable stool. If the bench is any higher, a stool doesn't work well. About 25 to 30 inches wide is good. Length is as long as you can comfortably fit, but at least four feet, with eight feet better. I have three benches in the shop and the one I gravitate to most often is 36 inches high, 27 inches wide and eight feet long. It has a shelf underneath and a smooth, painted top.

Any bench should be rugged and heavy. This is particularly true if you are going to have a vise or a barrel vise attached to it. You cannot build a bench too heavy. The heavier it is, the more stable it will be. It should also have a smooth top rather than planking, as small parts have a way of falling through the cracks. If you have a plank top, laminate a piece of one-inch plywood to it. That gives a better top and adds some weight. The best way is to glue it with construction glue and to screw it down every six inches. Send the screws up from the bottom if possible, so they don't show from the top. If that's not possible, put the screws in from the top and countersink the holes. Then fill them with Acraglas Gel. Sand it all smooth after the Acraglas Gel sets.

The last bench I made was for handloading, but the requirements are about the same. I used one-inch plywood and doubled it to create a two-inch-thick top. I coated the pieces with construction glue and used a screw every six inches. When the glue hardened, I squared the edges with a skill saw. I built a simple box frame from 2x6 lumber and used 4x4 timbers for the legs. I added a shelf on the bottom with one-inch plywood. The bench is so heavy that we moved it in two pieces, the frame and the top and then put them together on-site. But, it's a good design for a workbench or a reloading bench. Materials are relatively inexpensive and the construction is easy for anybody with basic tools and skills.

The other alternative is to buy a commercial workbench. I have a couple and they are fine for light work. Neither of mine is rugged enough to mount any kind of a vise on, though.

Finish the bench top with paint or polyurethane so that spilled oil or solvent will wipe up without soaking in and staining the wood.

STORAGE • You need plenty of storage in the form of shelves, drawers and cabinets. Those chests with multiple plastic drawers that are sold at the home supply store are very handy for small parts and tools. You can never have too many of them.

THIS IS A GOOD HEIGHT FOR A WORKBENCH.

1. Materials to build a bench. 2-4. Assembling the bench. 5. Using a skill saw to square the edges after gluing two pieces of plywood together to form the top of the bench.

shop cabinet

shop shelving

Parts cabinet

Pegboard is wonderful stuff. Hang it anyplace you have room and it will provide shelving and hangers for all kinds of tools and materials. There are hangers available for just about anything you can imagine.

I recommend at least one tightly sealed storage cabinet to keep things out of the dust and dirt that permeates all through any well-used shop. Also, include a few very strong shelf units for the heavy stuff. What you add depends a great deal on how much room you have and your budget, but I doubt you can ever have too much storage space.

You will also need a good toolbox. It not only will keep your tools protected, but it ensures that they have a place where they belong, which makes it much easier to keep track of them. Some delicate tools like micrometers or reamers should be kept in a closed toolbox and protected from contact with other tools that might damage them.

VISE • Every workbench should have a vise. You can get by with a small clamp-on vise that can be set up and removed on a temporary basis, but the best situation is a medium size, permanently mounted vise. About a four- to six-inch jaw size is good. The vise should be on a heavy and rugged bench so it has a strong foundation. Locate it on a corner so it's not in the way, but is easy to access when you do need it. Reinforce the bench top from underneath when you mount the vise.

Most vises will also have a flat section on the rear that will serve as a light duty anvil. Buy a set of magnetic soft jaws for the vise. These simply snap into place and will prevent marring any parts you are working on. They are inexpensive and incredibly useful. I picked mine up at Home Depot for about $15.00. The old standby is leather jaws. They work well, too, and Brownells still sells them.

Forester Products has a small vise they call the "Swiv-O-Ling Vise." It has a head that will rotate a full 360° and tilt up to 28° from the vertical. This small vise is very handy for working on small parts. Because it swivels in just about every direction, you can put the work exactly where you want it. I find it useful for stoning trigger parts and similar detail work.

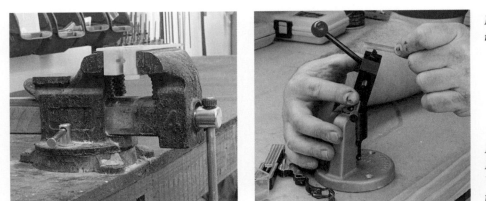

Far left: Bench vise with magnetic soft jaws.

Left: Using a Forester Products Swiv-O-Ling Vise to hold a trigger sear for stoning.

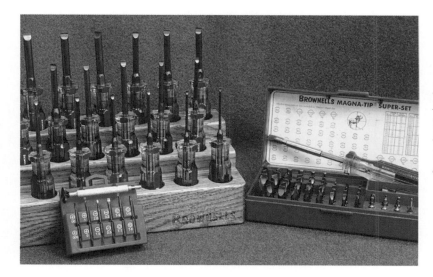

Brownells Fixed-Blade Gunsmith's Master Set screwdrivers (left to right), Magna-Tip 58 bit Master Super-Set Plus screwdrivers and the 12-In-1 Precision Miniature Screwdriver Set (front).

SCREWDRIVERS • Almost all gun work will require screwdrivers and it is extremely important that the proper screwdriver be used, both in design and fit. Never use a standard screwdriver on a gun. Most screwdrivers sold in hardware, home or auto supply stores have tapered sides. This allows them to fit a wide variety of screw slot sizes and it also adds strength. But they are a horrible choice for working on guns and they should never be used. The reason is that a tapered screwdriver will cam against the taper as you apply pressure and cause the screwdriver to ride up out of the slot, which will cause it to go skidding off and gouging anything in its path. It may be your hand, which will likely heal. Or it could leave an ugly gouge in the gun, which is forever. Either way it is guaranteed to ruin the screw, probably making it difficult to remove without drilling, and certainly unsightly. The pressure exerted by a screwdriver is amazing when it's applied to a very small surface. A tapered blade in a straight-sided slot contacts the screw only at the top of the slot. The forces applied to such a small contact area are enough to move the steel and cause the edges of the slot to round and strip.

A screwdriver must fit exactly in the slot of the screw it is being used on, both in thickness and in the width of the screw. I cannot stress the importance of this enough. The sides of the blade should be either hollow ground or with both sides parallel. A hollow-ground screwdriver will apply pressure to the bottom of the screw slot, rather than at the top as a tapered screwdriver does. This actually helps to "lock" the screwdriver into the screw as opposed to tying to cam it out of the slot like a tapered screwdriver will. A parallel side screwdriver will apply force for the entire depth of the screw slot, which distributes the force over a much larger surface area than a tapered screwdriver. A screwdriver that fits properly will fill the slot and have little slop and the maximum amount of contact surface inside the slot to distribute the forces being applied.

A properly fitting screwdriver will fill the width of the screw slot, which applies more leverage by moving the forces out to the very edges of the screwhead. This is a simple principle of leverage. With all else equal, it's much easier to turn a large wheel than it is a small wheel. There is little point in having a large wheel to allow more leverage

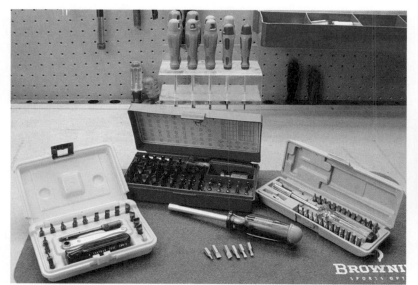

Working on guns will require specialized screwdrivers. There are kits available from a lot of different suppliers. These are from Chapman, Brownells, Midway and Lyman.

Tapered standard screwdriver on right and parallel straight side gunsmith's screwdriver on left.

and then only turning it from the halfway point which is closer to the axis and has less leverage. It turns easier when the force is applied to the outside radius, which is the farthest point from the axis. Think of the screwhead as the wheel that turns the screw. If your screwdriver only fills half the "wheel," you lose leverage. But if it fills the entire slot, it is turning from the full diameter of the "wheel" and is utilizing all the leverage possible.

In days past, gunsmiths spent hours filing the blades on screwdrivers until they fit perfectly. Today we have better options. Simply buy one or more of the many different screwdriver sets available that are designed for gun work. Some are fixed blade, but the most economical are the sets that use detachable bits with a single handle. This also allows you to have bits for Torx head, Phillips head and Allen head screws.

Lyman has one called the Magdriver. It features six hollow-ground bits and one $\frac{3}{32}$ hex bit that all store in the handle. Extra tips including Phillips and Torx designs are available. A magnetic hex tip allows easy changing of the tips. It's very handy for a range bag as well as on the workbench. They also have several models with more tips that are designed for shop uses.

Pachmayr, which is owned by Lyman, has a set of 10 fixed-blade screwdrivers designed specifically for gunsmiths. Each screwdriver has a rubber coated handle and a magnetized tip that is parallel ground. They are sided to fit Colt, Smith & Wesson, Ruger pistols and revolver screws as well as Torx for all scope rings and bases. A plastic stand is included that will mount on the bench or wall.

Chapman has a kit that includes a screwdriver handle, an extension and a ratchet handle. The #9600 also includes 14 hollow-ground bits, one .050 hex and two Phillips head tips. The #8900 has the same handles, 12 hollow-ground bits, 2 Phillips and 10 hex heads. There are also several extra heads that can be added.

Brownells has a huge variety of choices for screwdrivers, including the Chapman kits. In fixed-blade screwdrivers,

the best is likely the Fixed-Blade Gunsmith's Screwdrivers, which can be bought individually or in one of several sets. Their Fixed-Blade Gunsmith's Screwdriver Super Master Set might be the crown jewel of gunsmithing screwdrivers. It's a bit pricey, but worth the money if you are serious about this.

Brownells also offers several interchangeable magnetic tip screwdriver kits over a wide price range. Mine is the top of the line 58 bit Master Super Set. It includes two handles, one long and one short, 44 assorted hollow-ground tips, 10 Allen head tips, three Phillips head tips and a ⅛-inch square tip for some Remington butt plates. I added the four-piece Torx head bits as an extra. This is certainly one of the most complete kits available anywhere and at a cost far less than it would be for this many individual screwdrivers. It has been on my workbench for many years now and I don't recall a single problem or the need to replace any of the tips. That's a strong statement because these screwdrivers walk a fine line. If they are heat treated too much, they become brittle and will break, but too little heat treat and they will twist under pressure. At least on my set, Brownells got it exactly right. My only complaint is there are no Torx head tips included. But they can be added for just a few dollars more.

Midway USA sells the Wheeler Engineering Deluxe Screwdriver Set. This is a newer product and I have been using one for a few months now. It seems to be a very complete screwdriver kit. Wheeler's engineers measured the screws on over 100 modern and antique firearms to make sure that they offered bits for every situation. There are 54 hollow-ground flat bits that range in size from .120" x .020" to .360" x .070". That includes doubles in the thinnest sizes, because even the best will break now and then when they are this small.

The set also includes a complete selection of Phillips, Allen and Torx bits. There are 17 "specialty bits" that are included in the "professional" set. The set comes with two handles. The first is a regular size handle that's good for most jobs, and the second is a slimmer, shorter "Close Quarters" handle that is good for finesse work with smaller bits. It's all in a plastic case.

B-Square has a kit with 26 hardened steel bits in Phillips, Slotted, Hex, Torx, and Posi-Drive. There are no doubt many more screwdriver kits on the market, but these are what I have used and like.

You will also need a set of small "jeweler's" screwdrivers for some of the more delicate work you will encounter.

**Brownells Fixed-Blade Gunsmith's
Master Set screwdrivers.**

Again, I turned to Brownells for their 12-IN-1 Precision Miniature Screwdriver set. Finally, you will need a selection of "hardware" type screwdrivers. A long, thin, shank #2 Phillips head screwdriver is handy for removing recoil pads. Pick one that has a round shank and is polished and chrome plated. You want to be as smooth as possible to reduce the possibility of tearing the rubber in the pad. Also you will need a long (about 12 inches) and fairly large flat blade screwdriver to reach into the butt of shotguns and some rifles to remove the screw that holds the buttstock on. There are specialty screwdrivers on the market for this, but a high quality hardware store type will work fine for most guns.

Another screwdriver that I have found useful is a big wide tip that I filed a notch in for removing over-tightened nuts on Weaver Tip Off scope mount rings. The screw often extends out past the bottom of the slot and prevents the screwdriver from seating fully. The slot allows the screw to extend into the screwdriver so it can seat in the bottom of the slot. The big handle provides plenty of power to remove the nut, no matter how tight it was put it on.

FILES • Every gunsmith is going to need a selection of files and the ability to use them. The first you can buy, the second you must earn. The European gunmakers are said to test their students by asking them to make a perfect one-inch cube of steel with nothing more than a file. "Simple enough," I figured when I first read about it years ago. Then I tried it. After several attempts I concluded that success is elusive (at least for me) and secondary to teaching an aspiring gunsmith about using a file. It sounds easy in concept, but keeping all the sides even, parallel and square on this cube makes mastering Rubik's Cube look like kindergarten work. However, during any attempts you will learn a lot about how to use a file. Which may well be the point of it all.

Files have teeth that extend as continuous rows across the face at an angle. Files with rows of teeth going in one direction are called mill files. Files with rows going in both directions are called double-cut or flat files. Mill files generally provide smoother finishes than double-cut files and are more useful for gun work. The closer the rows are to each other, the finer the cut of the file in use. Coarse files are called bastard files. Medium files are called second-cut files. Fine files are called smooth files. Good files are expensive, so you will build your collection over time. For starting out, you will probably want at least one eight-inch mill file in smooth cut and another perhaps slightly larger, 10-inch in second-cut. A few more basic files you probably need include a round

BROWNELLS STARTER FILE SET

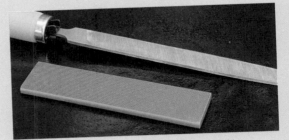

Not sure how to get started? Once again, Brownells to the rescue. They offer what they call a "Starter File Set," which includes the following:

1. Needle File Set (fine)
2. 3 Square Bent 60° File
3. 60° Sight Base File
4. 4" Barrette File (#1 cut)
5. 8" Half-Round File (smooth cut)
6. 8" Mill File (smooth cut)
7. 8" Hand File (smooth cut)
8. 6" Pillar File (#2 cut)
9. 8" Extra Narrow Pillar File (#2 cut)
10. 4" Very Extra Narrow Pillar File (#2 cut)
11. Six-pack File Chalk
12. Double Face File Card
13. 3 Needle File Handles
14. 2 Adjustable File Handles

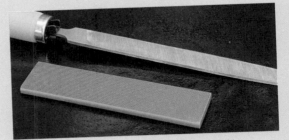

Draw file shown with a single cut mill file.

Mill or single cut (left) and double cut or flat file.

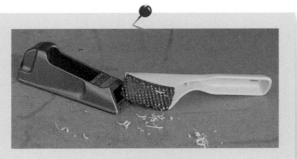

surform tools

Chalking a file.

Using a file card.

and a half-round in eight-inch smooth. Also a triangle file, six- or eight-inch. For working on dovetails, the best file is a 60° Standard Slot file designed for this work. This file has parallel sides rather than tapered, but with only one side with cutting teeth. The other two sides are "safe," which means they do not have teeth. The file can be used to widen dovetail slots in gun barrels without danger of inadvertently deepening the slot or damaging the edge not being worked on, because only one side cuts. As a parallel file, you have absolute control over the angle of the dovetail, which is all but impossible with tapered triangle files. This file should be in every gunsmith's shop.

If you are doing much stock work, you will add a few wood rasps, which are closely related to files. The teeth are different and they are definitely not interchangeable with files. Get one in each shape: flat, round and half-round. Also consider a couple of Stanley Surform tools,

which are sort of files. These are fast cutting wood rasps with replaceable blades. They are inexpensive and are handy for stock work where you need to remove material in a hurry.

You will also need a set of small "needle" files which are used in tight or small locations and for delicate work. Guns are full of tight and small locations, so they will see a lot of use. As you progress with your gun work, you will discover that you need many more size, shape and cuts of files, but these will get you started.

Always use an appropriate file handle whenever you use any size or shape file. File handles lessen hand and arm fatigue and give you more control of the file for more consistent, even cutting strokes which will improve the look, accuracy and final result of your work. File handles help you hold the file more securely and protect your hand from accidental injury caused by sharp, exposed file tangs. The tapered end of a file is made to fit in a handle, but it serves very well as a spear. All it takes is one slip and you have the file impaled in your hand. While a file handle makes the file easier to control and reduces hand fatigue, its most important function might be that it also keeps you from bleeding all over the guns.

To use a file, hold the handle in one hand and grasp the front of the file with the other hand. This allows more control over the pressure, direction and the angle of the cut. Check after every couple of strokes to make sure you are cutting what you want to cut and where you want to cut it.

When you get a new file, clean it with a solvent degreaser to remove any traces of preservative oil applied by the manufacturer. If oil or grease is left on the file, it will cause metal chips removed during filing to stick or lodge between the file teeth (this is known as "pinning"). Pinning inhibits the cutting effectiveness of the file and the pieces can score or scratch the surface of whatever you are working on.

After degreasing the file, rub file chalk into the teeth. The chalk collects between the teeth and helps prevent metal chips from sticking and building up on the file. To apply file chalk, simply rake the chalk back and forth along the face of the file. One or two strokes will apply sufficient chalk.

Never pull a file backward across the work piece, unless you want a useless and dull file. Push forward to cut, then lift the file clear of the work piece on the return stroke. Files cut on the forward stroke only. Maintaining pressure and pulling the files backward will roll the sharp edges of the file teeth and dull the file. Also be careful about what you use a file on; filing hardened or plated metal will also quickly dull your files.

A file card is a double-sided brush with fine nylon bristles on one side and bent steel bristles on the other. (Some also have short, stiff steel bristles on one side only.) This is a tool that is specially made to clean filing residue from between the file teeth. Use the file card frequently while working to keep the file teeth clean and clear of chips. Keeping the file teeth clean will enhance the cutting efficiency and smoothness of the cut. Thoroughly clean your files with the file card after every use and re-chalk after every cleaning and before putting them away.

Files should be stored so they never contact or touch one another. Files are very hard and very brittle. Contact between files can lead to chipped, broken or damaged teeth. Do not dump files together in a toolbox or drawer as that can dull or damage them. (I will plead guilty to this and speak from experience.) Wrap them in a shop rag to protect them and always protect a file from rusting. It's a good idea to make individual "sheaths" of cardboard for your files if they are to be stored in a toolbox. Given proper care, files will last for many years and provide excellent service. I have some that I have owned since the 1970s and they are still working fine. I have a few others that my wife's grandfather gave me that I suspect are older than I am. He was a tool and die maker so they saw a lot of use before I got them. They are worn and showing their age, but still working. Kind of like me.

A good rule of thumb to follow anytime you are cutting

or filing anything on a gun is to remember that you can always remove material from any part. But, replacing material after you screw up and remove something you did not intend to remove is extremely difficult and often impossible. Always pay attention, work slowly and look more than you file. Check your work from several angles. Often you think you are doing a great job when viewing the work from one angle as you file away, but when you see it from another viewpoint it becomes obvious that the file is cutting more in one location than another. That's one of the biggest challenges in making a cube with a file. The tendency is to file in something other than a square, flat plane. Pressure and stroke change as you move the file and a file has no conscience; it simply cuts what it is directed to cut.

STONES • Any gunsmith has got to have "stones." Not in the wise guy sense, although that helps the first time you start any new project, but abrasive stones. Much of gunsmithing is detail work and the stones are used for polishing and shaping metal parts. For that, you need a selection of different sizes, shapes and grits. There are several different types of stones that you can use. The first are natural stones. Most are silicon quartz which are mined in Arkansas and are usually called an Arkansas stone. One good feature of these is they tend to polish as they sharpen and for edged tools they remove less metal than man-made stones when sharpening.

These stones are mined from the earth and processed. There are several grades, but no true industrywide set standard. Norton may well be the largest supplier of abrasive stones and they use their own grading system for natural stones. They are as follows. Norton Soft Arkansas; this is an extra fine stone, but is still the coarsest grained of the Arkansas stones. Next is the Norton Hard

Above: Spyderco ceramic bench stone and ceramic file set.

Right: Stones from Norton and Brownells. The white stones are natural Arkansas stone or man-made ceramic; the darker stones are man-made India stones.

Air compressor

be cleaned with scrubbing powder and water.

Water stones are man-made stones used primarily for sharpening woodworking tools. They are named this because they use water rather than oil and so reduce the risk of staining a fine wood stock with oil transferred from a stone by the tools. They are soft and wear out fast. They often require "dressing" to keep them flat. If you are working with fine walnut stocks, a water stone that is dedicated to sharpening your carving tools is a very good idea.

Stones are like a lot of other tools in that you will find that they accumulate over the years. But to start with, you will need a good bench stone, preferably a double-sided one that has fine grit on one side and medium on the other. These are available from any hardware store. You will also need a selection of small Arkansas, ceramic and India stones in several grits and shapes. These are sometimes called stone files and are used in a lot of work in guns. Brownells has several kits to choose from and Norton has an excellent stone file kit that includes both natural and man-made stones.

Spyderco has a wide selection of ceramic stones including bench stones in three grits. They also have ceramic stone files, including a kit that has four stones, round, square, triangular and slip. They are housed in a leather pouch and are excellent for gun work.

Arkansas. They rate this as "superfine" but state that it's less dense than a hard Arkansas stone. Finally, they have a Norton Hard Translucent Arkansas. This stone is rated Ultrafine and is used for the finest finish and would be a good choice for trigger work and the like where polishing critical areas is the task.

Next are man-made stones. Norton calls their aluminum oxide stones "India stone." They have very hard and smooth cutting edges for close tolerance and are the best choice for most gun work other than polishing. They are usually orange in color and are offered in coarse, medium or fine and a wide variety of shapes and sizes.

Silicon carbide stones are also man made and they are a fast cutting stone, but do not give as nice a finish as the aluminum oxide stones. Silicon carbide stones are fine for removing material or sharpening tools, but not for polishing parts. Usually they are used in a bench stone. Again, they are offered in coarse, medium and fine.

Finally, there are ceramic stones. These are also man made and are less expensive than natural stones. They can produce a very fine finish and are very precise. They resist wear and retain their precise angles and shape well. Ceramic stones do not require oil during use as the other man-made and natural stones do and can be used dry or with water. This makes cleanup easier. When they glaze over, they can

AIR COMPRESSOR • It won't be long before you realize that you need an air compressor. It's used to blow dirt or solvent out of parts and mechanisms, to run power tools, for sandblasting, cleanup of dust and dirt and for spraying coatings. You will use it for a thousand other things as well, everything from blowing up your kid's bicycle tires to cleaning the dust out of your air conditioner when you get it out of winter storage.

I remember the air compressor my grandfather had in his garage when I was growing up. It was huge, noisy, nasty, dirty and a little scary. It was a complicated-looking contraption with lots of giant gears, spinning wheels and flopping belts. The beast filled a small room and probably cost as much as a car when it was new, which was well before my father was born. Today you can buy one that does everything that one did, but with less noise and commotion for about $300. (Although, they are still noisy!) One man can easily wheel it around and even load it in a pickup truck. I bought mine as a closeout on a floor model and got it for less than $200.

Make sure that the tank has enough volume for spraying and sandblasting applications, 25 to 30 gallons is good, 15 gallons might be adequate. Make sure it has at least 150 psi. Add a line filter to make sure the air is clean and free of water.

BELT AND DISK SANDER • It might be a toss-up between this and the drill press being the most valuable power tool in your shop. My sander has an eight-inch disk and a two-inch vertical belt. It will sand, shape, grind and sharpen. It will work metal as well as wood. I use it for everything from reshaping triggers to installing recoil pads. I recommend that you make this one of your first power tool purchases.

DRILL PRESS • I worked for years with just a hand-held drill. Then one year, my wife bought me a drill press for Father's Day and I couldn't understand how I ever survived without one. I use it for drilling, polishing, shaping and light milling (with a special vise). I have even used it as a makeshift arbor press to reassemble a double barrel shotgun.

In that circumstance, I needed a way to compress the hammer and its extremely stiff spring so that I could insert the hammer pivot pin. I needed to do this because I was dumb enough to dry-fire my old and much loved Lefever double barrel shotgun after cleaning it. When the right barrel snapped I heard the firing pin break, sending a fragment rattling out the bore. Just finding a new firing pin for that old shotgun was quite a challenge, but that was only the warmup for what was ahead.

Bench-mounted belt and disk sander

This was one of those projects where I thought I knew what I was doing when I decided to take everything apart. But when I pushed the hammer pivot pin out and parts and pieces went flying across the bench and scattered around the room, I knew I was in trouble. I tried to put it all back together, but Superman could not have compressed that spring by hand.

To do this required that the hammer be in place while you pressed on the hammer to compress the spring. The part of the hammer that was available for pushing was a radius and it was hard to find a place to press that was in alignment with the spring. The spring had to be compressed a long distance, and as the spring compressed and the hammer moved, it shifted the angle. Because of the radius, that would cause the relationship of the contact with whatever was pushing and the centerline of the spring to change. The force would suddenly be off center and something would slip and let loose. Parts would suddenly fly off to hide in my cluttered shop.

After about fifty tries, I knew I was in trouble. After about a hundred, I had skinned knuckles, a bad attitude and a wild look in my eyes. I also punched in the guts and panicked, "what the hell have I done now" feeling that every hobby gunsmith is going to experience every now and then. (A hint: When it happens, stop and go do something else for a while to calm down. You can probably fix it, but panic is not the route to an acceptable outcome. It will wait, so give it a day. Go fishing, wash the dishes for your wife or do anything except try to fix your blunder. Drinking works for me.)

Drill press

Ten minutes later I had my shotgun back together.

Of course, I got stupid and got to thinking whether there was a left and right to the hammers and if I had them in correctly. So, I took the shotgun apart again. Turns out that I had it right the first time. It also turns out that my idea about the drill press actually working was not a fluke and the gun went back together again with no major problems. Take my drill press away from me? Only when you pry it from my cold, dead hands!

HAND-HELD CORDLESS DRILL • These are not a replacement for a drill press, but rather a supplement to one. Actually, they are an entirely different tool and while there is some overlap, they serve a different function. I would like to see you building shelves in your shop using sheet rock screws and installing them with a drill press!

The new hand-held, rechargeable, cordless drills have all but replaced the old electric drills of the past. These variable speed, adjustable torque drills are not just for making holes. They also will turn screws, grind or polish parts and even mix you a drink if you are so inclined. Every shop should have one. Get the 18-volt model rather than the cheaper 12-volt. It will be more powerful and the battery will last longer. A spare battery is a very good idea. That way, one can be charging while you are using the other one.

DRILL BITS • A drill index with a complete set of drills should reside by your drill press. You will also need specialty drills as you move into some more advanced

When I decided to tackle it again a few days later, I called everybody I knew to ask what to do. After I explained the problem, most laughed hysterically and responded by saying, "What the hell did you do that for?" Nobody knew how to put the damn thing back together.

But one of the Brownells' "Gunsmithing Kinks" books (there are five volumes of the "Kinks" books and each is filled with lots of tips for the gunsmith) had a little blurb about using your drill press as an arbor press by raising the table against the part. That got me to thinking. I clamped the shotgun's action in a vise and clamped the vise to the drill press table. Then I ground the short leg of a large Allen wrench to fit the contour of the hammer. I clamped the long end of the wrench in the drill chuck. I lined it all up so that the Allen wrench was pushing on the hammer and then I raised the drill press table with the crank to compress the spring. It took a couple of tries to get the angle just right, but after that it worked perfectly.

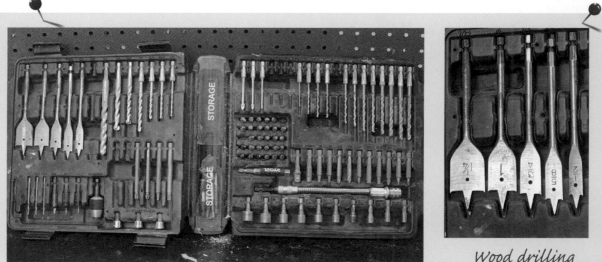

Drill set for metal and wood

Wood drilling spade bits

Author Bryce Towsley, in his shop (shown at right) cutting a stock off using a table saw.

projects, but an index that includes ¹⁄₁₆ inch through at least ⅜ inch is almost mandatory. Better yet is to go up to ½ inch. Try to get good quality as opposed to the cheap, discount drills. You might also add a selection of wood drilling spade bits.

TABLE SAW

TABLE SAW • I once picked up a gun in a trade that had a really odd-looking recoil pad installation. The guy had used a Skill saw to cut the buttstock off and a pocket-knife to whittle the recoil pad to fit. Not only did it look like a beaver had chewed the pad down more or less flush with the stock, but every angle was wrong on the recoil pad. It listed to the right and the top was cocked back at the gun with the toe pointing at the shooter. I didn't even bother trying to shoot it; I just traded off to another guy who said he didn't care.

The best way to cut off a buttstock for a new recoil pad installation or to shorten the length of pull is with a table saw. You will need a 40 tooth combination crosscut and ripping, general purpose blade for most of the work. But for cutting off stocks and other fine work, get a high quality 80 tooth carbide, trim and finish saw blade. They are expensive, but worth the money. They will make a clean cut with no chipping on the off edge. Don't use the blade for anything else except stock work and protect it like it was your first-born child. Never drop a carbide tooth (or any other) saw blade on a shop floor. It will break the teeth and ruin the blade. Don't use this blade for cutting anything except wood. If it hits a nail or anything else, it can ruin it.

With the appropriate blade, a table saw is also useful for other gunsmithing-related jobs dealing with wood or plastic. For example, I recently used mine to make wooden jaws for my vise to hold a rifle action.

You will also use a table saw for making shelf units in your shop, making gun racks for the shop and maybe

to remodel the bathroom. Perhaps you can live without a table saw, but it will be like living without good food. You can get by, but life is not as enjoyable. Every shop should have a table saw. You will be amazed at how often you will use it.

EYE AND EAR PROTECTION

EYE AND EAR PROTECTION • You can't hunt, shoot, work on guns or look at your wife and kids if you are blind. Every time you shoot a gun, run a power tool or use a solvent or chemical, you should be wearing safety glasses. Just a few days ago I was putting a 1911 pistol back together and something slipped. The recoil spring came free and bounced off my safety glasses, knocking them off my face and scratching the lenses. In the past forty years, that makes about a hundred times that glasses have saved my eyes. Broken end mills, shattered grinding wheels, carbide tips flying off saw blades, flying gun parts, they have all happened to me. I have also had a strip of primers blow up in my face and had a high-voltage power line short out and break my safety glasses with flying debris. (That one happened while I was standing on "hooks" 30 feet up a telephone pole.) It was actually one of those climbing hooks that caused the

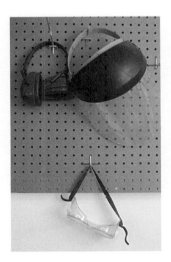

short, and the result was that the spike was burned off my climber. That was back in another life when I was a lineman for the telephone company. It was actually the first "real world" pole I climbed after completing climbing school. Not having the spike presented a big problem as there was no way to climb back down.

Safety goggles, face shield and ear protection.

I wasn't sure I wanted to anyway as the short caused an entire shopping center to lose power and there were a lot of angry people on the ground. One of my co-workers finally came up with a bucket truck and extracted me from my "position" on the pole. In the next decade I climbed a few thousand more telephone poles, but I never forgot to look where I was stabbing my hooks again. I lost the broken safety glasses, but I still have the climbing hook as a souvenir.

I have seen a lot of guys who think they can get away with "just a few minutes" without eye protection because they don't want to take the time to find it and put it on. They stand off to the side of a grinding wheel as they work and assume nothing will fly in their direction. They run the drill press without eye protection because it will only take a minute and they can't find the goggles. They squint as they run the power saw, to keep the sawdust out of their eyes. Most of the time they get away with it. But, I know at least three men who have lost their eyes in accidents where safety eye protection would have saved their vision. Not one of them feels the minutes they saved by not locating some eye protection was worth the price they paid. All three told me that it hurt like hell, too.

Every power tool should have goggles hanging by it, where they are convenient and easy to use. Every bench should have goggles or safety glasses on or near it. The power tools with a greater potential for problems, like grinders, saws, lathes or milling machines, should be run only while wearing a safety shield or goggles. If you sandblast, wear eye protection. If you are spraying coatings, wear eye protection. If you are working on spring-loaded mechanisms, wear eye protection. If you are running any power tool, wear eye protection. If you are working with dangerous chemicals, wear eye protection. When in doubt, wear eye protection.

Goggles can fit over eyeglasses. They are inexpensive and I keep several in my shop. A face shield will fit over glasses and help to protect your entire face; I have one adjusted to fit my head hanging near most of my power tools. I need reading glasses, so I bought a pair of bifocal safety glasses with side shields. The top part is clear, but the bottom is a 2.5X magnification. They allow me to be protected at all times and still see, no matter if I am working close or farther away. I wear these most of the time in the shop.

You should also have a pair of muff type hearing protectors in the shop. The rule here is simple: anything you are doing that is loud, put them on. That includes running most power tools. Hearing loss is cumulative and while you may not think you are damaging your hearing, you likely are losing a little bit every time you expose your ears to

A variety of punches

loud noises. The damage accumulates over the years until one day you can't understand conversations or what the actors are saying at the movies. Usually, I can ask my wife what the actor said about five or six times before she throws her popcorn at me and says, "He said to shut the hell up and watch the movie!" I don't mind her outburst and don't blame her, but popcorn is too expensive to waste.

It goes without saying that every time you test fire a gun you should have on both eye and ear protection.

PUNCHES • A gunsmith needs to know how to take a punch. Take it and fix a gun, of course! You will need an assortment of punches, both steel and brass. Brownells, Midway and others have kits that include most of the popular sizes. Start off with a kit for each steel and brass. You may need to add more specialty punches as you go along.

You will need a center punch for marking locations for drilling. I have both a conventional one that is struck with a hammer and a spring-loaded Starret model that is activated by pushing down on it. This spring-loaded punch is extremely handy because it will mark exactly where you want it to. Sometimes a conventional center punch will wander before you hit it with the hammer. It's not the fault of the punch, but more a case of ADD with the operator, but nevertheless it happens too often.

Punches are used to knock out pins and parts. They can also serve as a drift to help align parts when replacing the pins in guns. Drift punches have a long tip section with parallel sides. They are used for removing pins and should closely fit the diameter of the pin, but must not be larger, as they will not fit through the hole if they are. Drift punches should not be used for heavy work such as freeing a stuck pin, as they can bend easily. Once bent, you can never get them straight again. Tapered punches are just that, tapered. They are stronger and should be used to start stubborn pins. Select one that has a tip size close to the pin diameter. You won't be able to move the pin very far because the tapered punch will grow too large for the hole before it enters very far. But once the pin is broken free and started, it should move much easier. After the pin is started, switch to a drift punch to complete the removal. Keep your damaged punches, as you will need specialty punches from time to time and you can often make them from broken or bent punches. Chuck them in a drill press and use a file to reshape them to fit the job at hand.

A punch with a long, tapered, sharp point is handy for sometimes removing broken screws. If the screw is large enough, you can use the punch along the outside edge to bite in and turn the screw. Place the punch near the outside edge, angled so when it's tapped with a hammer it will bite into the metal and turn the screw counter-clockwise. This is an old mechanic's trick that sometimes will work on gun screws. It's always worth a try.

HAMMERS

HAMMERS • There are very few problems that can't be solved with a bigger hammer. Just remember that the outcome will not always be what you wanted.

Your shop will need several hammers. A small hammer with replaceable tips is probably the most useful. With a plastic tip on one side and brass tip on the other, this will be the hammer that sees the most use on your bench.

You will need a small and a medium ball-peen hammer and a big bludgeon type hammer. But, use that one only as a very last resort. Let it serve more as a reminder that brains over brawn is the best way to have a good outcome to a sticky problem. But when brains fail, get the bigger hammer. A good quality large rubber hammer will also be useful at times, as will a larger plastic-faced hammer.

GRINDER

GRINDER • A bench-mounted grinder is another "must-have" power tool. Buy the biggest and best you

Grinder with wire wheel

can afford, but nothing less than six inches. You will probably use this tool just about every time you work on a gun. A grinder will reshape parts, sharpen and modify tools, shorten springs and screws and even trim your fingernails. Although the last is usually accidental and is definitely not recommended.

Make sure you have a dressing tool to keep the wheel surface square. Most bench grinders will have two wheels, one on each side. In addition to the grinding wheel, you should also have a wire wheel which is used for cleaning rust or dirt off parts. Also have a cloth polishing wheel with a selection of polishing compounds. This will be used to polish parts for better operation or for finishing.

HAND GRINDER (DREMEL TOOL)

HAND GRINDER (DREMEL TOOL) • You will need a small hand-held grinder tool. Dremel is the most common brand and the name is often used generically to describe this tool. The grinder will accept a huge selection of grinding, cutting and polishing attachments. This little dynamo is one of the most-used hand tools you will have on the bench. It can shape stocks, modify parts, cut slots in screws, make parts, polish internal parts, cut off small metal pieces such as screws, and the list goes on and on. I have three of them. One industrial size and one Dremel brand date back to the 1970s, so they obviously hold up well. I also have a newer variable speed Dremel that's about five years old and still going strong. I will say that the variable speed is the way to go. I have not tried the cordless models, but I

An assortment of hammers

think one might be on the list of "new tools I need."

Plan on getting a good selection of bits and accessories. Brownells has a kit with all the most popular grinding stones. They also have another kit with felt polishing tools that work with polishing compound. Other polishing tools are made from rubber impregnated with abrasive; they are extremely useful for polishing. Dremel makes a few of these and Brownells has a kit by Cratex that

USING A CUTTING WHEEL ON A HAND GRINDER

1. Dremel hand grinder with assorted Cratex polishing tools from Brownells. 2. Polishing and grinding tip kits from Brownells for use with Dremel type hand grinders.

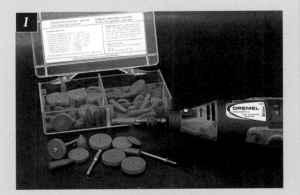

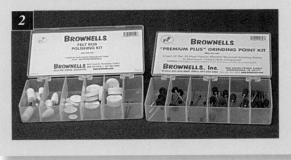

has several shapes and abrasive grits. You will also need some cutting wheels for cutting off screws, making slots in screws and that sort of thing. Metal cutting heads, either tool steel or tungsten, are used to shape inletting in stocks and remove material when needed. There are wire wheels for cleaning and tools for sanding, routing, engraving, carving and just about everything you want to do. There are even tiny little saw blades for cutting off small pieces.

GUN VISE • Every gunsmith needs a gun vise to hold long guns as they are being worked on or cleaned. The old style wooden Decker model was always a great choice, but, wood requires that it be finished or it will stain from solvent, oil or grease spills. Sinclair International now owns Decker and they have updated the Decker Gun Vise. It now features a heavy, machined polyethylene base with parts trays. This base is resistant to solvents and cleans easily. It adds a great deal of weight to the vise to make an extremely solid base. Rubber feet are screwed into the base to give a firm grip to the work surface. The forend rest is solid oak with padded leather upholstery.

The vise frame is powder-coated steel with leather padded vise jaws to ensure that the gunstock finish is protected and has solid oak trim surrounding the steel vise frame. This is a very classy gun vise. At 12.3 pounds, it stays put on the bench. There is also a version that is scaled down for use on handguns.

There are several plastic gun vises on the market of similar design, but less expensive than the fine wood vises. They work very well and are easier to keep clean.

The new Tipton's Best Gun Vise offers an interesting new approach. The vise was designed to accommodate a wide range of firearms for cleaning, maintenance or gunsmithing. It can be configured to handle bolt-action rifles, break-open shotguns, AR-15s, and handguns. A central aluminum channel lets the user move individual components to the ideal position for their firearm. Each component then adjusts to position for secure support. The rear base features two adjustable offset clamps for a tight grip on a wide range of buttstock configurations.

PARTS CLEANING TANK • A parts cleaning tank filled with solvent and with a filtering system is very useful for cleaning old gunk-filled actions and for removing the packing grease on new actions. In fact, it is useful for any kind of degreasing or cleaning job. Mine is 30 inches wide and holds up to 20 gallons of solvent. There is a filter and a pump that will spray the solvent from a nozzle to keep it circulating. I bought it at an auto parts store.

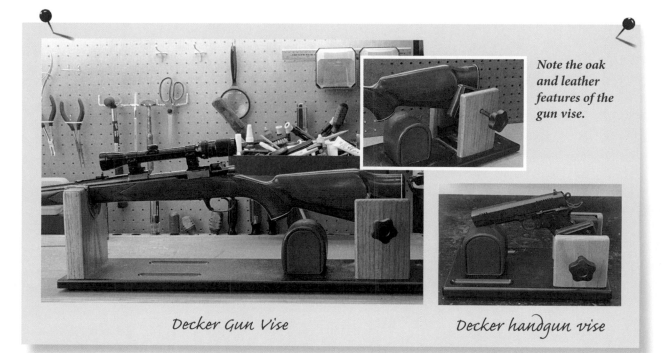

Note the oak and leather features of the gun vise.

Decker Gun Vise

Decker handgun vise

BENCH PADS • These are basically placemats for your bench. They protect the bench and the guns. They are padded, non-marring and help keep little parts from rolling off the bench. Every bench needs one.

WRENCHES & SOCKET • A ⅜-inch or a ¼-inch drive socket set like those sold for mechanics will come in handy now and then and is a good thing to have anyway. The same with a set of open-end and box-end wrenches. Every complete shop should have a basic set of each. It's not just for gun parts that they fit, but you will use these to adjust a lot of tools.

Socket sets and wrenches

DENTAL PICKS • Dental picks aren't just for cleaning teeth anymore. They are very handy for the endless reasons you need to get into the nooks and crannies of guns. They can dig out the crud, push a cleaning patch into mysterious places and dig out stuck things. These inexpensive tools are very handy and you should have a couple on every bench. I bought mine at the local hardware store.

WOOD CARVING CHISELS • Even if the extent of your stock work is glass bedding and fitting parts that can't be seen from the outside, you will need a set of hand chisels. They are so much handier and do a much better job than a pocketknife. Obviously, if you get into stock work on an advanced level, you will need to add to that list. Hand chisels or carving tools are extremely handy and are another "must-have." Brownells offers a set of six basic designs that will handle 90 percent of the jobs that you might encounter.

Nathan Towsley at a parts cleaning tank. Note use of Brownells' long apron to keep clothes clean.

Dental picks are very handy for cleaning guns.

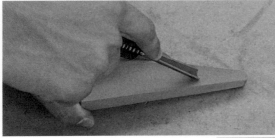

Inset: Using a Norton India slip stone to sharpen a hand chisel.

A set of wood carving hand chisels. Shown with a Norton India slip stone, and a larger Norton water stone.

HACKSAW

HACKSAW • From cutting off screws to cutting off barrels, the cheapest, easiest and safest way to cut metal is a hacksaw. Make sure you have a good one on hand with a good supply of blades of various tooth counts. Avoid the cheap hacksaws, as the frames are not ridged enough and they can flex allowing the blade to bend, break or come off the frame. This can cause a serious injury to your hands and can damage the gun. Spend a few bucks more and get a good hacksaw.

MEASURING TOOLS • Every gunsmith will need a dial caliper and a one-inch micrometer. You will also need a tape measure and a six-inch metal ruler.

The dial caliper will see a lot of use for most of your measuring. Don't skimp and buy a plastic model, get a high quality metal one. Digital models are more expensive and the batteries always seem to be dead when I need it most. The dial version works just as well and is not that much harder to read. Compared to the old vernier calipers, which required an advanced degree and a double helix nerd gene to understand, both the dial and the digital models are worlds ahead.

Micrometers are more precise than a caliper and are used when exact size matters a great deal. Traditional micrometers can be a bit tricky to use and read, but the newer digital micrometers, along with the ratcheting handles, have made them just about "dummy proof."

SCREW PITCH GAUGE • These are used to tell you the thread pitch of a screw. If you know the diameter (use your micrometer or dial caliper) and the pitch, you know what the screw is. Get one for U.S. (English) style threads and one for metric threads.

The English system is inch based and the threads are

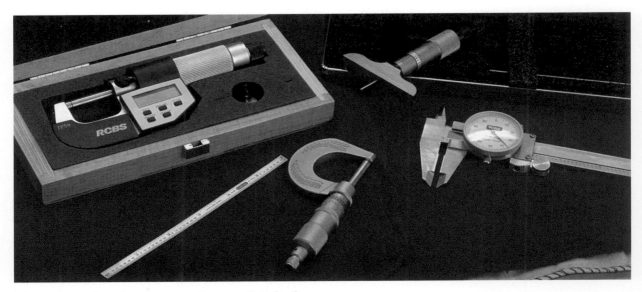

Measuring tools, micrometers, calipers and steel rulers.

specified by how many peaks there are in one inch of the length. They are specified as "threads per inch" written "TPI." The higher the number, the finer the thread. The diameter of the screw is measured and specified in thousandths of an inch. The diameter of a screw is the outer diameter of the thread, which is approximately equal to the diameter of the shaft before a thread was cut in it.

The size for U.S. screws is specified as a number for the smaller screws used often in gun work, or in a fraction of an inch for larger screws. Screws are described as 4-40, 6-48, 8-32, 10-32, 10-24, etc. (for numeric sizes, odd numbers are rare), or ¼"-20, ¼"-28, etc. The first number is the shaft diameter (numeric or inches) and the second number is the threads per inch.

A metric screw thread is specified by how far, in millimeters, the thread advances the part in one turn of the screw. For example, if one turn of a screw moves it one millimeter, the thread is called M1.0. This measurement is also the distance from one peak of the thread to the next one. The diameter of a metric screw is usually specified in millimeters (mm) prefixed by the capital letter M, as in "M5" for a 5 mm diameter screw.

TAP & DIE •

You will need at least one tap and die set, and probably two. One in U.S. or "English" threads and one for metric threads. Of the two, the U.S. is much more important and you will find that you can get by with only that one for most gun work. But some imported guns use metric screws and once in a while you will run into one. The trouble is while screw pitch gauges are inexpensive and are needed in both standards to identify unknown screws, tap and die sets cost a lot of money. It might be best to buy a U.S. set, which will do

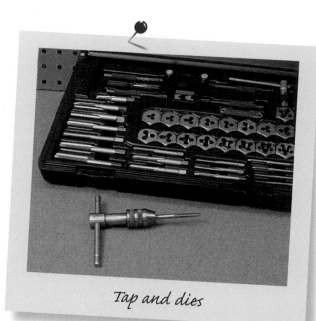

Tap and dies

99 percent of the work. Then get the individual metric taps or dies as the work comes up.

Plan on using 6-48 taps a lot, as that's the most popular screw size you will encounter in gun work. Taps are brittle and they break, so get a few extra in that size. Also, you will need tapered taps, plug taps and bottoming taps in the popular sizes. (Don't panic, they are not all that expensive.) The tapered tap will start easily. The plug tap will do most of the jobs, but cannot thread a blind hole to the bottom. A bottom tap has threads to the end and will cut to the bottom of the hole.

You will need a good T-handle tap handle as well as a tap wrench for the bigger jobs. You will also need a handle for the dies. You'll find that most kits include all of these handles.

Taps and dies are used to cut threads. As your gunsmithing skills expand, you will find that you are using them more and more for that purpose. For example, installing sights and scope bases, making screws, etc. But, you will also find that you will use a lot to fix damaged threads. This is called "chasing" a thread; you will do a lot of that in gun work.

BENCH BLOCKS •

Bench blocks are plastic or nylon blocks featuring various grooves and holes. They are used to support various parts during certain operations. For example, if you are driving a pin out, you can position the part on the bench block with a hole under the pin. Then you will be able to drive the pin out of the part and into the hole while the part is fully supported. Bench blocks are inexpensive and will come in very handy.

Screw thread pitch gauge

SHOP MATERIALS • There are some basic materials that you will need in your shop. Here are but a few suggestions.

SCREW KITS • Several companies offer kits that have a collection of the most commonly used gun screws. It's a good idea to have at least one and preferably several of these. It's not uncommon to be mounting a scope and have a screw break. If you have a kit, it's a small inconvenience. But without it, you will likely need to order another screw, delaying the job's completion for a week or more. The kits don't always contain exactly the screw you need, but they usually have one you can make into the screw you need. Without them you are stalemated, and don't count on finding any gun screws at your local hardware or industrial supply shops. I needed a screw a little while ago to repair my son Nathan's reproduction Winchester 1873 rifle. This is his Cowboy Action competition rifle and we had a shoot the next day. I live close to a medium-size city and we spent several hours looking, but never could find the right screw. However, back at the shop, one screw kit I had contained a screw that was close and I was able to modify it to fit. He took first place in the junior division the next day. After that, I ordered a few more screw kits. The low price is well worth the time they can save.

LOCTITE • Get a bottle of blue 242 Loctite and use it on just about every screw you put in a gun. You don't need much, just a drop or two, and a bottle will last a long time. The fact that most screws will stay put until you want to remove them is reason enough to use it. The 242 will allow you to remove the part later, something else that's important.

screw kits

Also consider the lower strength 222 for smaller parts as it's easier to take apart later. The 262 is a permanent application and should only be used on screws you have no plans to ever remove. The 290 is a wicking grade that can be applied outside the screw and it will penetrate the threads. Sometimes you will encounter a screw in a situation where removing it will cause all kinds of parts to spring out. But, you still want to lock the threads so it doesn't come out on its own. A wicking grade solves that problem, but note that it's all but permanent. The screw will require heat to remove it later.

I like the liquid, but they also offer medium and high strength in semisolid sticks called Quickstix. I have been using one on my bench for about a year, but decided I like the liquid much better.

SANDPAPER • Keep a selection of sandpaper and emery cloth on hand in several grits. You will need them often for sanding wood, synthetics or metal. Also keep a selection of different grades of steel wool. An assortment of Scotch-Brite pads is also useful for final polish.

Note that Scotch-Brite pads will remove bluing. Nathan found one in our sink and used it to remove some stubborn release agent from a rifle he just bedded. He thought it was just a scrub pad, but it took the bluing off. Fortunately, it was just on the floor plate and we were able to polish and re-blue the part.

RAGS AND PAPER TOWELS • Pick up a good supply of shop rags and heavy-duty paper towels. I buy mine at one or the other of the "Marts" and usually grab an armload at a time. The ubiquitous red shop rag is used for all kinds of things, and it looks cool hanging out of your back pocket as you work. Everybody knows that's the one true sign of a professional. Also look for some softer shop rags to use for rubbing down more delicate parts and finely blued guns. I usually buy some of the absorbent terry cloth shop rags as well.

I keep a roll of industrial grade paper towels over every bench and use them for everything from wiping down a gun I just sprayed with rust protector to cleaning up the many messes I seem to make.

APRONS • A shop apron will keep your clothes clean. For example, I recently spilled a cup of DuraCoat metal coating on a brand-new shirt. I ruined the shirt and stained my belly. The shirt is now a rag and my belly is interesting to explain at the beach. Anytime you are working on guns, you will be working with solvents, oils, sprays, paints and a lot of other things that can ruin clothing. An apron will protect them and keep you looking good.

Bench blocks　　　　Loctite　　　　Assorted sandpapers

Assorted shop rags　　　　Chemical-resistant vinyl gloves

I have two from Brownells, one short and one full length. The short one covers to just above the knees and the long one to below the knees.

LATEX AND VINYL GLOVES • Keep a good supply of throwaway latex and/or vinyl gloves on hand. You will need them for cleaning guns, handling stock finishing products, working with coatings, glass bedding and just about anything else that involves nasty or sticky substances.

You should also have a few pairs of long cuff, heavy-duty chemical gloves to use with parts cleaning solvents and degreasing tanks.

TRASH CANS • There is nothing more aggravating than needing to constantly cross the shop to throw away things. Keep a large trash can near every work station. At the very least, have one at each end of the shop. Use the heavy-duty contractor-style liner bags, as the thin bags will break and leak when you try to pull them out of the can.

Gun Safety

Bryce M. Towsley shooting prairie dogs in Montana with VarminATor bullets.

The destructive power of a modern firearm is incredible and once it's unleashed, it can never be taken back. It only takes a second of inaction for a gun to go off, but a lifetime of regret will never change the outcome.

First off, accept that if you handle firearms enough, sooner or later one is going to go off when you are not expecting it. I know that this statement goes against the "teachings" of gun safety protocol today, but it's the stark, naked truth.

But if you *always* have the muzzle pointed in a safe direction at *all times*, of *every gun* you handle, when this happens it will be embarrassing and it will scare the hell out of you, but nobody will get hurt. The number one rule of safe gun handling is to always consider every gun loaded, even if you know it is not, and to always have the muzzle pointed in a safe direction. Always, always, always, no matter what.

The only exception may be when doing some work on guns that requires the muzzle being pointed in a less than desirable direction. For example, it's difficult to re-crown a rifle muzzle without having body parts in the line of fire. In that circumstance the gun should be made inoperable by removing the bolt or other parts needed to function. At the very least, the action should be kept open.

The first stop for every gun that comes through the shop door is in your hands. Make it a habit to first check every gun to make sure it is unloaded. Open the gun and make a visual check to see that the chamber is empty and that you can see the magazine follower, which indicates that no cartridge is in the magazine. Then stick your pinky finger in the chamber to feel that it's empty. If the gun is a repeating design, point the muzzle in a safe direction and work the action several times, and then check again, both visually and by feel to be certain it's still not loaded.

Every time you pick up a gun, check it again. Even if you think you just did. Somebody could have loaded it when your back was turned. It may seem silly and redundant, but it is not. This does two things. First, it ensures that the gun is safe. Second, it forms a habit with you that after a while becomes second nature. If you automatically check a gun every time you pick it up, you will be less inclined to make a mistake or get an unpleasant surprise.

Never function test a gun with live ammo inside the shop. Use dummy rounds. These are simple to make by resizing brass and seating the bullet without powder or a new primer. Function testing with live ammo to ensure the gun fires, or that a semi-auto will cycle, should only be done at the range or in the shop with an infallible bullet stop such as the Savage Snail Trap Range System. The Snail Trap allows shooting inside and will safely catch

An automatic pistol with the slide pulled back and the chamber open. Every time you pick up a firearm, make a visual inspection to be certain that the weapon is unloaded.

To be doubly sure that the firearm is unloaded, insert your little finger into the chamber and feel to make certain that it is empty.

the bullets. I have two and the larger one will handle cartridges up to .50 BMG. The smaller "Gunsmith" model will handle cartridges up to the .338 Winchester. This system captures the bullet in a wet, lubricated steel spiral that sends it around and around until the energy is spent. Then the bullet drops through a hole in the bottom into a collection tray. Unless you have a range on-site, this is a very handy tool to have in your shop. It allows firing a gun safely inside a building or in an urban area.

To be blunt, if you fire even a single round at the shooting range or in your shop with the Snail Trap without high-quality eye and ear protection, you are a total moron. One simple question, how much hunting, shooting or tinkering on guns are you going to be doing when you are blind? I suppose you can still do most of that if you are deaf, but it won't be fun and your success will be less than sterling.

It takes about a millionth of a second to lose your sight and you can't know when it's coming. Your gun or the guy's next to you can blow up, it can potentially happen to any gun at any time. But the possibility of splash back from the bullet is just as real. My cousin

Philip can attest to that. He was hit in the leg by splash back and it penetrated through his new jeans and stopped when it hit his femur and cracked it. Philip is a big, rugged guy with muscular legs and if it penetrated to the bone on his thigh, it would certainly have taken out his eye with no problem.

Save your money, buy the best shooting glasses you can afford and wear them every single time you fire a gun. No exceptions.

Hearing loss is not so immediate, but is instead a cumulative effect. Every time you fire a gun without ear protection you lose a little more hearing. If you don't think that can add up, ask an old shooter from your grandfather's generation when they rarely wore ear protection. But write the question down, because I doubt he will hear you.

I have been lucky to meet several of the old gun writers whose work I had been reading for years. They all seemed to have the same limited vocabulary.

"Huh?"

"What?"

It makes for lousy conversation.

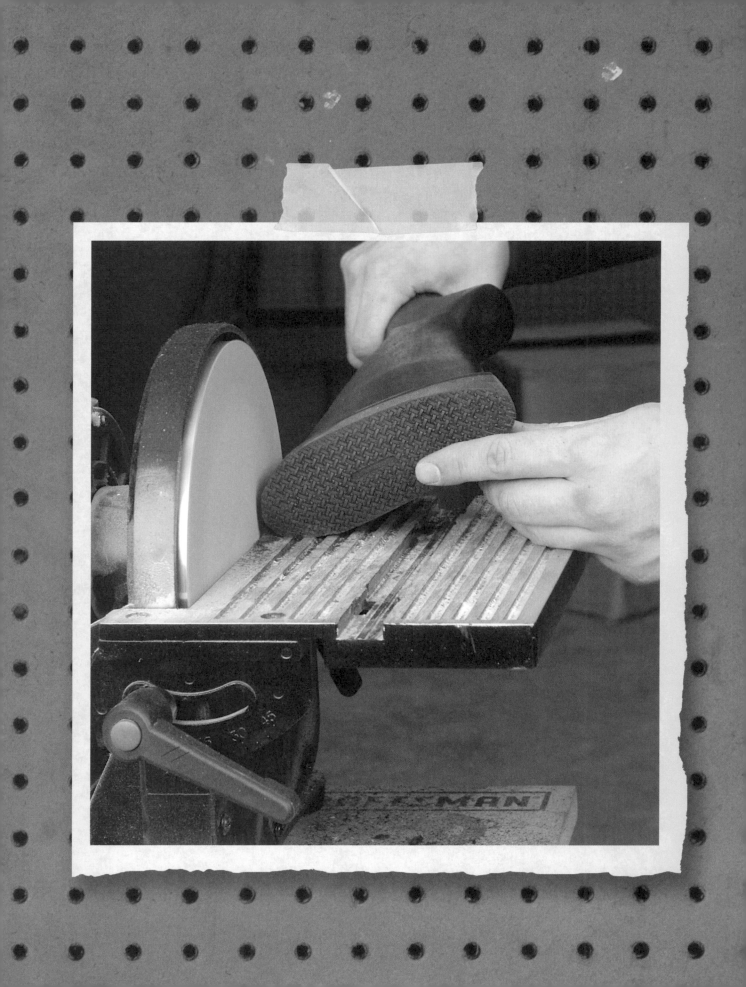

How We Learn
Chapter 2

Most hobby gunsmithing consists of small projects like installing a set of sling swivels, mounting a scope, installing a recoil pad or perhaps adding a new trigger. These are the core of this hobby and are also how we learn the craft. You can't expect to jump in with both feet and build a rifle if you don't even know how to run a drill press or read a micrometer. These small to moderate size projects are how we develop our skills. They make up the day-to-day work that builds familiarity with the tools and processes and breed confidence for bigger jobs.

I am not sure when I first began hobby gunsmithing, but the first project I recall was when I was about ten years old and someone at school sold me a BB gun scope. It was a side-mounted affair and not made to fit my gun. But I had a plan. I glued the mount to the side of my lever action Daisy. But I forgot one important thing, the scope was not lined up with the bore and there was no way to adjust the sight enough to compensate. But now I had the thing permanently epoxied to my gun. With my father's help I managed to get the scope off, shim it until it lined up and put it back on with a couple of screws. I was envied by all of my buddies, who I neglected to tell about my attempt to mount the scope by myself. My next project was refinishing the stock on my first .22 rifle. The outcome was very good and inspired me to keep trying.

There were more small projects, like repairing a broken rifle stock for one of my teachers, or fixing the safety on a Marlin .22 pump-action rifle. I mounted sights and scopes and did several stock refinishing jobs

and I was starting to get a little cocky. Then I got into another problem trying to drill and tap a .22 rifle for one of my buddies. I didn't have a clue what I was doing and was too stubborn to ask for help. The result was a mess, and it haunts me to this day. But this is how we learn, by doing. My biggest mistake was doing it on someone else's gun. My other mistake was in not wanting to ask for help, or at least learning all I could before starting. In the end, the best I can say is it was a learning experience.

Don't be afraid to fail, but don't be too proud to look for help. Think more than you act, not all projects will be raging successes, but each will teach you something. Even the masters had to start someplace and you can be sure that they made mistakes along the way, too.

My friend and master gunsmith Mark Bansner just built a rifle for a fund raiser for the Grand Slam Club/ Ovis. The rifle was named the Transcaspian Urial Ultimate Classic Rifle, the first in a series of four unique rifles. It recently sold for $38,000, a testament to Mark's gun building skills. But he wasn't born with them. He learned by doing many different things with many different guns. No doubt he made some mistakes along the way, but he learned from them and went on to build some of the finest rifles made today. None of us on the "hobby" side will likely attain Mark's skill level, but we should always strive to be the best we can be at what we do.

I plan to send an inscribed copy of this book to my old junior high buddy along with an apology for messing up his .22 rifle and a thank-you for a lesson that stuck.

Installing a Recoil Pad
Gunsmithing Project No. 1

A finished recoil pad installation on a Stoeger Coach Gun.

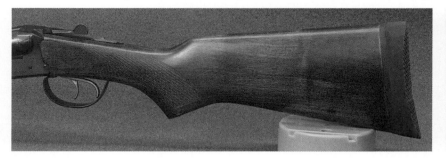

Can hobby gunsmithing books or magazine articles have a cliché? If so, installing a recoil pad is a candidate for the top of the list. It's been "done to death" as they say, but it's still a viable project.

While there are some recoil pads on the market today that are "pre-fit," they are mostly for the very popular model firearms and we will proceed on the assumption that your gun is not a candidate.

Measure the butt of your gun and order a recoil pad that is slightly wider and slightly longer. Make sure it's the style and design you want. In years past, you could have red-ventilated or black-ventilated, today there are lots of options. Some of the new high-tech recoil pads like the Pachmayr Decelerator do a wonderful job of reducing felt recoil and I highly recommend them, even though they cost a bit more. The recoil pad must be larger than the gunstock at all points around the parameter and have enough extra to carry the lines of the toe and heel out to the edge of the recoil pad. However, do not get a recoil pad that is too big, as some contain an internal metal frame and if you sand enough of the recoil pad away, the frame will show. (I learned this the hard way!) Here is a tip that might save the job. If a small amount of the metal frame is exposed on a black recoil pad, you can coat it with liquid electrician's tape. Apply several overlapping coats to the rubber on the recoil pad, and when it's dry, sand it flush to the recoil pad. It will likely show as the color will be slightly off, but it's far better than the metal showing.

Remove the stock from the gun. If you are built like my buddy Pete Lajoie and are six feet six inches tall with arms longer than my legs (his son Colin is seven feet two inches!), you probably need the extra length of pull that a new recoil pad can add to a rifle or shotgun. However, for those of us constructed more like normal humans, the next step will be to cut the stock off.

If you want to adjust the length of pull longer or shorter, now is the time. Just remember to add for the recoil pad length to your final measurement. If you want to retain the same length of pull, you will need to cut the same amount off the stock as the thickness of the recoil pad. If the pad is one inch thick, you need to cut one inch off the stock to maintain the same length of pull.

This pad shows careful installation on a high-tech synthetic stock.

Measuring the length of pull on a shotgun stock with a Brownells Pull & Drop Gauge prior to installing a recoil pad.

The best way to cut the stock off is with a table saw. Use a high quality 80 tooth carbide trim and finish blade. Keep this blade just for this type of work and protect it from any damage or misuse. This blade will help to keep chipping on the off side of the cut to a minimum. I have read that wrapping the stock with masking tape will also help reduce chipping, but in the couple of times I tried this I have not noticed that it helped and the tape can gum up the saw blade.

Set the ripping fence on the table saw to maintain the correct distance for the amount you wish to cut off. Remember to measure from the opposite side of the saw blade to allow for the width of the cut. The ripping fence provides a positive stop for the stock to maintain the correct length to be cut off, and it also provides a square surface to index the butt against. The butt should fit flat and square against the ripping fence to ensure that the cut exactly follows the lines of the stock. Use the crosscut guide to push the stock, and angle it so that it is pushing the stock with the butt perfectly square to the saw blade. It's likely that the front of the stock will require a shim or two underneath to raise it up to keep the butt square with the ripping fence. That's because the stock is thinner to the front than in the rear. If left to just lie on the table, the cut would not be square to the centerline of the stock. So, take a little time and make sure the stock is leveled so that the butt remains square to the ripping fence. It's a good idea to tape the shim to the stock to keep it in place. Lower or remove the saw blade and try pushing the stock along the path you will use to make the cut to ensure that everything is going to work the way it should. Shims have a way of slipping; things catch, shift and move. Find this all out and correct any problems before you start the cut. Check and recheck everything until you are absolutely certain it's perfect. You can't replace what you cut off and if you do it wrong, you are screwed! So check twice, cut once.

Of course, if you are planning to change the angle or pitch of the butt pad, you will not square with the ripping fence, although the cut must still be 90° with the centerline of the stock. Making this change is something to consider. Most rifles have the recoil pad at an angle, but a butt pad that is ninety degrees to the bore will reduce the felt recoil of a rifle. If you elect to make the change, always make your measurement from the longest

Top: For the best cut on a gunstock, use a carbide 80 tooth saw blade.

Using a table saw to cut a shotgun buttstock.

Cutting the stretched rubber of a recoil pad to allow inserting the screws. Always use a new razor blade or a fresh utility knife.

point to ensure that the length of pull is correct.

It goes without saying, or should, that you need eye protection when running the saw. Start the saw and carefully make the cut. It should be perfect but if it's slightly off, you can square it up and clean it up later on a disk sander. Make sure to check the table on the sander for square before working.

It's a good idea at this point to seal the wood before proceeding. Use polyurethane that has been thinned according to the instructions on the can. The wood should soak up the first couple of coats. When it stops absorbing the thinned polyurethane, finish with a couple of coats of uncut polyurethane. This will slow the job down due to the drying time, but will give a much better end result by protecting the stock from water damage. Among other things, water can cause the stock to swell which will ruin the fit of the recoil pad. Also note that some older Remington pump-action rifles and perhaps other guns used compressed wood on their stocks. The stock was somehow compressed into shape and then coated with a "bowling alley" finish to seal it. Once you cut the stock, and particularly if you do not seal it again, the stock will swell. The recoil pad you fitted so carefully is mysteriously too small a few months later. I am not sure of the answer here, except to seal the stock and hope for the best. Or perhaps to leave the recoil pad slightly oversize and then trim it to fit a few months later after the stock has had a chance to stabilize.

Some recoil pads will be warped slightly. If so, you can square up the base on a belt or disk sander. Most recoil pads will require that you cut the rubber to allow the screws to enter. Push a punch that fits in the hole through from the back so it stretches the rubber on the recoil pad side. Use a small, thin, new and sharp utility knife or razor blade to make a small vertical slit centered in the stretched portion of the recoil pad. After making the cut and releasing the pressure from the punch, the slit should not be visible. Do the same for both holes. Lubricate the holes generously with liquid dish soap and carefully insert the screws. You will need a screwdriver that has a round shank and the best would be chrome plated and very smooth. A square or rough shank will tear the rubber where you made the slits and damage the recoil pad. A round, smooth screwdriver that is well lubricated with soap should not.

Odds are the screw holes for the recoil pad will not line up with the existing holes in the stock. Generally, one or the other will line up enough to use. If that's the case, install that screw. You may need to lengthen the screw hole in the stock first to allow for the length that has been cut off. Snug that screw up and carefully align the recoil pad.

When the recoil pad is centered, put the punch or large nail through the other hole and tap with a hammer to mark the location to drill for the other screw hole. If neither of the existing holes line up, carefully center the recoil pad and mark the location for both new holes. If they are too close to the existing holes, you may need to fill the old holes. Drill to ¼ inch and insert a piece of ¼-wooden dowel that you have coated with epoxy. Cut the dowel off and sand or file it flush to the stock. After the glue has set, you can drill the new holes.

Drill the holes with the correct size drill bit for the screws. Make sure the holes are deep enough, as a screw that bottoms out will not hold the recoil pad tight. If you try to force it past the end of the hole, it can damage the stock.

Install the recoil pad on the stock. It will be oversized and should overlap the stock all the way around its perimeter. There are a couple of ways to go from here. One is to scribe a line all around the recoil pad at the edge of the stock. Then use a jig to do the grinding. This keeps all the grinding operations off the stock and eliminates the possibility of damaging the wood or the finish. Unless you are planning to refinish the stock, this is the safest way to go. It's easy to hit the stock with the sander; one small contact and the damage will be done. That can't happen if you do the sanding with the recoil pad off the stock.

To use the jigs made by B-Square or Miles & Gilbert, mount the recoil pad on the jig, back side up and set the toe angle as explained in the instructions. Hold the base of the jig on the platform of the sander. It is a good idea to check the platform for square before starting. Sand the recoil pad on a disk or belt sander until just taking scribe line. Remember the line was made outside of the stock, so you must sand to the inside of the scribe line for the best fit. This is tricky, so work slowly and be careful. Once the toe is shaped, reset the jig angle for the heel. Then sand the heel re-set the jig and the sides to the scribe line, again just taking the line. You may want to finish with a hand sanding block. Finally install the recoil pad.

The other method is to sand the recoil pad on the stock. This gives the best fit, but subjects the stock to danger of damage. Simply sand the recoil pad, following the same lines as the stock, but be very careful not to hit the stock with the abrasive. Make sure that you carry the lines of the stock out to the end of the recoil pad. There is a tendency with novices to want to sand the recoil pad edges at a ninety-degree angle to the back of the recoil pad, which, of course, will ruin the pad. Follow the lines of the toe and heel all the way to the end of the recoil pad. This will result in the edge of the pad being at an angle something other than 90 degrees to the back.

INSTALL A RECOIL PAD

3. Pad in Miles & Gilbert recoil pad sanding jig.

1. Masking tape wrapped on the stock to protect the finish while sanding the recoil pad. 2. Scribing a line on the recoil pad along the edge of the stock to allow sanding the pad on a jig.

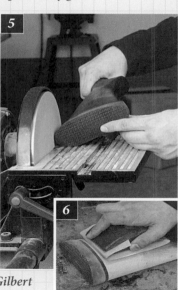

4. Sanding a recoil pad in Miles & Gilbert recoil pad sanding jig. 5. Shaping a recoil pad attached to the stock. 6. If the stock is going to be refinished, the best fit is by sanding the recoil pad and the stock at the same time.

7. Shaping a recoil pad on a disk and belt sander. Note safety glasses and mask.

Wrap the stock near the recoil pad with masking tape. Use two layers and cover the top layer with marks from a permanent felt marker or pencil. When you start to see these marks disappear, you know you are getting close as the sander is hitting the tape. At that point it's best to stop using the power sander and work with a hand sanding block. Finish with a single layer of tape that is marked and sand until those marks are starting to disappear from sanding. Be very careful not to sand through the masking tape. If you are going to refinish the stock, you can forget the tape and sand the wood and recoil pad at the same time for a perfect match.

Make sure you add more soap when installing the recoil pad and make sure the screws snug it down tight. Clean up the left over soap.

That's it, you are done.

Modifying a Shotgun Stock
Gunsmithing Project No. 2

Shooting the shotgun to check for proper fit as the stock is modified.

When shooting a shotgun, the shooter's eye is in effect the rear sight. If it is not lined up properly, you will not hit what you are shooting at. The comb is the top line of the shotgun's stock and it's the part that supports the shooter's face and controls the position of the eye. If the comb is too high or too low, the gun will shoot high or low. If it's too much to the left or right, the gun will shoot left or right.

My son Nathan's Stoeger Coach Gun shotgun had this problem. The Coach Gun is an inexpensive and incredibly tough double barrel shotgun that we bought for him to use in Cowboy Action Shooting. This short barreled gun has thousands of shotshells through it in three years of intense competition and it has never failed. Nathan likes it so well that in spite of a vault full of options he also uses it for hunting, skeet and our informal sporting clays sessions.

But the comb was too high and that created a tendency to shoot high. This was particularly true in the fast moving game of Cowboy Action Shooting. If Nathan missed, it was always because he was shooting over the targets.

There are some options on adjusting the stock. Remember that the key to sighting in a gun is that you move the back sight in the direction you want the bullet (or in this case the pattern) impact to move on the target. So if the gun is shooting high you will want to move the point of impact down, which means the "back sight," the shooter's eye in this case, must move down. If you are shooting to the left, the back sight must move to the right, hitting right, move the sight left.

If the comb must be higher, the only way to correct it is to add material. There are aftermarket pads that stick on the stock to raise the comb or you can replace the stock with one with the correct dimensions, or even laminate a piece of wood to the top and reshape it. In this case the gun was shooting high, so the stock's comb had to be lowered, which is the easiest of the possibilities. Also, the comb was a little too thick, so the shooter's face was a bit too far to the left (for a right-handed shooter) and it needed to be thinned a little.

Note how the shooter's eye is positioned incorrectly. This indicates the comb height is correct. (Note: This gun is disabled and cannot shoot.)

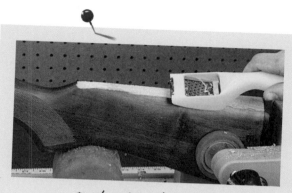

Reshaping the comb.

Checking the stock for fit.

Before starting, we used a Brownells Pull & Drop Gauge to get some baseline measurements. This is an "L" shaped measuring tool with the short arm movable. The tool is made from cherry wood and not only is functional but looks good hanging on the shop wall as well. It is used to measure the length of pull and the drop of a shotgun stock. With it, we knew what the stock measured for drop when we started, so we could keep track of how much we were removing by measuring with the tool again as we progressed.

The first step is to shoot several patterns over the course of several days before making any changes to ensure that it is indeed a gun problem and not a shooter problem. Ideally the shooter's eye should be looking down the barrel's rib when it's properly aligned, but don't depend on that. I have a couple of double barrel shotguns with combs that are too high and my eye is positioned high so that I am looking down at the rib. Yet, I shoot them well and the patterns hit where they are supposed to hit. So, use your head position as a guideline, but do not make any changes until you shoot the gun several times over the course of several different days. Don't force the aiming. In fact, don't aim at all; shotguns are pointed, not aimed like rifles. Just shoot the shotgun as you would naturally. In this case I had Nathan shoot at steel plates in a simulation of a Cowboy Action Shooting match. I painted the plates between shots so that each pattern impact could be seen. Just as it always had, the gun continued to shoot high and a little to the left. So we decided to go ahead with shaving the comb down and making it thinner.

To shape the stock, we simply took a Stanley Surform pocket plane and a Surform shaver and slowly worked the comb to remove material and make it lower, while being careful to preserve the lines by taking an equal amount of wood off the entire comb. At the same time we thinned the comb a bit, keeping both sides equal to preserve the aesthetic balance.

The Surform is a replaceable blade tool that works like a wood rasp to remove wood. The blade has several formed teeth which cut the wood as the tool is moved along the surface. It will remove wood quickly, so care

Checking the fit will require test firing the shotgun as the stock is modified. Note the pattern on target, not perfectly centered but better than when we started.

is needed to not go too far.

We lowered the comb and thinned it slightly. Then we would try the gun to see how it positioned Nathan's eye along the center rib. When we thought we were getting close, we took the gun out to the range and shot several targets. Then shaved a little more, shot more targets, shaved, shot, etc., etc., until we got it perfect. Just to be sure, we waited a few days and shot some more until we were satisfied that the stock was correctly sized and shaped to align Nathan's eye perfectly. Because we were also fitting a new Pachmayr Decelerator recoil pad, all the work was completed at the same time.

Of course, this cutting down will require that the stock be refinished as it's all but impossible to blend

REFINISHING A SHOTGUN STOCK

stripping the old finish off a stock.

Sanding the stock.

Finishing the stock.

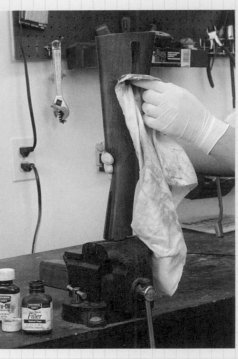

the color of any new finish to the old finish. So we stripped the old finish off with paint and finish remover and then sanded the stock. After sanding, we stained the stock with a walnut stain. When that was dry, we applied several coats of Birchwood Casey Gun Stock Sealer & Filler, using steel wool between coats. Then we followed with several coats of Birchwood Casey Tru-Oil

stock finish; again, lightly polishing with fine steel wool between coats. The stock looks better now than it did when the gun was new.

Nathan could count on several missed shotgun targets in any CAS match before we did this work. With three matches under our belts since modifying the stock, he has yet to record a miss. I would say we got this one right.

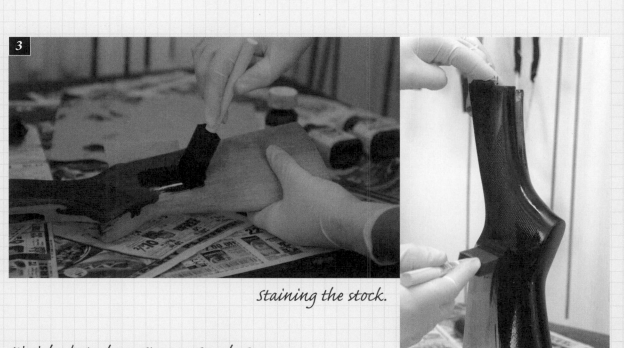
Staining the stock.

Finished stock on Stoeger Coach Gun.

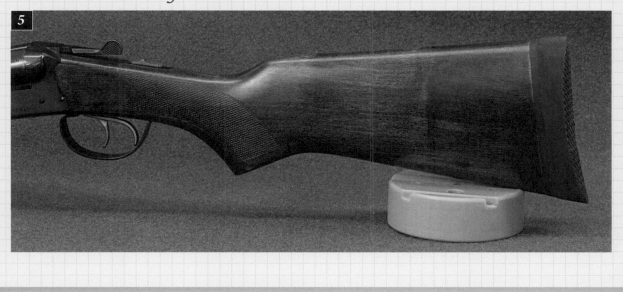

Stripped Allen Head Screws
Gunsmithing Project No. 3

small vise grips holding broken screw.

MATERIALS LIST	
• gun vise	• frozen screw
• screwdriver	jack
Torx or Allen	• vise grips
bits	• Dremel tool
• plastic	
hammer	

The tiny hex head or Allen head screws used on scope mounts have an annoying habit of stripping at just the wrong time. (Kind of a dumb expression isn't it? When is exactly the "right time" for a screw to strip?) This is particularly true when removing a scope mount that's been installed for a while. The screws might be a little rusty from years of hunting and there usually is a bit of corrosion between the screw and the ring threads. Also, the screws were often overtightened when they were installed. It's very common that the screw was damaged during installation by the wrench slipping and buggering up the head. All this adds up to screws that are very tough to remove.

When trying to remove existing scope mounts, it's asking for trouble to use the cheap "giveaway" Allen wrenches that come with scope mounts. They are soft and will strip and round the edges. Usually this will damage the screw at the same time. They are barely acceptable for new installations where everything is new and exactly as it should be with clean threads and where you are in charge of how much torque will be applied to complete the job. But when you are removing old screws that may be rusted in place, very well could have been overtightened when they were installed and may already be damaged from the installation, these cheap wrenches are a poor choice. Use only a good, high quality hardened steel bit in a large diameter screwdriver handle. This also allows you to keep the torque centered on the axis of the screw. With the L-shaped Allen wrenches, the tendency is for the torque to

B-SQUARE SCREWDRIVERS

The giveaway Allen wrench that is often packaged with new rings or bases is more likely to damage the screws than a new high quality screwdriver bit.

B-Square screwdriver set.

✳ **B-SQUARE has a tool called a frozen screw jack. This uses replaceable screwdriver tips which it clamps into the screw by force. Then it is turned with a wrench to apply a lot of force. This ensures that the screwdriver won't slip out of the screw, but it's not a guarantee that something will not break. However, if the screw has a prayer of being removed with a screwdriver, this tool is your best option.**

be twisted off center and cause the wrench to tip in the screw, which leads to slipping and stripped screw heads and rounded wrenches.

You are only going to get one shot at this, so take some time and get it right. Hold the gun in a gun vise so it's solid and you don't need to worry about holding on to it while you work. Select a hex bit that is in good shape without rounded or worn edges. Make sure the hex in the screw is clean and free from debris so that the bit can enter all the way to the bottom of the screw. Insert it into the screw and tap it into place with a plastic tipped hammer. A few solid whacks with the hammer on the screwdriver handle not only seats the hex bit in the screw, but may also help to loosen the screw. If the fit is sloppy at all, put a little Drive Grip on the wrench. Using two hands push down straight on the screwdriver with one hand and turn with the other. Keep the screwdriver perfectly in line with the center of the screw; do not allow it to tip. Be careful about how much torque you apply as these are small, rather delicate screws. You are not building a bridge here or bolting a new cylinder head on a truck engine, keep that in mind. If the screw doesn't loosen, back off. Try again while tapping on the screwdriver handle with a plastic hammer and applying constant torque to the handle. This is easier to do if you have some help. One person taps on the handle with the hammer while the other keeps the screwdriver straight and applies the torque.

If one screw is a problem, remove the rest of them first. Sometimes there is a misalignment of parts so that when all the screws are tight, the part is applying pressure on one particular screw. If you remove the rest of them, that pressure is relieved and often the screw can then be removed.

If the screw is in a scope base that is sitting on a flat receiver, you can sometimes use a plastic hammer to tap on the base and turn it on the gun enough to loosen the screw. Remove all the other screws, and then tap the corner of the base so that it will drive the base counter-clockwise. It's not necessary to turn it very far, just a partial turn will often break the screw free. Sometimes working the base back and forth with the hammer a few times will also break the screw free. Be careful about doing this on rounded receivers like the Remington 700, as tapping the mount will cause it to cam against the receiver and jam the screw tighter or break it off.

Sometimes you can do everything right and the screw still strips. The base I just removed from a Remington 700 .35 Whelen is a perfect example. The scope was installed sometime back in the late 1980s.

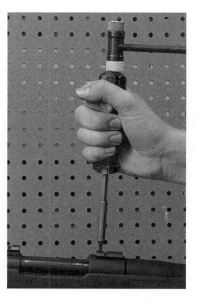

Tapping the screwdriver with a hammer seats it in the screw and can help loosen the screw.

Sometimes to loosen a stuck screw, remove all the other screws, then tap on the corner opposite the stuck screw to turn the base. This works best with flat receivers.

The first three screws came free just fine, a testament to the fact that I use only high quality bits for this kind of work, but the last one stripped. I thought it could handle the amount of pressure I was applying, but it had been damaged during installation and the hex stripped easier than it should have, catching me off guard.

I switched to a bit designed for a Torx head screw that was slightly larger than the stripped hole in the screw. Keeping it straight, I tapped the screwdriver with a hammer to drive the Torx head wrench into the screw, effectively cutting the metal with the bit. That allowed me to remove the screw. Of course, the screw is no good anymore and it sometimes damages the Torx bit, but a new bit is only a couple of dollars, far less than the cost or time needed to drill out the broken screw and re-tap the hole. I always keep a supply of screws on hand anyway because it's very common to need a replacement. Brownells and B-Square offer

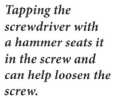

Brownells Rosin

Shows Torx and Allen type tips screwdriver set.

kits of assorted scope mount base and ring screws.

Sometimes nothing will work and you must drill out the screw. Clamp the gun in a vise and use a drill press, which will give you a lot more control than a hand-held drill. Select a bit that is slightly smaller than the head of the screw. Drill just far enough to remove the head from the screw. Once the drill bit hits the bottom of the wrench socket, it should be centered and it will drill to the shank of the screw. This removes the head from the shank. This will free up the base and if you are lucky leave a small amount of the screw shank sticking out from the gun. If it still will not come out easily and if you have time, it wouldn't hurt to keep this screw saturated for a few days with penetrating oil before attempting to remove it.

Use a new pair of small and high quality Vise Grips to clamp onto the screw and try to remove it. New, so that the teeth are clean, sharp and the jaws are perfectly aligned. Sometimes you get lucky. If there is not enough screw protruding to grip with Vise Grips you may be able to very carefully cut a slot in the screw with a cutting wheel on a small hand-held grinder. Tape off the gun with several layers of masking tape, as the cutting wheel can catch and fly off the screw and mark the gun. Be very careful and hold the hand grinder very firmly when doing this, as it will tend to have a mind of its own. Use very little pressure and a delicate touch. Let the wheel do the work and do not try to force it, as that will cause it to grab and run off to have great adventures with your gun's finish. After cutting the slot, use a flat bladed screwdriver that fits the slot to try and remove the screw. If the screw was rusted or stuck, this slot probably won't be strong enough to remove it. But if the screw was overtightened and jammed, sometimes removing that pressure by drilling the head off will allow you to remove it this way. It may help to gently heat the receiver with a heat gun.

The final solution is to drill out the screw and re-tap the hole. This is a bit tricky and I don't recommend trying it on a rifle receiver until after you have some experience with less critical applications. If you do not have any experience with drilling out broken screws and rethreading the screw holes, a rifle receiver is not the place to practice. Take the rifle to somebody who knows how and has the proper equipment. I have seen several ruined receivers and more than one hole drilled through the barrel by people who didn't believe that advice.

Using Dremel cutting wheel to cut a slot for a screw.

Trigger Talk
Gunsmithing Project No. 4

The trigger has been ground off shorter, reshaped and blued to fit a narrow guard.

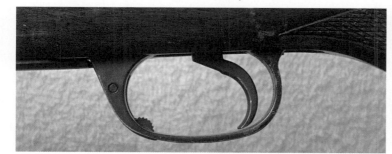

MATERIALS LIST

- file
- Allen wrenches
- pliers
- Dremel tool
- trigger pull gauge
- calipers
- punch
- cold blue
- aluminum black
- cleaner/ degreaser
- grinding wheel

One of the undeniable truths about buying used guns is that sometimes you get surprised. The surprises are not always good, and like everybody else I have been burned a time or two. But sometimes the surprise is in your favor.

WHAT A DIFFERENCE A TRIGGER MAKES •
Not too long ago I bought three guns from a family friend as a package deal. The one I really wanted was a 16-gauge Fox Stirlingworth side-by-side double barrel shotgun. No surprises there, it's a lively, light and well-made shotgun. One of my great pleasures in life is in rambling the fall New England woods in pursuit of ruffed grouse. The sharp cold and clean air is filled with the smell of autumn, the trees are at their peak color and the anticipation of flushing birds is like no other feeling in the world. For that, a man really ought to use a double barrel shotgun and to be truly

proper, they should be stacked side by side. That's what this gun was born to do, that's what I bought it for.

The second gun is a Savage Model 1907 semi-auto handgun in .32 ACP. It's a compact little handgun that so far seems to shoot surprisingly well. No surprise here, either.

But the third gun was the surprise. I bought it simply because the price was right and because it was part of the "deal," but I held little hope that it would prove to be much of anything interesting or useful. It's a "Pasadena Firearms Company, Inc." rifle built back when guns were trendy and socially acceptable with the "in" crowd and when the state of California still liked them. This sixties-era rifle is based on a Mauser action and is chambered for 6mm Remington. It's a simple bolt-action rifle in a plain walnut wood stock with checkering and whiteline spacers on the grip cap and the buttplate. It has open sights and is topped with a Realist 1.4-4.5 scope, another relic of the sixties, in Weaver mounts. The scope was weeping grease inside the adjustment caps, which made me think of problems. But I cleaned it up and took the gun to the range.

In spite of a horrible double-digit pull-weight trigger with about a foot of creep, the gun turned in some excellent groups. The scope responded well to corrections and seemed to be working fine. I thought it showed some potential so I went home and ordered some ammo. Then I ordered a new trigger. Changing the trigger was a simple job. If not for the fact that I had to modify the trigger portion to fit inside the trigger guard, I would have

Bold trigger from Boyds Gunstock Industries on a Mauser action.

Sean Dwyer, Remington VP of ammo, checking zero in Argentina. Remington Model 700 triggers are adjustable.

completed it in about fifteen minutes with only a few simple tools. The gun has a very shallow trigger guard, so the bottom of the trigger hit the trigger guard. That required that I grind off about a quarter-inch from the bottom of the trigger and reshape the end. I polished the metal and cold blued it. This fully adjustable trigger was easily set to a crisp, clean, three pounds.

The bedding on the stock was appalling but with no time to mess with it, I put it all back together and headed for the range. The gun shows a definite preference for 100-grain bullets and with either Remington Core Lokts or Federal Premium with Nosler Partitions it will group right at one inch at one hundred yards. Later, I glass-bedded the action and the groups shrunk a little more. Handloads brought them down a bit more and in the end this "clunker" gun was shooting like a finely tuned varmint rifle. The rifle may not be all that pretty, but from a shooting standpoint it is a jewel and a pleasant surprise. The single biggest change came from simply replacing the trigger.

The single most important key to good shooting is in the trigger. In a test I did with two rifles of every action type a few years ago, I used six shooters of different abilities and tested for speed and accuracy under hunting conditions. One clear point, perhaps the only clear point, that emerged was that for accurate shooting, the trigger is

the key element. Yet most factory guns today have triggers designed to keep the lawyers happy, not the shooters. I think this has been going on for so long now that a complete generation of shooters has never known a good trigger on a factory rifle.

Triggers can be adjusted and some will give a satisfactory result. For example, the Remington Model 700 rifle still has an adjustable trigger and it can almost always be tuned to a very acceptable result. But, most of the gun companies have caved to the trial lawyers and installed nonadjustable triggers or "adjustable" triggers that are a joke on their rifles. They may advertise them as adjustable and I suppose it's accurate, but they are often adjustable from eight pounds down to five pounds, hardly acceptable to a discerning rifle shooter.

FACTORY TRIGGERS •

It's a rare factory rifle that is shipped today with a really great trigger, and while some claim to be adjustable, few offer enough adjustment options to achieve an exceptional result. Yet, a good trigger pull is one of the most important things you can add to any firearm.

Achieving greatness in a rifle trigger is almost always going to require some gunsmithing work. Trigger work is one of the most specialized and tricky gunsmithing areas you can get into. It's also one that can create a dangerous condition if you get it wrong. My advice is if you don't know what you are doing when it comes to modifying or adjusting a trigger, don't even try. The best approach for now is to take the gun to a competent professional gunsmith and ask if he will let you watch and learn.

If you understand what makes a good trigger, you will be able to communicate better with the gunsmith about what you want on your rifle. There are four important points to trigger pull. First is the let off weight. This is simply how hard you need to pull on the trigger to make the gun go bang. Big game hunting rifles should have about a three-pound trigger pull. Competition or varmint hunting rifles might require a much lighter trigger pull.

Next is how smooth the trigger pull is. A rough trigger

Installing a Timney trigger on this Weatherby Vanguard rifle has greatly improved the trigger pull.

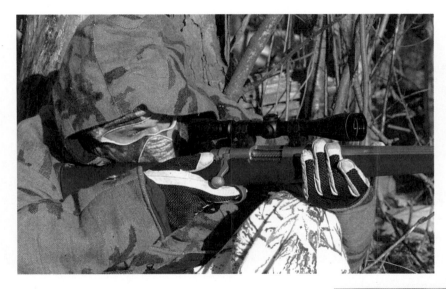

Nathan Towsley shooting a .223 Remington Model 700 LV SF with a Leupold Vari-X I 4-12X40mm scope. A good trigger pull is important for accurate field shooting.

will actually feel like it pulls harder than it does and a smooth trigger will feel lighter than it actually is. A trigger that hitches and catches as you pull it will never allow precise trigger control for the shooter. A good trigger should pull smoothly with little discernable movement and then break cleanly. The term "breaking like glass" describes the crisp, clean release of a good trigger.

Creep is the amount the trigger travels before it releases. The best rifle triggers have little or no discernable creep.

Finally is overtravel. This is the amount of distance the trigger can move after the sear releases. It's important because that movement occurs during a critical time when the gun is firing and can disturb the aim.

Most adjustable triggers will have three or less adjustments. One will be the tension on the trigger return spring. This is the spring that pushes the trigger back into position after you pull and release it. Every time you pull the trigger, you are pulling against this spring. The idea is to have the minimum amount of spring tension needed to return the trigger into position. That way you are not pulling against more pressure than is necessary. If you get the spring too light, the trigger will not reliably return to position for re-cocking. It might be fine in the shop, but out in the cold, wet, dirty, cruel world it could stop working just when you need it most. So, it's always best to leave at least a little cushion of insurance in the trigger return spring tension. Adjust for the minimum of spring tension needed to return the trigger to position, and then add another turn of the screw to be sure.

Some triggers have a sear engagement adjustment. This one is very dangerous to mess with and if you get it wrong it can result in an unsafe rifle. It's best to leave it alone.

Many triggers have an overtravel stop adjustment. Leave this adjustment for last. After all the other

Adjusting a Timney trigger.

Adjusting the trigger on .458 Winchester Mauser. Wrenches are from Brownells.

Using a Dremel grinder to remove stock material to allow a Timney Trigger to fit on a Weatherby Vanguard rifle.

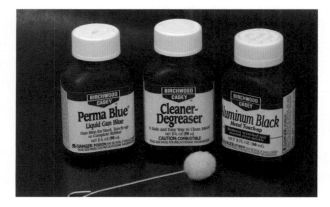

Birchwood Casey Perma Blue Cold Blue, Cleaner-Degreaser and Aluminum Black.

adjustments have been made, turn the overtravel adjustment screw in until the gun will not dry fire. (It should go without saying that you have made absolutely sure that the gun is empty. That is the first step anytime you pick up a gun for any reason.) Then back it off while holding pressure on the trigger until the gun dry fires. Now turn the screw one-half turn more and lock it down. Check several times to make sure that the gun will fire. If not, add another half-turn on the adjustment screw.

If these adjustments are not enough to provide an acceptable trigger pull, the next step is to take the trigger apart and polish the engagement surfaces with a very fine stone. This is tricky work that can result in an unsafe firearm if done incorrectly. My advice is do not attempt to modify or otherwise change the internal parts of a trigger. Some things are best left to the professionals.

While modifying and tuning a trigger is a complicated project, and not recommended for most hobby gunsmiths, usually replacing the trigger is simple and is an easy

project. Companies like Timney, Boyds and others offer aftermarket triggers that are well made, fully adjustable and usually very easy to install on most factory rifles.

Usually it's a matter of taking the action out of the stock and removing a screw or backing off on a set screw and removing a pin that holds the trigger group on the gun. Then reverse the process with the new trigger. Usually it's about ten minutes' work.

Sometimes you need to modify the stock a little bit to allow room for the new parts, as the trigger may not have the exact same external dimensions as the old trigger. That was the situation when I put a Timney trigger on my new Weatherby Vanguard in .257 Weatherby. I had to use a Dremel tool to remove a little bit of stock material in front of the trigger to allow for slightly wider trigger housing. That caused the job to take about twenty minutes.

When installing a Timney trigger on a Charles Daly Mini-Mauser, it was necessary to make a choice between modifying the slot in the trigger guard or modifying the trigger, as the trigger was too thick to fit through the slot in the bottom metal. I have done it both ways, but the easiest is to simply thin the actual trigger (the part you pull on) on a belt grinder or with a file until it fits. Then polish the metal and cold blue. With this trigger, putting on the safety causes a pin to pop out of the other side of the trigger assembly and it was necessary to remove a bit of wood for clearance. It was also necessary to bend the

ALLOWING SPACE FOR A WIDER TRIGGER

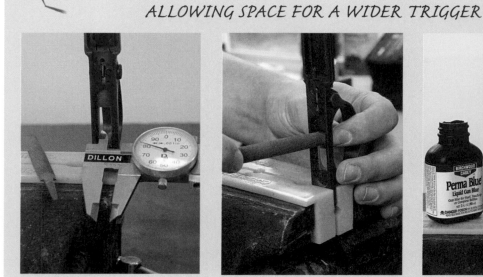

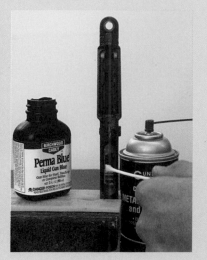

Measuring the trigger guard on a Mini-Mauser to allow for a wider trigger.

Using a file to open the space in the trigger guard on a Mini-Mauser to allow for a wider trigger.

Rebluing the trigger guard with cold blue after the space is enlarged.

safety arm with a pair of pliers so that it would clear the bolt shroud. Some material had to be removed from the stock to allow the safety to operate without interference. In the end, the job took about an hour the first time. But I had an excellent end result.

My point here is to illustrate some of the problems of installing a trigger and how to deal with them. They are mostly problems dealing with fitting the new trigger into the stock and trigger guard, which are not very technical, but do require patience and skill. Each rifle will be slightly different in the problems it presents, but by talking about those I have worked on recently, I can illustrate some of the approaches to solving those problems.

Changing a trigger is almost always easy and fast and will result in a far better trigger pull. Contrast that with the last full-blown trigger job I did on an existing trigger, a Ruger M-77, when I had about three hours invested to create a very good trigger pull. A few months later I had to send the gun back to Ruger for a replacement barrel and they took my trigger off and replaced it with another "Ruger" trigger that pulled seven pounds of creepy crud. Sometimes you just can't win.

NEW TRIGGER FOR MINI-MAUSER

Measuring a Mini-Mauser trigger.

Timney trigger on a Mini-Mauser rifle in a Boyds stock.

Using pliers to bend the safety on a Timney trigger so it will clear the bolt on a Mini-Mauser rifle.

NEW TRIGGER FOR WEATHERBY

Installing a Timney trigger on a Weatherby rifle.

Installing a new trigger is often as easy as loosening a screw and pushing out a pin, then reversing the process. The pin is indicated by a pointer, and the screw by a screwdriver.

Chamber and Bore Polishing
Gunsmithing Project No. 5

Using a Brownells chamber flex hone to polish a shotgun chamber.

If you are competing in Cowboy Action Shooting with a double barrel shotgun, you need to be able to reload quickly. The SASS rules state that the gun must not have ejectors, and one of the most frustrating things I dealt with early on was trying to get the empty shells out of my double gun in a hurry. I learned by watching the top competitors and I noticed that they all just dumped them out, or some simply opened the gun and thrust it forward suddenly, ejecting the empties. I tried both with my shotgun, but it didn't work. So I started asking questions. It turns out that they can do it because they have chambers that are polished and this allows the empty hulls to slide out easily.

Brownells makes an inexpensive tool to polish the chambers called a chamber flex hone. This tool has hundreds of abrasive "balls" mounted on a flexible shaft that will polish the chamber. Always use their Flex Hone Oil, as any other oil can damage the hone. Keep lots of oil on the hone and make sure you are prepared for a mess. The oil will run out the bottom of the barrel as you work

The Brownells chamber flex hone, shown attached to a drill, is used for polishing a shotgun chamber.

and make a mess on your shoes and the floor if you are not careful. The hone will fling oil from centrifugal force each time it exits the barrel. I like to do this outdoors and to let the oil drain onto a wad of paper towels. Wear old clothes and/or a shop apron. Always have on eye protection.

Clean the chamber and bore first, making sure you have all the fouling out. The plastic fouling from wads can be tough to remove, but you must get it all out as it can damage the hone. Use a wad fouling solvent and a wire brush, and keep scrubbing. A while back, my son Nathan called my cell phone while I was off on a hunting trip. He had just cleaned his Stoeger Coach Gun shotgun with a wire brush and when he looked through the barrel, it was all peeling away. He was sure he had ruined his shotgun and was very upset. Of course, it was just all the plastic fouling that had collected after a long season of Cowboy Action Shooting and a lax cleaning program. I had him switch to the proper solvent and he had the barrel looking great in no time at all. We try to stay on top of the fouling better now and clean after every match with the right solvents.

Remove the barrel from the shotgun. Chuck the flex hone in a variable speed electric drill and wet the hone with Brownells Flex Hone Oil. Start the drill on low speed and insert the hone into the chamber. Run it up to about three-quarter speed, or about 700 rpm to hone the chamber, as it cuts a slurry of abrasive and oil develops to help speed the cutting action. Avoid excess pressure and slowly keep the hone moving front to back.

I usually take this a step further and after using the Brownells hone, I finish the chambers by using a brush wrapped with cleaning patch material and impregnated with jeweler's rouge. Or, if I can find them, an oversize chamber mop, for example a 10-gauge mop for a 12-gauge gun. I simply impregnate these with jeweler's rouge and polish the chamber by moving the tool in and out. I then reverse the direction of the drill, and replenish the jeweler's rouge often. This gives me a very smooth, polished finish in just a few minutes.

Brownells also offers a Flex Hone which is a diameter to fit the bore and, of course, has a longer shaft so it can reach the entire barrel. Polishing the bore will clean up the barrel's bore and reduce fouling as well as potentially help patterns. It also makes cleaning the barrel much easier. Another hone is designed for the forcing cone if you want to cover all the bases.

After completing the work, clean the barrel with a degreasing spray to flush out all the slurry. Then clean with patches wet with solvent followed by dry patches. Finish with a rust protector.

This is not only a good treatment for a CAS competition shotgun, but polishing the chamber and the bore is also a great way to improve any hunting or clay target gun that does not have chrome lined barrels. The gun will shoot better and will clean easier. If it's a semi-auto, extraction will be improved and as a result, the gun will function more reliably.

Plus, there is a certain satisfaction in looking down a shotgun's bore and seeing all that shiny, perfect finish and thinking, "I did that."

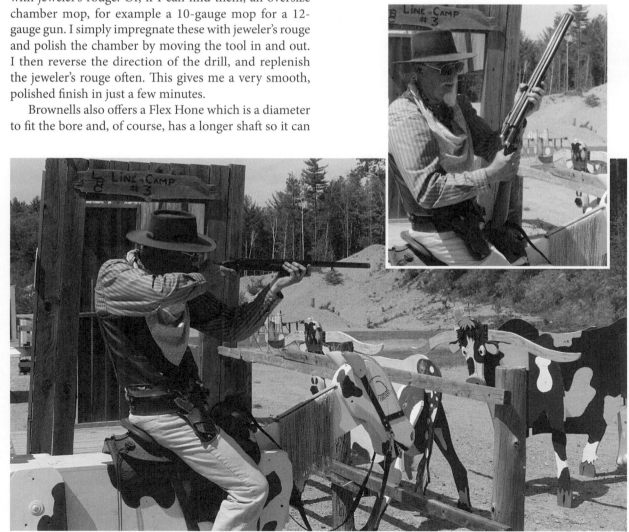

Note how this CAS shooter is dumping the empty hulls from his shotgun.

Installing Sling Swivel Studs

Gunsmithing Project No. 6

A sling swivel stud installed on the forend of a bolt-action rifle.

MATERIALS LIST

- tape measure
- screwdriver
- electric drill
- drill press
- bits
- glue
- electrician's tape
- bit alignment tool
- brass punch
- plastic hammer

The old saying that "you carry your rifle a lot more than you shoot it" has a ring of truth to it. A sling on a rifle makes it a lot easier to carry the rifle and can be used as a shooting aid. Not all guns are shipped with sling swivel studs, but installing them is an easy project for the hobby gunsmith.

The following instructions work well for both wood and synthetic stocks. You will need a set of sling swivels designed to fit your rifle. Perhaps the best known supplier of these is Michael's of Oregon. You will also need the correct size drills. You can buy drills designed specifically for this job, or use standard drill bits you probably have in your shop.

It's important to remove the stock from the rifle. This not only makes it easier to handle, but helps prevent damage to the metal. The first step is to mark the location for the rear stud about 2¼ inches to 3 inches from the toe of the butt pad. If you use a drilling fixture like the Miles & Gilbert shown in the photos on page 56-57, draw a pencil line along the centerline of the stock to help align the fixture. Otherwise, use a prick punch to mark a hole in the exact center of the stock at the location where you want to mount the swivel stud.

Uncle Mike's recommends a .157-inch drill (⁵⁄₃₂ inch) for the rear swivel stud screw. It is critical that the drill be exactly centered on the stock and that it is at a 90-degree angle to the bottom edge of the stock. The drill fixture will keep the 90-degree angle, but will not guarantee that the drill is centered. It is best to clamp the stock in a padded vise and use a drill press but if you are extremely careful, a hand-held drill will work. Make the hole deep enough to accommodate the full length of the rear swivel stud screw and ⅛ inch more. If you are using a hand-held drill, wrap a piece of electrician's tape around the drill to act as a marker or stop for when you are deep enough. With a drill press, set the stop on the press for the correct depth.

The top shank of the screw is not threaded and so a slightly larger hole must be drilled to allow it to pass without splitting the stock. Uncle Mike's suggests a .220-inch drill (⁷⁄₃₂ inch). Be very careful to only drill deep enough to accommodate the shoulder of the screw and no deeper. If you are using a hand-held drill, it's a good idea to wrap the drill with vinyl electrician's tape to act as a stop, as the drill bit can catch in the wood and pull the drill in too deep without some sort of mechanical stop. If you are using a drill press, set the stop to prevent the bit from drilling too deep.

Finally, the stock should be squared to accept the swivel stud base and, if you elect to use one, the white spacer. It's best to use a cutter designed for that job. Uncle Mike's offers a counterbore that is .373 inch. But if you do not have that, you can do it with a ⅜-inch drill bit, although this is a distant second choice. Be very careful as you only want to "kiss" the wood and not actually drill to any depth. This simply squares up the face of the stock and gives the swivel base a solid foundation to tighten against. Sometimes, running the drill in reverse first will help to compress the wood and "pre-stress" it in preparation for the actual drilling.

Seal any exposed wood with stock finish or polyurethane and let it dry. Coat the threads of the swivel stud with glue and carefully screw it into the hole. Make sure that you have it square and aligned correctly with the hole. Use a pin punch, a nail or an Allen wrench to screw the stud in. No matter which you select, be very careful that it doesn't contact the stock as you turn it, as this can scratch the wood. An Allen wrench is usually available and will work, but the wrench can turn and the short leg can scratch the stock, so be very careful. Or better yet, use a pin punch. When the swivel base is tight, it should sit square and tight against the stock and should be aligned in the center. Make sure, too, that the hole through the swivel stud is ninety degrees to the centerline of the gun.

Bolt-action rifles have the forward stud mounted in the stock about 2 inches to 2½ inches from the forend tip. You must remove the stock from the rifle for this one. Carefully mark the stock in the exact center with a prick punch. In this case, we are drilling a hole that the machine screw for the front swivel will pass through, so the hole has to be slightly larger than the screw. For Uncle Mike's sling swivels, use a .190-inch (³⁄₁₆-inch) drill bit and drill all the way through the stock.

Turn the stock over so that the barrel channel side is facing up. The hole must be counterbored with a larger drill to allow the swivel nut to be inserted far enough to be below the surface of the barrel channel. Uncle Mike's suggests a .388-inch counterbore or a ⅜-inch drill bit will work. Be careful not to drill it too large, as the edge of the nut is serrated and it must be a tight fit in the hole for those serrations to grip and hold the nut against turning.

Coat all exposed wood with stock finish or polyurethane and let it dry. Using a small brass or plastic hammer, and/or a brass or nylon punch, tap the swivel nut into the hole with the rounded side down. Work carefully, making sure the nut doesn't twist or get out of alignment with the hole. Make sure that the top of the nut is below the surface of the barrel channel in the stock. Now screw the swivel stud in from the other side and tighten. Make sure that the screw does not protrude above the barrel channel in the stock. If it does, remove it and grind off enough to bring it below the stock. Reassemble the rifle and install the sling.

Pump action, semi-auto and lever action rifles often use a band type front swivel stud. In the Uncle Mike's style, these are wrapped around the barrel or magazine tube and a hollow screw is threaded through to pull the two sides together. The sling swivel's pin will then pass through the hollow screw. These bands can be a bit aggravating to install and persistence is your best tool. Position the band as close to the top of the forend as possible. However, the diameter of the tube or barrel often will limit how far down the band will slide. Be careful not to force anything, as you can easily scratch the bluing.

A few tips. Smooth the inside of the ring and polish a small radius on the edges. This will help it slide up and down easier for positioning and reduce the risk of marring the bluing. Make sure that the holes on the two sides are in perfect alignment before attempting to install the screw. A padded vise can help correct any misalignment. It is easier to remove any sights and barrel bands to allow the band to slide down the tube or barrel than it is to bend the ring around them and then try to bring it back into alignment.

If the swivel will not close all the way after installation, use a file to carefully cut the sides of the stud to reduce the thickness until the swivel will close and lock.

FIXING MISTAKES • If you screw up and drill the rear swivel hole slightly off center, Larry Weeks at Brownells explained that there may be a way to correct the mistake.

Redrill the hole using a larger drill, but make sure that

Tools and materials for installing sling swivels on a pump action rifle. Drills, alignment tool and swivels.

it is smaller than the base diameter of the swivel. Try to correct the alignment problem as much as possible while drilling this hole. You may also try using a small cutter in a Dremel tool to open the hole on the side that is off center.

Coat the swivel stud and screw with a release agent and allow it to dry. Paste wax will work, but the best is the release agent that Brownells supplies with their glass bedding kits. They also sell it in three-ounce or one-quart bottles.

Clamp the stock in a vise to keep it level and cover the stock around the hole with masking tape. Fill the hole with Brownells Acraglas Gel bedding compound and insert the swivel stud into the hole. Wipe up any excess gel and keep the swivel stud aligned; use a piece of tape to hold it if necessary. It's a good idea to dye the Acraglas Gel as close to the color of the stock as possible. After the Acraglas

INSTALLING STUDS ON WOOD AND SYNTHETIC STOCKS

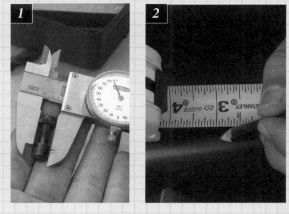

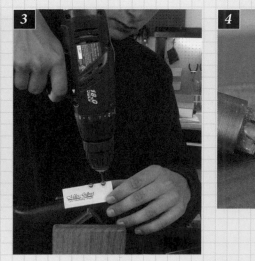

1. The drill selected to countersink the hole in the forend of a bolt-action rifle's stock must be slightly smaller than the knurled nut used so that it will be a tight fit to grip the nut. 2. Marking the location for the rear sling swivel stud.

3. Using a drill alignment tool as a guide while drilling a rifle stock to install a rear sling swivel stud. When using a hand-held drill, care must be taken to keep the alignment correct. 4. This cutter squares the stock for better alignment of the sling swivel stud.

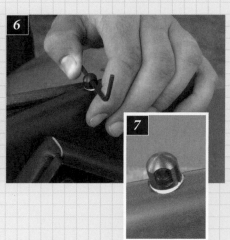

6. Using an Allen wrench to install the rear sling swivel stud. Be very careful to not contact the wood with the Allen wrench, which can gouge the stock. 7. Shows a correctly installed rear sling swivel stud. In this installation the optional white spacer was included.

5. A dab of glue on the sling swivel stud screw will help keep it in place.

Gel sets, you can remove the stud by unscrewing it. Clean up any excess gel and carefully sand flush to the stock contours. Reinstall the swivel stud and wait a week before using it, to allow the compound to set completely.

You can also repair a rear swivel stud that has pulled out and stripped the wood using this method. Drill the hole just enough larger to clean it up and give you a clean wood surface for the Acraglas Gel to adhere to.

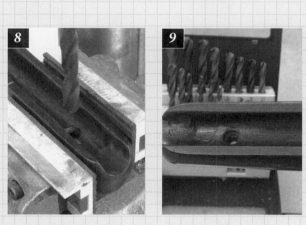

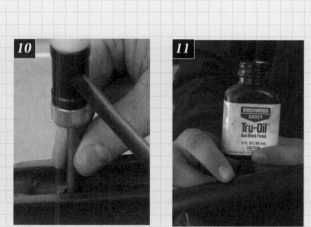

8. This shows a rifle stock clamped in a vise in a drill press in preparation for drilling. 9. Proper drill size is important to a quality installation of a sling swivel.

10. Using a brass punch to tap the knurled nut into place for installing a sling swivel stud on the forend of a bolt-action rifle. 11. All exposed wood should be coated with stock finish.

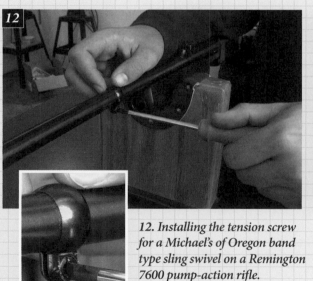

12. Installing the tension screw for a Michael's of Oregon band type sling swivel on a Remington 7600 pump-action rifle.

13. A completed installation of Michael's of Oregon band type sling swivel on a Remington 7600 pump-action rifle.

Installing a Marble's Tang Sight
Gunsmithing Project No. 7

Marlin 1894 rifle with tang sight.

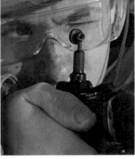

There is something inherently "American" about hunting with a lever action rifle. After all, the lever action is the "gun that won the West." It's the gun our grandfathers hunted with and for many of us it's the gun we first lugged into the deer woods. Returning to those roots has a certain appeal, but for a lot of us the open sights are not as sharp as they were when our eyes were young. A peep sight is much kinder to eyes of any age and a tang-mounted peep sight is a nostalgic return to the roots of lever action rifles and is extremely popular with Cowboy Action shooters.

Installing a tang-mounted peep sight on a lever action rifle is a simple "do-it-yourself" project for any hunter with a few basic tools. Both Lyman and Marble's offer tang sights to fit Winchester and Marlin lever action rifles. In this case we will be mounting a Marble's tang sight on a Marlin Model 1894 rifle.

Clamp the rifle in a cradle like the Decker Gun Vise. Remove the tang screw and place the sight on the tang. Make sure that you use a gunsmith's screwdriver that exactly fits the screw slot and has parallel sides. Do not use a standard screwdriver, as the tapered sides can cause the screwdriver to ride out of the slot and gouge the rifle. One of the best investments you can make is a set of gunsmith's screwdrivers available from Brownells, Lyman or Chapman.

Shooting a Marlin with a tang sight.

Install the longer tang screw supplied in the rear sight in the hole and tighten enough to hold the sight, but also to allow it to move when tapped gently with a plastic hammer. Center the front of the sight on the tang by tapping it gently with a plastic hammer or with a hammer and a nylon or brass punch.

Using a center punch, mark the tang in the exact center of the hole. A spring-loaded center punch like the one made by Starret makes the job a little easier, as it eliminates the use of a hammer and is easier to control. If you plan to on installing more sights in the future it will be worth the extra cost. A shotgun bead drill fixture sold by Brownells is designed to center a drill on a shotgun rib. It can be used to ensure that you are exactly in the center of the tang.

Remove the tang screw and remove the sight and the buttstock. Clamp the rifle in a vise with padded jaws and place it in a drill press. Chuck the proper size drill in the drill press. In this case we will use a #21 drill for a 10-32 screw. (The screw size information will be included with the sight.) Make sure that the tang is square to the drill and that the drill is lined up exactly with the punch mark in the tang. Double-check everything and when you are certain it is correct, carefully drill through the tang.

Select the correct tap for the screw supplied with the sight, in this case a 10-32. Put the tap in a tap handle. Make sure that the tap is square with and centered in the drilled

INSTALLING A TANG-MOUNTED PEEP SIGHT

1. Center punch marks location to drill.

2. Starrett spring-loaded center punch.

3. Brownells' shotgun bead drill fixture to center drill.

4. Drilling the new hole.

5. Tapping the new hole.

6. Tightening the screw.

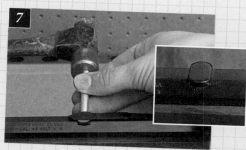

7. Using a brass punch to install a plug in the dovetail where the rear sight was.

8. New tang sight installed on Marlin Model 1894 rifle.

hole and that you have applied plenty of cutting oil. Carefully turn the tap clockwise to cut the new threads. Make sure to reverse the tap often to clear the chips every turn or so. The tap should turn easily and cut cleanly. If it binds or chatters, stop, something is wrong. Do not force it as taps are very brittle and can break easily if misused.

After you have the thread the full depth of the hole, wipe the tang clean of cutting oil and chips. Install the buttstock and the sight. Replace the tang screw, but do not tighten. Install the front screw and snug it down. Tighten the rear tang screw, then tighten the front sight screw. A drop of blue Loctite on the threads of each screw before installing will help ensure that the screws stay tight.

Use a brass or nylon punch and a hammer to remove the open sight from its dovetail. Install a dovetail slot blank by tapping it into place until centered with a brass or nylon punch. If you use brass, it may mark the metal. Wipe this with a patch wet with copper removing bore solvent and it should remove the brass smear. The front sight bead should be fine, but you may consider one that is higher or lower.

The sight is now installed. All that is needed is to zero the gun at the shooting range and enjoy it.

Repairing a Ruger Trigger
Gunsmithing Project No. 8

Ruger Vaquero single action handgun

By the end of World War II, Colonel Colt's famous six-gun was yesterday's news; everybody knew that, even Colt. In 1947 Big C had announced that they would no longer make single action handguns. With that, the design became obsolete. The future, they said, was in double action revolvers and semi-auto handguns. One Colt executive snidely told Bill Ruger, "You'll find that out."

But, as Ruger said about the people running Colt at the time, "They really saw no fun in the gun. To them it was a chore and a bore. . . " Ruger was a gun guy and he decided that a single action still would appeal to the public and set out to prove that with a new single action .22 rimfire revolver. Pete Kuhlhoff ran a small announcement about this new single action .22 LR in *Argosy* magazine, and the Southport, Connecticut, post office was flooded with mail. That left little doubt that the public didn't share Colt's views on the role of single action revolvers in the mid 20th century and it launched Ruger into the single action revolver business.

Sturm Ruger introduced the Single Six, single action .22-caliber revolver in 1953 and from that grew to be the single largest producer of single action handguns in America today. The Ruger single action handguns are legendary for strength, reliability, accuracy and durability. In recent years they are also legendary for the poundage of their trigger pulls. As my cousin and local shooting philosopher Philip Baker said, "It takes three men and a hairy dog just to pull the trigger on those guns!"

With lawyers setting the rules for so much of American life these days, a good trigger pull on a factory shipped gun is as rare as an honest politician. They exist, but most folks have never seen one in its natural habitat. Yet, like honesty, a quality trigger pull is perhaps the number one prerequisite for straight shooting.

I am not sure what we can do about honesty in politics, but putting a good trigger and a smooth action in a single action Ruger handgun is pretty simple. It can be done by any hobby gunsmith with a few tools and a mechanical aptitude that is at least a little higher than Michael Jackson's.

Your workbench should be clean, free from clutter and have good lighting. You will need a pad to work on to prevent scratching the gun. There are lots of excellent commercial pads, but an old bath towel works well, too.

The Ruger Vaquero handgun with some of the tools and parts needed to improve the trigger pull and smooth up the action.

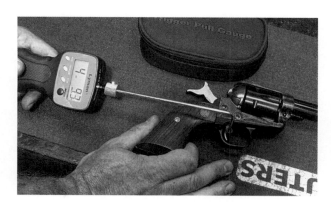

*The Ruger Vaquero handgun
showing the "before" trigger pull
on a Lyman trigger pull scale.*

One excellent investment anytime you work on guns is a book that shows an exploded parts drawing of the gun you are going to be working on. I can't tell you how many times I have been saved by this. It's easy to take a gun apart, but sometimes not so easy to put it back together, and a drawing showing how it all goes back in place is a pretty good embarrassment antidote.

Most of the Ruger single action revolvers are pretty similar, but there can be some differences. The gun we are working on here is a Vaquero chambered for .357 Magnum. This is basically the same gun as the Blackhawk, but without adjustable sights. As the slimy VCR salesman on the old SNL skit said, "same guts." It's is also essentially the same as the Super Blackhawk and the New Model Single Six. The parts are not interchangeable, but the design is pretty much the same.

One trick that will save you a lot of trouble is to clear a space on your bench away from where you are working. As you remove the parts from the gun, place them in the relative location where they go. Orient the gun as you would hold it to shoot as a reference. Place the top screws on top, left screws on the left, etc. Do the same with internal parts, keep them in the relative position they are removed from.

If course, it goes without saying that you should make sure the gun is unloaded before doing anything. Open the loading gate to free the cylinder. Depress the lock for the base pin located in the front of the frame and remove the base pin by sliding it forward. On some guns it will hit the ejector rod before it's completely clear of the frame, so you can't completely remove it without removing the ejector rod housing. However, this is not necessary as the pin should be far enough forward to remove the cylinder, which is the goal here. After removing the cylinder, close the loading gate. Remove the grip screw and remove the grips. If they are sticking, replace the screw but leave it slightly high. Then gently tap the screwhead with a small plastic hammer. This will break the off-side grip free. Remove the screw and the grip panel. Reach through the grip frame with a large punch and gently tap the other grip to free it.

Cock the handgun. Sometimes the cylinder advance pawl will catch on the frame if the cylinder is not in place, preventing the gun from being cocked. If that happens, simply reach into the frame with a small screwdriver, push back on the pawl and the gun should cock.

Inside the grip frame, the hammer strut should be protruding outside of the hammer spring by a considerable margin. Notice the small hole in the hammer strut. Insert a nail or pin punch into that hole and pull the trigger while holding the hammer, then slowly lower the hammer. The mainspring seat will hit the nail or punch you inserted and will hold the tension off the hammer. Remove the five grip frame screws. The top screws first, the front bottom screw next and then the rear bottom screws. Make sure you place them on the bench in order so you know exactly where each screw fits. Note that the screw on the bottom right has an extension that mates with a groove in the hammer pivot pin, so it must be replaced in exactly the same hole. Pull the grip frame slightly to the rear and remove. Remove the hammer strut and spring assembly from the grip frame. Make note of the orientation of the strut, as there is a top and bottom and it must be correct when reinstalling it.

If you are planning to change the hammer spring, you would skip the step with the nail and simply remove the grip frame with the spring under tension. For any hunting handgun, there is little reason to replace the hammer spring; however, a lot of Cowboy Action

Replacement spring kits

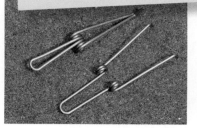

The replacement spring (bottom) is shaped differently from the factory original spring.

DISASSEMBLE THE GRIP & FRAME

1. *Tapping the grip screw on a Ruger Vaquero Single Action Handgun to knock the grip loose.*

2. *Punch shows the location of the hole in the hammer spring strut. The pin (or a nail) can be inserted in this hole when the gun is cocked. This keeps the spring in place during disassembly.*

3. *The bottom, right screw on the Ruger Vaquero has an extension that mates with this groove in the hammer pivot pin to lock it in place. Use a stone to smooth the surface of this groove to help ensure a good trigger pull.*

Shooting competitors replace the hammer spring with a lighter spring so that the gun will cock easier. There may be a slight tactical advantage in doing that as it will be slightly faster. Also, the gun will be slightly less difficult to cock and so it may prevent a few "missed" cocking cycles. But, a lighter spring risks misfires and for most shooters the factory Ruger hammer spring is probably fine. I have seen springs so light that the competitors have to use not only a specific brand of primer, but even a specific lot of that primer. That seems a bit ridiculous to me. If the gun misfires even once, you will lose more points than a lighter spring will ever gain for you. For what it's worth, I left the factory springs in my Cowboy Action competition guns. I don't think it takes a bit longer to work the action and with the adrenalin flowing as it is in competition, I never notice the difference and my guns go off every time.

If you wish to replace the hammer spring, have all your proper swear words lined up and ready to go, because you will need them. Clamp the mainspring seat in a soft jaw vise and turned so that the side of the hammer strut will show the nail hole when it's inserted. That is so that the flat of the hammer strut will be horizontal. That way the hole will be in a position so that you can insert a punch or nail when the hammer strut exits the mainspring seat. Put the new spring on the hammer strut, pad your hand with a shop rag and push the strut into the mainspring seat as it's held firmly in the vise, compressing the spring as you go. You will need to hold the spring with your off hand to keep it aligned and not twisting and turning. Push the strut in far enough that it exits the mainspring seat enough to allow you to insert the nail in the hole. This keeps the spring compressed. It's pretty simple reading it here, but can be frustratingly difficult to pull off with less than three hands.

When removing the grip frame, be careful not to lose the cylinder stop plunger and spring from the grip frame; or the cylinder hand spring and plunger from the hole in the upper left of the main frame. Use needle nose pliers to unhook the two legs of the trigger return spring from the cross pin in the grip frame. Use the correct size punch to tap out the trigger spring retaining pin and remove the spring. Replace it with the spring from your new kit and replace the retaining pin. Hook the legs of the spring over the cross pin and reassemble the handgun in the reverse order. You will need to push up on the spring arm as you slide the grip frame into place to allow the trigger spring to enter the slot in the back of the trigger. A small screwdriver and the same three hands make this easier. If you have trouble, unhook the legs of the spring from the cross pin until the grip frame is in place, then hook them back on the cross pin to tension the spring.

1. Installing a new hammer spring. Hold the mainspring hammer seat in a vise, install the new spring on the hammer strut and push it into the seat until you are able to place a nail or pin through the hole to hold the tension. Note the

padding on the hand and the small Allen wrench on the vise ready to be placed in the hole. 2. Punch shows the location of trigger spring pin. This pin is removed to change the trigger return spring.

3. Shows pliers being used to unhook the trigger return spring arms from the cross pin. 4. Using a small punch to knock out the pin that holds the trigger return

spring in place on a Ruger Vaquero. 5. The pen points to the groove in the Ruger trigger where the trigger return spring rides. If the surface inside is not

smooth, the spring will bind, causing the trigger to pull hard. Use a stone to smooth the surface of this groove to help ensure a good trigger pull.

Usually, this is enough to show considerable improvement in the trigger pull. But if you are still not a pound or two lighter than before, look at where the tab of the spring slides into the trigger. Sometimes this is rough and if it is, you will never attain a proper trigger pull until you fix it. That's because the spring will bind when the trigger is activated. It is rare, but I have encountered this on a couple of Ruger handguns. To correct it, use a thin stone to reach inside this groove and polish the surface that engages the spring. It's far easier if you remove the hammer, which requires taking the rest of the action apart. But if you are planning on working on the action, you will need to take the gun apart anyway.

The trickiest part of disassembling the handgun is removing the trigger/cylinder latch pivot pin. It's locked into the frame by the loading gate spring. You must compress this spring and push the trigger pin out at the same time. Again, it's easier with three hands. Remove the loading gate spring and the cylinder stop. Then remove the trigger by detaching it from the transfer bar. Push out the hammer pivot pin and remove the hammer from the bottom. The cylinder hand should come with it, make note of how they fit together, because it's much easier to remember now than it is to figure it out later. Finally, the transfer bar can be removed.

This is a good time to polish all the contact surfaces on the moving parts. Work very carefully with hard Arkansas stones and a buffing wheel on a hand-held Dremel type grinding tool until they are smooth. Don't remove any metal, just polish and never change the shape, dimension or contour of any part. Be very careful with any edge or corner as it's easy to round them off

REMOVING THE TRIGGER/CYLINDER LATCH PIVOT PIN

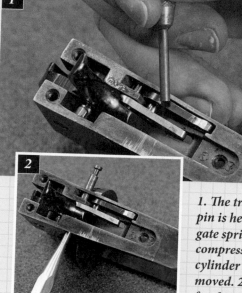

1. *The trigger/cylinder latch pivot pin is held in place by the loading gate spring. This spring must be compressed for the trigger/cylinder latch pivot to be removed. 2. The groove in the pin is for the spring to lock it in place.*

Also note the brass punch (from Dillon) used to push out the pin without marring the metal.
3. For the best results, polish all the contact surfaces on the internal parts. This will smooth up the action.

without realizing that you are doing it. All you are doing is polishing off the rough spots on any contact areas, not reshaping any parts. Be sure to polish any moving part that contacts any other part. The smoother they are, the easier they slide. Polish the hammer pivot pin and the trigger/cylinder latch pivot pin. This can be done by clamping them in a drill press and using the polishing wheel on the pin as it rotates. Have the polishing wheel turning in the opposite direction as the pin in the drill press. Then turn it around and do the other end. Again, and this is important, do not remove metal from any part, simply polish what is there. That means only the finest compounds on the polishing wheels and only the finest stones. I even polish the hammer strut and round the edges very slightly so that it slides through the mainspring keeper better. This is the only place I remove any metal or change contours. Then polish the end that fits into the hammer. Look at every single part and see if it moves, or has another part moving against it. If it does, polish the contact surfaces. Also polish anyplace in the frame where a moving part contacts it. A selection of different sizes and shapes of hard Arkansas stones works best for this as they are easier to control than a power tool. But some places are just hard to get at with a stone. Use a hand grinder with a rubber tip that is impregnated with abrasive compound for those places. Finish with a buffing wheel and buffing compound until the area is smooth and bright. Work slowly and very carefully, being certain to not change any angles or remove any

metal. The buffing wheels with red buffing compound are pretty safe as they are not all that abrasive, but the impregnated rubber tips from Dremel or Cratex can remove metal, so caution is urged.

Use an oversize chamber mop impregnated with jeweler's rouge to polish the inside of the chambers so that the empty cases will drop out easily.

Put the gun back together in the reverse order. Starting the trigger pin past the loading gate spring is tricky. You must compress the spring as you insert the pin and push the pin past the spring and line it up with the cylinder latch and the frame. With plenty of patience (and a handy third hand) it can be accomplished.

After the gun is fully assembled, check it for function and put a few drops of good lubricating oil on the key parts and you should be done.

Nothing you can do will improve your handgun shooting more than a good trigger job and you will be absolutely amazed at how much better you will shoot. One word of advice, though. Keep it a secret. If your shooting buddies find out you know how to do this, they will all want you to "fix" their guns, too. Then you will be spending all your time in the shop, instead of on the range.

SMOOTHER ENGAGEMENT SURFACE •

Stoning the engagement surfaces of the hammer sear and trigger will help smooth up the trigger pull considerably. This not only lightens the pull weight, but polishing the engagement surfaces also helps to smooth up the trigger pull by eliminating hitches and glitches.

But this is pretty tricky work and if you don't know how, it's best to just leave it alone. Simply changing the springs will usually make a big difference in the trigger pull. It will be better with the engagement surfaces polished, but not enough better to risk a dangerous gun if you do them wrong.

However, if you choose to disregard my advice to hire a professional and are planning to work on the sear, you will need some stones and possibly a jig to keep the alignment. Also, some sort of magnification tool for viewing your work is very handy.

The key is to never change the angle, shape or contour of the surface. What you are doing is simply polishing the contact surfaces without removing any more metal than needed to smooth the surface. This is the same concept as the polishing you did on the internal parts, but at a more critical level.

Do not use the felt polishing wheel. They will wear at the edges of the part and cause a slight radius rather than a perfect corner. Because the cloth polishing wheels are flexible, they are difficult to control and a wheel is not the best shape for this job. Select a hard Arkansas stone or one of the new extra fine ceramic stones that will allow you to make contact with the entire surface and to keep the surfaces flat and the edges square. Use only a new stone that is in good shape and not worn. Make sure that it is very flat with square edges. The trigger will require a flat stone, but the hammer may require a knife edge stone so that it has enough clearance on the hammer notch. Use the stone with plenty of oil to smooth and polish the engagement surfaces on the trigger and hammer. Move the stone in a linear motion across the surface. Work slowly and carefully, making sure to check the progress often and to ensure that the stone is making complete contact with the surface. Wipe the oil off the surface each time before doing the visual check so that you are looking at the metal and not an oil coating. It helps to use a magnifying eyepiece to visually check the progress. I often use a 5X to 11X photo loupe to look at the surface. Polish only enough to smooth the surfaces and no further. Hold the part in a vise while you work. Better yet, hold the trigger in a jig such as the Power Custom Inc. Series I Universal Sear Stoning Fixture sold by Brownells. This will keep the trigger and the stone aligned to maintain the correct angle at all times.

When the engagement surface is polished to a glass smooth finish, you are done. Reassemble the gun with the new lighter trigger spring and feel the magic.

By mounting the trigger and hammer on the pins inserted in the side of the revolver frame, you can see how the trigger works. This is an aid in knowing which parts need to be polished to improve the trigger pull.

When working on small parts like this hammer, it's easier to hold it in a vise. This vise is made by Forester and the ball head will pivot to any angle.

This Universal Sear Stoning Fixture is sold by Brownells. It maintains the correct angle when stoning the trigger sear to polish it.

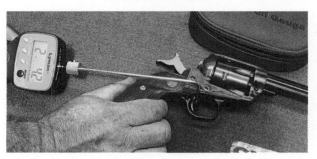

The Ruger Vaquero handgun showing the "after" trigger pull on a Lyman trigger pull scale.

Scope Mounting Made Easy
Gunsmithing Project No. 9

Using a bore sighter inserted in the barrel, this shooter adjusts his scope enough to "get it on paper" before making final adjustments by shooting at a target.

MATERIALS LIST

- Torx head screwdriver
- Loctite
- gun vise
- torque wrench
- file
- aluminum rod
- alignment rods
- ring lapping kit
- soap
- screws

It is so rare to see a rifle in the field without a scope these days that everybody feels compelled to mention it. While working on a book a few yeas ago, I hunted in northern Maine with a Remington 7600 pump action rifle mounted with a Williams peep sight. My choice was entirely intentional and made with good and sound reasoning. I was there to study the art of deer tracking with the legendary Benoit family and because they believe that this setup is the best available for that style of hunting, I wanted to see firsthand if they were indeed correct. The question if they were right paled in comparison to the many times I had to explain why I didn't have a scope on my rifle. Everybody outside of the Benoits' circles that I ran into had to know. It would almost have been easier to have a card printed, so I could hand it to them without needing to explain again verbally.

This only serves to illustrate that scopes are a fixture on today's hunting rifles. One primary factor in how well they will perform is in how they are installed. Improper installation can affect accuracy, reliability and even the life of the scope. Mounting a scope is not all that hard to do it right and with a minimum of tools, anyone who is reasonably handy can can do it on a rifle so that everything works properly. This is one of those projects that works as well on a kitchen table as it does in a fully equipped shop.

As with any job, it is important that you have the correct tools. In years past, a lot of the mounts used Allen head hex screws and many still do. These are an improvement over slotted screws, but they still will strip if too much pressure is applied. The line between a tight screw and a stripped head is pretty fine and care must be taken when tightening this (or any) style of mounting screw. They will require a new wrench with clean, sharp edges that haven't been rounded by previous slippage during use. The cheap throw away wrenches that come with the ring sets are not the best choice, as they tend to be soft and will slip and strip too easily. It's far better to use an Allen head tip with a high quality gunsmithing screwdriver set. These are hardened steel and will not strip when tightening the screws.

The current trend is to use Torx head screws which are much better. These require a special six-point "star" shaped wrench which provides more gripping surface that allows

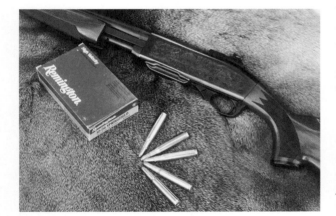

Remington 7600 Carbine pump in .30-06 with a Williams peep sight. Some hunters, particularly in the Northeast, still cling to iron sights. Certainly it's a personal choice, but any argument that they are faster than scopes for shooting at game lacks credibility.

more power to be applied to the screw without stripping.

Almost all gun work will require screwdrivers for slotted screws and that still includes a lot of scope mounts. Although it's a lot rarer than in the past, many mounts still use slotted screws and to the eyes of some shooters, they are still the most aesthetically pleasing. However, it is imperative that the proper screwdriver be used. The sides of the blade should be either hollow ground or with both sides parallel. Most screwdrivers sold in hardware stores have tapered sides and should never be used for working on guns. A screwdriver must fit exactly in the slot of the screw it is being used on, both in thickness of the slot and in the width of the screw. I cannot stress the importance of this enough. The reason is that a tapered or poor fitting screwdriver will ride out of the slot as pressure is applied and is guaranteed to ruin the screw, probably making it difficult to remove without drilling. Also, the screwdriver can fly off uncontrollably. This is, of course, dangerous as it can easily stab into important body parts. I heard of one poor fella who stabbed his left wrist and hit the artery. He almost bled to death because of using a cheap screwdriver on his scope mount. The screwdriver flying off will also often add custom, although less than artistic, engraving to your rifle as it gouges the wood and metal without discrimination. The first time you do that to one of your favorite rifles, or a gun you just spent a month making pretty, you will feel like slashing your wrists anyway.

A hollow-ground screwdriver will apply pressure to the bottom of the screw slot, rather than at the top as a tapered screwdriver will. This actually helps to "lock" the screwdriver into the screw as opposed to trying to

cam it out of the slot like a tapered screwdriver will. A screwdriver that fits properly will fill the slot and have the maximum amount of contact surface inside the slot to distribute the forces being applied. It's amazing how much per-square-inch force is applied by the screwdriver blade. A poorly shaped screwdriver will tend to concentrate the force on the small contact area, which increases the chances of damaging the screw or having the screwdriver slip. Also, a properly fitting screwdriver will distribute the force over a larger area and allow more leverage on the screw. A screwdriver that is turning from the edge of the screw slot will have more leverage, because the force radiates further from the axis, than one that is narrower and is applying pressure closer to the center of the screw. It's simply the physics of a lever in action.

A product that I have found helpful when using screwdrivers or Allen wrenches on a worn screwhead or a stuck screw is called Drive Grip. It has fine abrasive in a gel carrier that when applied to the contact surfaces between the screw and screwdriver or wrench helps in gripping. Another alternative is to use a little powdered rosin to help the tool grip better. Brownells sells powdered rosin for use with barrel vises, but it also has plenty of other applications around the shop.

Another handy tool is a gun vise to hold your rifle while you work. The first time you slip while trying to loosen a stubborn screw and stab your hand or, worse

Tips for three commonly used screwdriver bit types. It is very important to use a screwdriver that fits and has parallel blade sides when working on guns.

Putting Drive Grip on screwdriver.

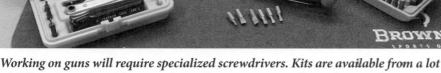

Working on guns will require specialized screwdrivers. Kits are available from a lot of different suppliers. These are from Chapman, Brownells, Midway and Lyman.

Adding Loctite to any gun screws is an important step. Make sure you use the kind that allows later removal of the screw.

Tightening a scope ring screw with an Allen wrench.

yet, gouge a chunk out of your rifle, you will agree. There are lots of gun vises on the market for a very reasonable price and every bench where long guns are worked on should have one. I have several in my shop, including one that is in two pieces.

It's a bit of a long story, but it illustrates what not to do with a gun vise. Back in my hungry days I would take any magazine assignment that paid in black ink and whittled a little at the mortgage. They weren't all smart, but the

dumbest one I ever said yes to was to test every 12-gauge 3-inch and 3½-inch turkey load on the market in three different guns. It worked out to firing an average of eight shots from each gun with each load and the number of loads seemed limitless.

For those of you not bitten with the turkey hunting addiction, I will note that these things kick. The 3½-inch loads have a recoil level that is equal to an elephant gun when used in firearms of equal weight. The problem is that a turkey gun weighs about two pounds less than most elephant guns, so they actually kick the shooter harder. The other problem is that, following my standard operating procedure, I waited until just before the deadline to start the project, and so had to rush to get it all done. After two long days of shooting at the bench, I was suddenly hit with a wicked headache and found myself vomiting beside the shooting bench. Turns out I had a mild concussion caused by my brain bouncing around inside my skull from the recoil. I had to finish the project, so it was time to get creative. I tried duct taping a 25-pound bag of shot to the barrel, but the tape ripped off in a few shots. I hung the shot bag over the front of the bench from a rope tied to the trigger guard. But that broke the trigger guard after a few shots. (Dumb, I know, but I had the "brain damage" thing going on.) Then I got the bright idea to clamp a Decker wooden gun vise to my bench and lock the shotgun in it. The first couple of shots drove the C-clamp in the back of the gun vise into the recoil pad; in turn, driving the recoil pad into the hollow synthetic stock on the pump shotgun and damaging the buttstock. I fixed the pad and the stock,

ALIGNING A SCOPE BASE

Many scope mounts do not have any way to adjust for windage problems. I recently encountered this when mounting a scope on a new muzzleloader. I didn't have enough scope windage to adjust it using a Leupold

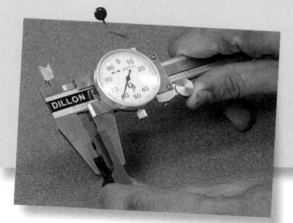

Magnetic Bore Sighter. Usually, when this happens I'll double-check with another bore sighter to make certain the problem is with the mounts and not the bore sighter. Sometimes I find that the end of the barrel is not square with the bore and this can affect the reading on magnetic bore sighters that attach to the face of the barrel.

I ran into this problem a while ago with a bolt-action .243 Winchester. The gun was out of production, so I had to modify a newer scope mount. The front base was fine, but the rear base was too thick, so I had to thin the rear base to bring the elevation in line. I thinned the base by working carefully on a belt grinder. I checked the thickness often at several points with a dial caliper (*at left*) to ensure that I was removing metal evenly so that and then I made a plate to cover the clamp and distribute the recoil forces over the entire recoil pad.

I wasn't concerned with pinpoint accuracy, but only with keeping the pattern on the paper. My finger was taking a beating while pulling the trigger, so I rigged up a string to accomplish that chore. This "poor man's universal receiver-bench test gun" worked pretty well for a while and the testing progressed nicely.

Then it rebelled. I had my portable shooting bench set up in front of the kid's four-foot-deep swimming pool in my yard and after about a dozen more shots, the front part of the cradle stayed clamped to the bench, but the back half, complete with my Browning Gold shotgun, flipped through the air and splashed down dead center in the swimming pool.

The recoil forces had broken the gun vise in the center. When I ordered a new one from Decker, they suggested that I might want to restrict its use to mounting scopes and other gun work. That broken vise stays around as a reminder of the fact they were obviously correct.

Before mounting the scope, you should clean all the screw holes, contact surfaces, screws, rings and bases with a good spray degreaser. Degreasers are nasty, so use them in a well-ventilated area, protect your eyes and wash off any contact with your skin right away. I usually take everything outdoors, if possible, for degreasing. You can also use isopropyl alcohol. I don't

Torque wrenches made by CDI Torque Products and available from Sinclair International.

think this works quite as well, but it is a lot less offensive. The key is to use a degreaser that dries without any residue, leaving the metal clean.

Mount the base or bases on the receiver of the rifle, making sure to use the correct screws in the proper holes, as some bases will use different length screws for each of the holes. Leave all the screws loose and then tighten them one at a time, checking to see that the screw will tighten the base until you cannot move it. Then back out that screw and try the next one. This is to ensure that none of the screws are bottoming out instead of clamping the base. At the same time make sure that none of the screws are projecting past the end of the hole. If they are, take them out and recheck that you have the correct length screws in each hole. If you find the screws are placed correctly, grind or file a little off the end. Make sure to carefully round the end of the threads so that they will start into the holes properly. The best way to do this is to chuck the screw in a drill press, and use a hand-held file to shorten and shape the screw. Make sure that the file has a handle installed as it can catch and be thrown by the power of the drill press, and the sharp tapered end designed to fit in the handle can cause serious injuries. This is not as likely to happen with small parts like mount screws but if you get in the habit, sooner or later you will use a file without a

the base was the correct thickness at all points and the bottom was parallel with the top. I finished with emery cloth on a flat surface, polishing the mount over that to ensure that the bottom was perfectly flat. I blued the base with Birchwood Casey Super Blue Liquid Gun Blue and oiled the steel to stop the bluing process and protect it from rust. I shortened some screws to the correct length and installed the base.

It worked perfectly, as far as it went. But after getting the elevation correct, I couldn't get the windage to zero on the bore sighter. I switched to a bore sighter with an internal spud and found that the face of the barrel was not cut square. After adjusting with an internal arbor bore sighter, the gun was less than two inches off at 100 yards when I test fired it. I figured I

had the same problem with the muzzleloader. But, I didn't have a bore sighter with a large enough spud and decided to shoot the gun to see what was going on. I discovered that it shot a foot to the left with all the right windage the scope would allow.

The base was a simple two-piece "Weaver" style with the recoil slot in the center. So, I removed the bases and turned them around 180 degrees. Using a bore sighter, I was able to get it back on the paper. I was now able to sight in the rifle and the scope was much closer to the center of adjustment. Either the receiver, or one, or both of the mount bases had been drilled off center.

Try every combination you can think of before giving up. Something as simple as reversing a scope base solved what at first appeared to be a big problem.

Using a one-inch aluminum rod to turn in a dovetail front ring. Inset: It is a good idea to add lubricant to any dovetail rings before installation.

ALUMINUM ROD ALIGNMENT

1. Using a one-inch aluminum rod to check the alignment of the two scope rings. 2. Sleeved scope alignment rods for use on 30mm as well as one-inch rings from Brownells. Note that by lining up the points, the rings are in alignment with each other. 3. Using a Sinclair International lapping tool to lap the rings. Note the lapping compound in the small white container.

handle on a bigger part and be wondering why it's sticking through your arm. Be safe, use a file handle.

Put a drop of Loctite on each screw before installation. I prefer the blue #242 because it allows the screws to be removed later. Once you are sure all the screws will tighten the base properly, go ahead and snug them up. Move from front to back or back to front so that the screws will draw the base down smoothly and firmly. Apply torque until all the screws are tight. This requires a balance and a certain feel. The screws must be tight, but you need to be careful not to strip or break them. Some sources recommend tapping the screwdriver with a hammer as you tighten the screw, but many now discourage this practice and I have found it unnecessary.

Leupold recommends that 6-48 screws in a ring or base be tightened to 18 inch-pounds and 8-40 screws be tightened to 28 inch-pounds.

Chapman says that with their screwdriver's relatively small handle and full hand pressure, most men will achieve 17 to 50 inch-pounds. With the thumb and first two fingers, most will apply 10 to 17 inch-pounds. But that is subjective at best. I can apply a lot more torque with this method than my son can and we are both pretty much grown men. I just outweigh him by about 60 pounds. The only true measure of how much you are tightening a screw is a torque wrench.

A torque wrench has the capability of reading how much torque you are applying to any bolt or screw. I used a big half-inch drive torque wrench for years when working on engines. For example, the torque applied to cylinder head bolts was important to ensure that the engine worked correctly, particularly on some of the high performance racing engines we were building. The same principle would apply to working on guns, particularly in mounting scopes, but on a smaller scale.

Recently, I have been using two torque wrenches made by CDI Torque Products and available from Sinclair International. One is The Adjustable Plastic Handle Micrometer Torque Wrench. It looks like a long handle ratchet wrench for use with socket wrenches. This ¼-inch drive torque wrench is designed for action screws and the like. It has a range of 30.0 inch-pounds to 150.0 inch-pounds. This puts it above the range needed for most scope mounting operations. It is, however, useful for a lot of other gunsmithing applications.

The smaller model is the Micrometer Adjustable Torque Screwdriver. This is designed for scope mounts and rings. It uses a screwdriver type handle and will accept any of the common screwdriver, Torx or Allen style bits. This tool has a range of 8.0 inch-pounds to 50.0 inch-pounds, which is perfect for scope mounting.

Brownells Rosin

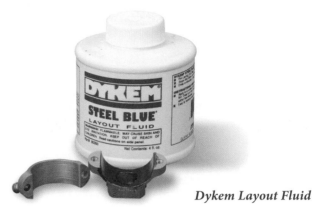

Dykem Layout Fluid

It shocked me when first using this precision tool by just how much I have been overtightening my base and ring screws all these years. These torque wrenches will really open your eyes to the mistakes you have been making and they will ensure that you don't continue to make them in the future. They are expensive and I recognize that most hobby gunsmiths will never buy one. That's probably OK; I mounted hundreds of scopes before I got mine. However, they do make for a better end result and will help to educate you a great deal on how much is too much when it comes to these small screws, so if you can afford one I would consider it money well spent.

Over-torqued screws can cause all kinds of problems, like broken screws or stripped threads. Also, stripped sockets for the wrench in Allen or Torx head screws. Also, twisting the ring screws too tight can damage the scope. It can result in bent or dented scope tubes and misaligned internal parts. The adjustments may not work correctly in a scope that has the tube distorted, making it impossible to sight in or in some cases to retain zero. It's a fine line between getting it tight enough so that things stay in place and so tight that things break. The best way to do this is with a torque wrench. That's not to say you absolutely need one to mount scopes on guns. Like I said before, thousands are mounted every year by people who have never heard of a torque wrench. But, for the very best job and for an eye-opening look at how much torque is correct, a torque wrench is the only answer.

In years past when mounting scopes on heavy recoiling firearms, I often would use a film of Loctite 242 between the base and the receiver as well as on the screws. This helps to fill in the gaps and provide a full contact area to aid in preventing slipping. But it would still allow the rings or bases to be removed. However, the Loctite is very difficult to remove from the rings, bases, rifle or scope. Because of this difficulty of removing the Loctite, if I want to reuse the rings, bases, rifle or scopes again, I find that I am more cautious about applying this practice. (I can deal with occasionally trashing a scope base or a set of rings,

but the rifles were getting expensive.)

One alternative is to use powdered rosin on the rings to aid in gripping. I have only tried it a few times, but so far the results with some very hard recoiling rifles are promising and this might be a better alternative. I questioned Larry Weeks at Brownells about that practice and he said that a lot of gunsmiths use powdered rosin on the rings with good results. However, for the vast majority of scope installations I do these days I use nothing for a grip enhancer. I simply lap the rings for good contact and tighten them correctly. I can't remember the last time a scope slipped after doing this. That includes heavy recoiling guns as well as the pipsqueaks.

After tightening all the base screws, clean all excess Loctite off the rings and bases. Don't forget to clean inside the action where the screw holes come through as the Loctite can drip through and cause problems if it's not cleaned up.

Now mount the rings on the bases. On dovetail turn-

Bryce Towsley takes aim with a Knight Revolution ML while hunting whitetails in South Dakota in 2004.

An extension ring

in type rings, add a bit more lubricating grease to the dovetail before installing the ring. Never use the scope to turn the ring into place. Instead use a one-inch aluminum or steel rod or a Leupold Ring Wrench. If you use a rod, always have the top of the ring screwed on before you apply torque to avoid springing the bottom section of ring, causing it to misalign with the top. If this happens, you will have trouble starting the screws and the ring won't fit the scope correctly.

Use the one-inch aluminum rod to make sure that both rings are aligned properly before installing the scope. If you can lay the rod in the rings and turn and slide it back and forth without any of the edges or corners shaving or dragging and the rod lies on the bottom of both rings, you have them properly aligned.

Better still, buy a set of scope alignment rods from Brownells or Wheeler Engineering sold by Midway. These are pointed on one end and after mounting one in each ring, you adjust the rings until the points are in perfect alignment with each other.

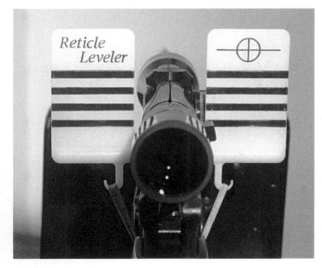

Reticle Leveler

After you have the rings in alignment, it is a good idea to lap them. Due to variances in manufacturing the rings, bases and gun receivers, there can be some subtle differences between the front and rear rings. Lapping eliminates those differences and brings all the surfaces to the same plane. This improves the mounting job and adds to the gripping surface, which can be important for hard recoiling guns. Lapping works best with steel rings. Aluminum is soft enough that it can wear away too fast and it can imbed the abrasive grit from the lapping compound and scratch your scope.

Brownells, Midway and Sinclair International all offer ring lapping kits. They are simple to use. Coat the one-inch steel lapping rod with compound and place it in both rings on the base only with the top removed. If you are lapping 30mm rings you will need a lapping rod of the correct diameter for that size ring. The rod must be exactly the same diameter as the scope body.

Lapping works best with horizontally split rings that have a top and bottom. The rings that split vertically can be lapped, but not easily and some designs do not work well with any approach to lapping. An inquiry to Warne reported that they do not recommend lapping their rings at all.

Move the lapping tool back and forth while rotating slightly and applying downward pressure. Check often to see how much of the ring is being lapped and stop when you have at least 75 percent contact on both ring bases. More contact is better, but 100 percent is all but impossible and you do not want to remove so much metal that the ring is too big. If that happens, you can sometimes file a little off the contact shoulders of the rings to allow them to close a little tighter. However, this will only work for a slight adjustment. Usually, rings that are opened up too far will require replacement, because they are too big and are no longer round. So, work carefully and check your progress often.

It's easy to tell if you are getting enough contact on blued rings as the shiny metal will indicate where lapping has taken place. On stainless steel rings it is not as apparent. Before starting lapping on these rings, coat the surface with Dykem layout fluid. This will abrade away on the high spots, showing the contact surface as shiny. Or you can do the same with a felt-tip marker by coloring the ring surface.

The Reticle Leveler in use. This clever device makes aligning the crosshairs during a scope installation much easier.

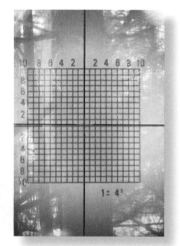

Most sources say that it is not necessary to lap the tops of the rings, as they are springy enough to compensate for slight misalignment. However, I do usually like to break the edges with a round fine India stone. This will remove any "cutting edge" and help to lessen the chance of marring the scope while moving it inside the rings for final positioning. I simply put a slight radius on the edges of the rings, paying particular attention to the corner where the rings split.

After completing lapping, clean the rings to remove any lapping compound. If any is left in place, the abrasive will make adjusting the position of the scope in the rings difficult and it can scratch the surface of the scope tube.

Place the scope in the rings and tighten the screws until there is a little drag on the scope but it can still be moved. Keep the rings evenly tightened so that the gap between the top and bottom ring is equal on each side.

Adjust the scope forward and back until the eye relief is correct for you. With a variable scope, make certain that you check it at both ends of the power spectrum. To check, hold the rifle in a natural shooting position while looking through the scope. Move your head forward until you start to see a black ring around the outside edge of the scope's field of view. Make a mental note of where your head is located on the gun's stock. Now move your head back slowly until the ring disappears and continue moving back until the ring reappears. Make a mental note of that position. The ideal "eye relief" is halfway in between. It often takes a couple of trips up and down the stock to find exactly the right spot.

The ideal scope position is when your head is in the natural position for shooting and it is exactly halfway between the two spots the scope starts to black out. Obviously, you move the scope forward or back to adjust for that. If the center of the eye relief is too far forward, move the scope back. If it's too far to the rear, move the scope forward. Remember to check eye relief when

dressed in hunting clothes. Setting the eye relief in a T-shirt and then trying to shoot a buck next hunting season while bundled up in several layers of thick clothing may bring some surprises and allow the buck to die of old age.

Sometimes there simply isn't enough room to move the scope without hitting the rings with the objective, power ring or adjustment turret. The answer is an extension ring. This is a ring that is offset with an extension so that the ring can be farther in front of or behind the base. This allows more latitude for adjusting for eye relief. Extension rings are also handy when the gun has a short receiver that puts the scope bases too close together or a long receiver where they are too far apart for the scope you want to mount.

Perhaps the most difficult part of mounting a rifle scope is aligning the crosshairs. The vertical crosshair should be in line with the axis of the bore, but on a huge number of rifles that I look at, it's tilted. This can make it difficult to properly sight in your rifle and can even affect your shooting in the field. The Reticle Leveler from Segway Industries solves that problem. It's one of those "why didn't I think of that?" gadgets. It indexes to a flat surface, usually on the scope mount base, and allows alignment of the crosshairs with the bore. It is remarkably easy to use and surprisingly accurate. However, this tool will not work with all guns or mounts. It must have a flat surface that is square with the bore to index off. Sometimes the mounts are too compact and there is no surface to index off. I have also run into guns on which the holes for the mounts or the receiver itself is off center, causing the scope bases to tilt slightly. But, in the vast majority of installations the Reticle Leveler works great.

To use it, put the two halves together in place and place them on a flat surface close to the rear of the scope. A rubber band hooks on either side and runs underneath the gun to keep tension on the tool. Look through the scope and use your peripheral vision to see the relationship between the scopes' horizontal crosshair and the lines on the Reticle Leveler. Any misalignment will be instantly apparent and can be corrected by turning the scope in the rings.

Another tool that works very well with most rifles is

The rear base is for windage. Note the damage caused to the screw by using an improper screwdriver.

Wheeler Engineering Level-Level-Level being used to square scope crosshairs.

Using the Level-Level-Level to align an aimpoint red dot sight.

the Wheeler Engineering Level-Level-Level (Hey, I don't name them, I just report on how they work). This tool uses a magnetically attached level that indexes off the bolt rails in the action. Another level is placed on the top adjustment cap on the scope. When both are reading perfectly level, the scope is in alignment with the bore. It works very well, but will not fit on some rifles because of the action design.

There are several other theories about how to make sure the scope is square to the bore by visually checking the horizontal crosshair. I do it by looking through the scope at a white wall as I hold the rifle, being careful to not cant the gun. I also check to see that the vertical crosshair is centered on the barrel or receiver. I recheck this several times to make sure I am not inadvertently twisting the gun. Another method is to place the gun in a gun vise and step back, away and behind the rifle. You can't see through the scope, but if you get the angle just right, you can see the crosshairs. Visually check to see

if the vertical crosshair is aligned with the centerline of the butt plate.

When the crosshairs are aligned correctly, tighten the ring screws in an alternate pattern, left to right and front to back.

When you cleaned and degreased the mounts, you left the metal without protection; so now is a good time to spray the rings and bases with a metal preservative or oil to prevent rusting. Be careful not to get any on the lenses, as you don't want any oil on the optics.

I have used this method of installing scopes on rifles up to .458 Winchester without a single problem. However, in really hard kicking rifles (yes, there are some with more recoil than the .458 Winchester!) you might consider epoxy on the bases and epoxy, rosin or another grip enhancer on the rings. Just remember that epoxy is pretty permanent; you can remove it with heat but that's difficult and tricky when you have optics involved. Too much heat and your scope can be damaged.

Boresighting can be accomplished by clamping the rifle, minus the bolt, in your gun vise and sighting through the bore at a distant object and then without moving the rifle make the adjustments by turning the scope adjustments until the crosshairs are aimed at the same object. A much easier way, in fact the only way for rifles such as lever actions that don't allow you to look through the breech, is to use a commercial bore sighter. Many use an arbor that fits in the bore, but a few years back Leupold brought out a bore sighter that has a magnet to attach it to the front of the barrel. One downside is that it had to be pointed at something bright

SCOPE SHIMS

In years past, you often needed to shim scope bases to make them fit correctly. That was because manufacturing tolerances were a lot more "loosely interpreted" and one receiver might not be the same as the next. Because of computer controlled machines, today's guns and scope bases are so well made that this is almost a thing of the past. But, once in a while you will encounter a mount that needs a shim. The shim must be metal and steel is best. Never use cardboard or wood. The traditional way is to make a shim which takes a lot of time

and never works out the way you had hoped.

Another approach is to use a pre-made shim. Brownells has a kit called the Brownells Scope Shim Kit. The kit contains 10 blued steel shims for each of the various hole spacings and thicknesses—a total of 80 shims. They are .600-inch and .860-inch center-to-center hole spacing. The thickness is .006 inch, .008 inch, .010 inch, .012 inch. The shims are sold individually in packs of 10 each.

The holes are large enough to allow some shifting for alignment and even if there is not an exact shim to fit your specific need, these are easy to modify.

If you install a shim, you may need to replace the screw with a longer one to make up the distance. This is particularly important on the blind holes on the front of most receivers. They are not all that deep to start to work best. But that model was recently replaced by an updated version with an internal light. These are fast and accurate if the muzzle is square with the bore. I have run into some guns where the muzzle is not cut square and that skewed the readings. In that situation I simply got out my old bore sighter with the arbors that fit in the bore and that took care of business.

If you do not have enough adjustment in the scope to boresight, then the mounts must be moved. Vertical adjustments can be made by placing a shim under the front or rear base as needed. Horizontal adjustment is easiest with the "Redfield JR" type of mount that captures the rear ring with two screws. This style of mount is sold by many other mount manufacturers, including Leupold. Simply loosen one screw and tighten the other to move the rear ring left or right. The front ring is in a dovetail that can pivot slightly to keep the scope from becoming twisted. If you are not using this type of base and do not have enough horizontal adjustment, you now have a problem. Try switching the rings and if possible the bases. Also try turning them around. Often, there can be a slight misalignment that self-corrects with a different position. If the misalignment is so bad that nothing works, switch to a scope mounting system that allows horizontal adjustments.

The goal is to have the scope's adjustments close to the center of their range when the gun is boresighted. To find the center of the adjustment range, turn the adjustment screw in one direction until it stops. Now turn it back in the opposite direction until it stops again, making sure to count the turns. Go back in the opposite direction again to exactly half the number of turns it took to go from stop

to stop and that's the halfway point. Try to get as close to that as possible, both vertically and horizontally when the gun is boresighted.

Just remember though, boresighting is only to "get you on the paper." You must shoot the rifle to completely sight in the rifle.

If you follow these simple instructions, you should have years of trouble-free service from your scope and rifle.

And a lot fewer questions to answer.

Bryce Towsley with a caribou taken in Manitoba with a Knight .52 caliber muzzleloader.

with and because the front base absorbs most of the recoil forces, it's important that the screw fit all the way to the bottom so that every available thread is utilized. A few thousands of an inch probably won't matter, but if the base required multiple shims for a thick shim pack, you will need a new screw.

Fitting the screw will probably require cutting off a long screw and grinding it for a perfect fit. The easiest way to cut it off is with a pair of electrician's wire strippers with a screw shortening capability. The final fit should be done by carefully grinding off a little at a time and trying the screw until it firmly locks the base in place, without bottoming out in the screw hole.

Chuck the screw in a drill press and work it carefully with a file. File a small amount off the bottom of the screw, round the bottom edge slightly to permit it to start in the threads and try the screw.

If it's too long, the base will be loose after the screw is tightened. The screw is hitting the bottom of the hole and not the base. With through holes, you can see the screw protruding below the surface of the action. If it's too long, remove the screw and take a little more off the end. When the screw firmly locks the base to the receiver or is flush with the receiver in a through hole, you are done.

With front screws, I try to have a slight relief between the screw and the bottom of the hole after the screw is tight. To check, coat the bottom of the screw with Dykem and tighten it with the base in place. If the Dykem indicates that the screw is contacting the bottom of the hole, take a few more thousandths of an inch off the end and try it again. When the Dykem is not marked, there is no contact between the screw and the bottom of the hole.

Cutting Off a Barrel
Gunsmithing Project No. 10

Measuring and marking a barrel in preparation for cutting it off.
Note that a quarter inch is left to make up for a cut that is not square.

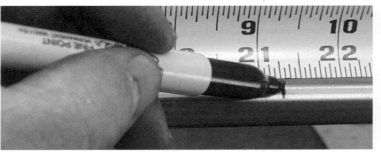

MATERIALS LIST

- felt marker
- hacksaw
- muzzle facing/ chamfering tool
- drill
- chuck adapter
- stop collar system
- muzzle radius cutter

I remember several things in my life that were hard to get started. Like jumping off a high bridge into the river, back when I was ten years old. I stood with shaking knees through several false starts. But after my buddies jumped, I couldn't chicken out, and I finally dove into the thin air and made the long drop to the cool water. Throwing a punch at the school bully took some determination. He was bigger than me, liked to fight, and was dead set on fighting with me. I had most of the fourth grade watching, so I couldn't chicken out. That would have hurt more than a bloody nose. The first time I flew a hang glider required more courage than I thought I had, but we had a couple of good-looking girls watching, so not doing it was never an option. However, when I recently took a hacksaw to cut off my new Douglas rifle barrel, it might have been harder than all those things combined.

A hacksaw? On a brand-new, top quality rifle barrel?

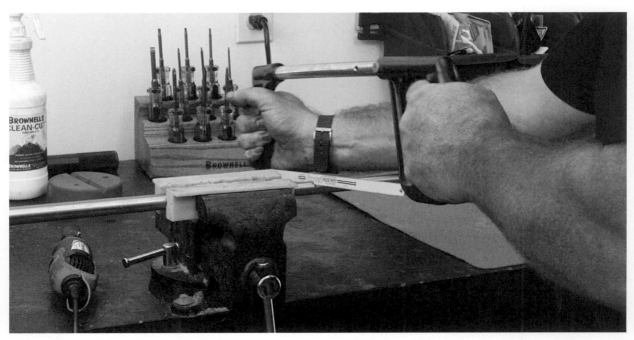

Shortening a rifle barrel with a hacksaw.

Isn't that against the laws of man? Or at the very least a venial sin? It was pretty scary to think of the consequences if things went wrong. With that other stuff, my bruises would heal over time, but a ruined barrel is forever. On top of that, I didn't have any audience for this and I seriously considered chickening out. But who on earth would build a .358 Winchester rifle with a 26-inch barrel? It had to be done and this was the only way, so I took a deep breath, closed my eyes and pushed on the hacksaw to start the cut.

Yes, I know professional gunsmiths take the barrel off the action and chuck it in a lathe to shorten it. But if you don't have a lathe, there is another way. One with results that are just as good, and in fact it's a way that I think is a lot easier. Removing a barrel from the action is hard work and it runs the risk of a marred finish from the barrel slipping in the barrel vise or the action in the action wrench. Avoiding it altogether is a rather inviting alternative.

There are lots of reasons to cut off a rifle barrel. In this case, I wanted a new deer rifle in one of my favorite cartridges. I have been a fan of 35-caliber rifles for most of my hunting career and I have used most of them at one time or another in the hunting fields. I learned decades ago that the .358 Winchester is one of the best woods cartridges for deer and black bear ever conceived. I have had a couple of them over the years, but currently found that my gun vault had a serious deficit of rifles in that chambering. I suffered the pains of withdrawal for as long as I could bear, and then caved in to the urges. I decided the only cure would be a new bolt-action rifle in .358 Winchester well before deer season opened. Because the .358 Winchester is no longer offered in any bolt-action rifles, I decided to build one of my own. I ordered one of the new Remington Model 700 SPS rifles in .308 Winchester and removed the barrel before firing a shot. After stripping the action and sandblasting it in preparation for a new DuraCoat finish, I fitted a short chambered Douglas .358 Winchester barrel that I ordered through Brownells. These barrels come "full length," which is 26 inches, with the expectations that they will be cut to the desired length. In this case, I wanted a short and handy rifle for hunting in the thick brush, and I wanted it to be just a little bit different. So, I

End of a rifle barrel after cutting it off with a hack-saw. Note below how it is uneven.

cut the barrel off to 21 inches.

Of course, building a rifle is just one of many reasons you may wish to cut off a rifle barrel. Perhaps there is crown damage and you need to remove the end section. Or perhaps you simply want a shorter barrel on your rifle. It's also a way to enhance accuracy. For years Browning engineers knew that if a rifle was returned with accuracy complaints and nothing else worked, if they cut a little off the barrel the accuracy was often improved. That knowledge led to the BOSS system that allows the "length" of the barrel to be adjusted by moving a threaded weight in or out on the end of the barrel. So, if you have a gun that's not shooting as well as it should, before you install a new barrel or trade it to somebody you don't like, it's worth a try to cut half an inch off at a time to see if the accuracy improves.

No matter what the motivation, this is an easy project with the right tools. There is no need to remove the barrel from the action. Remove the bolt and mark where you will be cutting the barrel. Then run a tight plug of cleaning patch material into the bore, leaving it a few inches from where you will be cutting. This will prevent chips from traveling down the barrel and into the action.

Once you know how long you want the barrel, clamp it in a vise with soft jaws and start "hacking" with a hacksaw. Try to keep the cut as straight and square as possible, but don't worry if it's not perfect and trust me, it won't be.

Once again, it's Brownells to the rescue. You will need a 90-degree muzzle facing cutter, larger than the diameter of the barrel's muzzle and a pilot to fit the bore of the rifle you are working on. The pilots are offered in steel or brass. I chose brass simply because I think there is less chance

Brownells' 90-degree muzzle facing cutter and
Brownells Muzzle Facing/Chamfering Tool
Stop Collar System block.

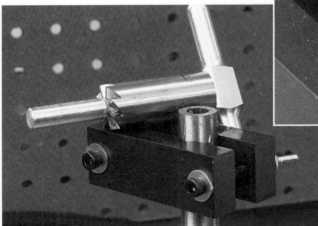

Rifle barrel muzzle
after facing it off with
a Brownells' 90-degree
muzzle facing cutter.

of damage to the rifle's bore. The cutter comes with a T-handle to turn it and you can certainly use that to do the job. But, it's much easier and faster to buy the Muzzle Facing/Crowning Cutter Drill Chuck Adapter. Long name, amazing results. This little inexpensive adapter allows you to chuck the cutting tool in a hand-held drill. This makes things go much faster and easier. Simply turn the drill to its lowest RPM setting, and remember to use plenty of cutting oil. The cutter will soon have the face of the barrel a perfect 90 degrees to the bore. But, be careful as this cutter works fast and you can shorten your barrel more than you planned if you are not paying attention.

One problem with doing this job without a lathe is that the cutter has a tendency to chatter. The cutter blades then tend to follow the contours of the chatter, which deepens the valleys and makes it worse. Once that starts, it becomes all but impossible to correct while using the cutter either by hand or in the drill.

Chatter creates marks in a regular pattern that appear on the cutting surface of the barrel as the muzzle is chamfered or faced. Chatter is a low frequency vibration that may be initiated by hard or soft spots in the steel, causing a cutter flute to dig in or bounce. It can also be caused by uneven pressure on the cutter against the barrel. With a lathe, it's easy to control the pressure on the cutter and the depth it can cut, but when you are hand holding the cutter, that level of control becomes almost impossible.

The answer is the Brownells Muzzle Facing/Chamfering Tool Stop Collar System, which is a long way to say this is a stop that will control the depth the cutter can travel. When this system is used, the cutter is physically blocked from continuing to cut in the low areas caused by chatter, so any high spots will be cut down until the entire surface is even.

The Stop Collar System is made of steel and consists of an adjustable ring to surround the cutter and a stop clamp for the barrel. Two different tools allow using either a cutter that is larger than the barrel or one that is smaller than the diameter of the barrel. Simply loosen the adjustment and move the stop until the gap is set for the desired depth of cut.

Cut until the Stop Collar touches either the muzzle or

Brownells Muzzle Radius
Cutter in drill. Finished
rifle muzzle.

the Stop Blocks, depending on your setup. Make sure you frequently clean all metal chips from the cutter and the bore because they can accumulate quickly and can cause scoring of the barrel. Each time the cutter and pilot are removed from the barrel, clean the muzzle, bore, cutter and pilot and check for chatter marks. If they start to develop, don't worry! When the face of the Stop Collar reaches the face of the barrel or the rim of the Stop Collar reaches the Stop Blocks, simply continue cutting until the chatter marks are removed. Always turn the cutter in a clockwise direction. Reversing the cut will roll the edges of the blades and ruin them.

Now switch the 90-degree cutter to one designed for cutting the crown. My choice on the .358 Winchester was a 79-degree cutter that was slightly smaller than the diameter of the barrel, which gave me a recessed crown. The 79-degree cutter is designed for what is commonly called an 11-degree crown, which is considered very good for accuracy. (The name is a result of 90 degrees, or the angle between the bore and the muzzle, minus 11 degrees equals 79 degrees.) Again, I adjusted the stop for the depth I wanted and ran the cutter until all the chatter marks were gone.

Finally, a radius on the outside edge of the muzzle gives the barrel a "finished" look and removes the sharp edge. For that I used a Brownells Muzzle Radius Cutter, designed to put the finishing touch on the barrel crowning job. This tool removes the sharp outside edge that remains after shortening a barrel or cutting a new crown with a cutter wider than the barrel. The cutter comes in three sizes and each cutter covers a range of diameters. Simply order the one with the diameter range that your barrel falls into. Chuck this cutter in the hand drill and make a few turns on the end of the barrel until the desired effect is achieved and you are done.

Obviously, the barrel is now raw steel. You can leave it like that, which is a good approach with stainless steel. Or if it's carbon steel, you can refinish it with cold blue. In my case I was applying DuraCoat to the entire barreled action anyway, so the finish, or lack of it, was not a problem.

One key to exceptional accuracy is a good crown that is perfectly square to the bore. My .358 Winchester was shooting minute of angle groups the first trip to the shooting range. I guess I can live with that, and I doubt a barrel cut off and crowned on a lathe would do any better.

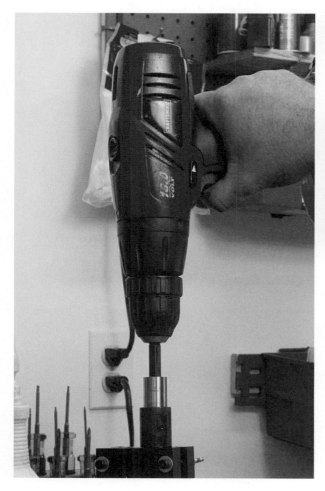

Left: Brownells 79° crown cutter being used in drill to add a radius to the outside of the barrel's muzzle. The finished muzzle is shown above.

Cleaning & Maintenance
Chapter 3

This Mauser .30-06 for years
was thought to be a mediocre shooter
at best. But a proper cleaning of the
bore brought out its accuracy.

In my family, my grandfather was really the only avid shooter. Others hunted and owned guns, but he was the one who built his life around them.

In our blue-collar, lower middle-class, small-town world his was an awe-inspiring collection. While he favored old lever-action Winchester rifles and well-balanced side-by-side shotguns, his collection pretty much ran the category from odd and unusual to modern and common.

One of the nicer rifles was a .30-06 Mauser sporter with a half-octagon barrel, a full rib and a front sight ramp all milled from a single piece of steel. It was always a source of Gramp's pride but every time he showed the rifle, he felt compelled to mention that it never shot as well as he liked.

Like most of his guns, it was sold to a famous baseball player after he died more than two decades ago. I thought I had seen that rifle for the last time when they took it out the door of Gramp's suddenly hollow and empty house. The collection was cherry-picked and some of it was sold off. The better pieces like this Mauser went to private collectors and were not offered for sale to the public, while others were sold to dealers. It was heartbreaking to see some of Gramp's guns show up on the tables at gun shows over the next several years. Even more so, given that my financial status at the time prevented me from doing anything more than looking at them. A few years ago my uncle Butch was able to buy the Mauser from the man who had owned it for the last 18 years. He brought it to me soon after when he was having some trouble with cases sticking in the chamber. We cleaned up the gunk that was the problem and at the same time I kept the rifle for a few days and properly cleaned the bore, which proved to be badly clogged with two generations of metal fouling. It took me two days of scrubbing to get all the gunk out of the rifle, but with that small change it's now an amazingly accurate rifle. It wasn't that the rifle was inherently inaccurate, it was just dirty!

Gramp started shooting in the early days of smokeless powder and was "old school" in much of what he believed. Because they favored low velocity cartridges that didn't foul much, once noncorrosive priming was introduced he and many others of his generation thought that a gun barrel did not need to be cleaned often. "More guns are ruined by cleaning than are by shooting" was the conventional wisdom heard often around the deer camps of his time, and they were probably right. Bad technique, poor cleaning rods and soft steel in the old barrels led to spoiled rifles and a propensity not to clean.

Today we know better.

Got Accuracy Problems? Clean the Bore

Cleaning the bore correctly and often is the key to a correct rifle break-in.

It might seem odd to have a chapter on gun cleaning in a book on gunsmithing. But more than just about anything else you can do to a rifle, knowing how to clean it correctly will restore and maintain accuracy. If you do not know how to do this, nothing else you will do to your rifle will make it accurate.

If you want your rifle to perform to its ability, you must clean it properly and often. Many of today's shooters get the "often" part right, but fail badly on the "properly" side of the equation. With today's "bigger-better-faster" trend in cartridge design coupled with parallel trend for better terminal performance bullets, this has never been more important. Just because you made a couple of swipes with a patch down the barrel doesn't mean you have the rifle clean. You must remove all metal and powder fouling to

call a bore "clean."

I suspect that a lot of barrels that were replaced as "shot out" in years past simply needed a good cleaning. In my grandfather's time they didn't have the super solvents that we have today and removing metal fouling was difficult. I have long suspected that the .220 Swift's reputation as a barrel burner was more likely because it was a barrel fouler. Sure it would burn out a barrel quicker than other cartridges of that era; this was a cartridge that was topping 4,000 fps in an era when 3,000 fps was still awe inspiring. When it was introduced in 1935 it was the hottest thing around and that performance always comes with a price. But, they didn't have the bullet materials or the powders that we have today and I suspect that the metal fouling was horrendous. Without the means or the knowledge to properly clean that

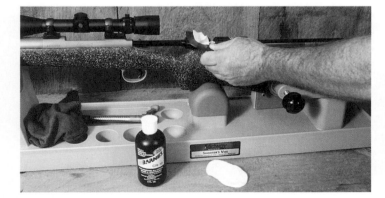

Starting a patch using the Bore Tech Patch Guide in the bore of a .358 UMT rifle. These bore guides are inserted through a rifle's receiver after removing the bolt. They keep the cleaning rod aligned with the bore while protecting the action from dripping solvent. They also make it easier to start a patch.

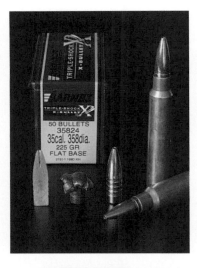

Barnes Triple Shock bullets are one example of the new generation of high-tech bullets.

This three-shot, 100-yard group was fired with a .358 UMT and Barnes VLC X-Bullets. For the best accuracy from any rifle, you need the bore clean.

of barrel, you know there is some serious "stuff" going on inside. Modern cartridges generate as much as 65,000 pounds per square inch of pressure. That pressure is developed by burning powder which creates rapidly expanding gasses. This process also generates a tremendous amount of heat. The heat, combined with the expanding gasses, is like a blow-torch in the barrel, pushing on the bullet and everything else. Also consider the friction that is generated as the bullet is reshaped to fit the rifling and then is pushed at an extremely high rate of acceleration down the barrel. It's a wonder we don't simply melt down the bullets in the barrel!

Today's high velocity big game cartridges not only drive a bullet very fast down the barrel, but they also demand a lot when that bullet contacts the target. The bullet makers have responded with "super" bullets that expand over a wide range of impact velocity and still retain weight for penetration. Many of them are made from material that is more prone to metal-foul the bore than more "common" bullets. The problem is compounded when we practice shooting with gilding metal jacketed bullets and then switch to copper jacketed bullets for hunting. Gilding metal is harder than the copper and the fouling in the rifle barrel actually will "weld" with the softer copper as it passes by, greatly escalating the speed of fouling. The only answer is to completely clean the bore after every shooting session and always before switching bullet types.

When I have a rifle come into my shop that is having accuracy problems, the very first thing I do to it is clean the bore completely. More often than not that will correct the problem, just as it did with my grandfather's old Mauser. However, even if it does not fix the problem, it will eliminate one more possibility in the checklist of what is causing the accuracy trouble.

Many shooters run a few patches through the bore and maybe make a pass or two with a brush and assume that they have cleaned the rifle. But, the truth is that a fouled bore is tough and time consuming to clean properly and because fouling is cumulative, each time that you fail to clean properly, the fouling left behind is added to the collection and the problem is compounded and grows over the weeks, months or years. If you shoot 20 rounds, but only clean enough to remove the fouling from eight rounds, and then do this repeatedly, after a dozen shooting sessions you have the accumulated fouling from 144 rounds. It's no wonder the gun is not shooting accurately. The only solution is to completely clean the bore to the bare metal, each time.

Running a few patches with some solvent through the barrel is not enough. You must clean the barrel down to bare steel and remove all powder and metal fouling each time you clean. If you can accomplish that with a few patches,

fouling from the bore, I am guessing a lot of poor shooting barrels were labeled as "shot out" and replaced. The label "barrel burner" stuck and the Swift never recovered from the bad publicity. It ruined the Swift's reputation and all but killed the cartridge in the marketplace. It's funny that when the .22-250 was introduced by Remington as a factory cartridge 30 years later, it had similar ballistics, but wasn't labeled a "barrel burner." That was probably due in part to advancements in barrel metallurgy and propellant technology. But, also in great part to better bullets and far better cleaning solvents. Today the Swift has seen a small comeback and I don't hear anybody complaining that it shoots out barrels faster than any other high performance varmint cartridge. I have owned three and have not seen any premature barrel failure from any of them.

The high velocity of today's rifles comes at a price and the currency is pressure and heat. When a bullet is accelerated to three or four thousand feet per second in two feet or less fine, but it doesn't happen often. I have a custom rifle with a Krieger Barrel that is that easy to clean. In spite of the fact it is chambered for an extreme wildcat, the .358 UMT, which pushes a 35-caliber 250-grain bullet to more than 3,100 fps, the bore on this gun is so good that it rarely fouls and when it does it's very easy to clean. But, that's at one very lonely end of the spectrum. Most rifle barrels, particularly factory guns, are somewhere closer to the other end of the bell curve, and they will take more effort to clean. I can't say how many patches or how many swipes of the brush will be required to clean any specific rifle, nobody can. What I can give you is some guidelines on how to do it correctly and how to tell when you are done.

A PLACE TO WORK • You must have a solid surface like a workbench or a table and it's always best to hold the rifle in a cradle or gun vise of some sort. There are lots of commercial rifle cleaning cradles and gun vises on the market. Having one on your workbench will be money well spent.

The chemicals used for cleaning guns are powerful and nasty. How could they not be, they are designed to dissolve metal fouling. Do you really think that warm milk would do the job? When you clean your guns, take measures to not ingest or absorb these solvents. Make sure that you have good ventilation. Keep a supply of latex or, better still, vinyl gloves to wear. Some gun cleaning chemicals will damage latex, but vinyl seems immune to more of them. Safety glasses or goggles are a good idea. I can tell you from painful experience that the aggressive copper eating solvents we use on a rifle bore are not pleasant to have in your eyes. Another smart product

would be a shop apron to keep the mess off your clothes. You will need lots of shop rags and I always keep a roll of shop grade paper towels on a hanger above the bench. Wipe up spills and when you finish put all the rags and used patches in a sealed container like a Ziploc™ bag before putting them in the trash. Keep a large trash can close to the bench with a contractor's grade liner bag. That allows you to keep the mess to a minimum and to tie up the bag at the end of your session to help trap the fumes from the solvents.

A very handy product is the Patch Hog made by Bore Tech and sold by Brownells'. One end screws onto a half-gallon plastic soda bottle and the other end slips over the muzzle of the gun. One size fits all, even over the front sights. The bottle catches the patches and when it's full, you simply unscrew it, put a cap on the bottle and dispose of it. It eliminates solvent dripping on the bench and the need to pick up those crud-covered patches. It also helps to contain the fumes. When using a brush, the bristles will "spring" forward as they exit the bore and this sprays solvent all over everything, but with the Patch Hog, it's all contained in the bottle. No mess. It's a great product.

THE ROD • Cleaning rod wear, caused by the rod excessively contacting the rifling, particularly at the crown, is one source of barrel damage. It's what led to the common idea in Gramp's time that cleaning was a bad idea. This is particularly true when a cheap aluminum rod is used to clean from the muzzle. Soft aluminum rods pick up and imbed grit to become, in essence, a file that grinds away at the muzzle crown.

The best cleaning rods are one piece. Jointed rods

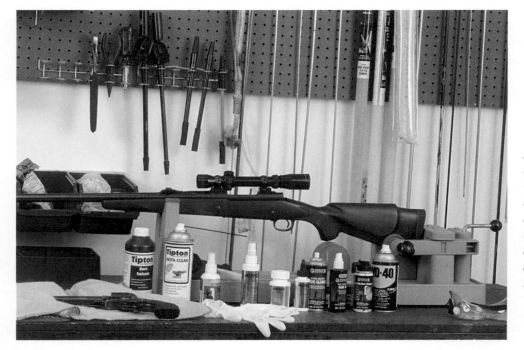

A good, well-equipped place to work can make gun cleaning chores a lot easier. Note the wide variety of chemicals used for cleaning and maintaining guns.

have more flex and the joints provide potential areas for embedded particles or sharp edges which can harm barrels. There are two schools of thought concerning the design of one-piece rods: some like hardened steel rods, while other shooters prefer plastic coated rods. The theory is that a hard steel rod will not embed grit and become a "file." Other shooters prefer a coated rod because it's soft enough not to damage the bore and will not imbed particles as easily as aluminum. There is also a theory that as a rod flexes inside the bore, it continuously hits the edge of the lands on the rifling. The theory is that a steel rod will continuously hit the barrel at the flex point and "peen" the rifling as it pushes the patch through, while a coated rod provides some protection against that. If a steel rod is damaged, it can develop a burr that can damage a rifle bore. For what it's worth, most serious shooters I know use coated rods. More recently, graphite rods have become popular. They are soft like coated rods, have less propensity to embedding grit than aluminum and they are relatively inexpensive.

The rod should also fit relatively snugly in the rifle bore. Forget "all-purpose" cleaning kits and buy a rod specific to each bore diameter. The cost is small compared to the benefits it will bring.

Wipe the rod clean of solvent and debris often during the cleaning process. Keeping the rod clean preserves its useful life and also helps reduce the chance of bore damage.

GUIDES

• If possible, always clean from the breech and use a rod guide. This is a tool that inserts into the action after you remove the bolt. It will fit into the chamber and extend out past the back of the action. This provides a pipeline from the front of the gun to the bore. The best guides not only keep the rod aligned with the bore, but also protect the action from dripping solvent and crud. Trying to keep a patch lined up on the jag as you push it through the action can be frustrating enough to make a grown man cry, and one other big asset of a bore guide is it will also make it much easier to start a patch.

Some rifles such as semi-auto, lever-action or pump-actions must be cleaned from the muzzle. A big danger here is cleaning rod wear. Years ago I traded a shotgun I didn't like for a Winchester Model 94 carbine in .44 Magnum. The guy who owned the Winchester had taken the gun apart and could not figure out how to get it back together, which put me in a good bargaining position. I put all the parts back in place, but the darn thing never shot all that well. A careful examination and a few questions to the former owner revealed that he had been very exuberant about cleaning the gun. The rifling was damaged and worn on one side of the muzzle from an aluminum cleaning rod constantly rubbing on it.

It is important in any "clean from the muzzle" situation to use a muzzle guide to align the rod with the bore and to protect the delicate crown from cleaning rod wear. A muzzle guide is a cone-shaped piece of plastic or brass with a hole through the center. The cone is inserted into the

ROD GUIDES

A selection of bore guides. These bore guides are inserted through a rifle's receiver after removing the bolt. They keep the cleaning rod aligned with the bore while protecting the action from dripping solvent. They also make it easier to start a patch.

Shows starting a patch, using Bore Tech Patch Guide.

These muzzle guards fit into the rifle's bore and align the cleaning rod with the bore, preventing it from contacting the crown and causing damage.

With rifles that must be cleaned from the muzzle like this Marlin 1895, it's a good idea to place the gun upside down and put a rag in the action to catch the solvent. A gun vise will make cleaning any rifle much easier.

muzzle and the rod is run through the hole in the center. The guide keeps the rod centered in the bore so it will not contact the muzzle and cause wear or damage. The downside of a muzzle guide is that the hole is usually rod size and so you can't push a patch through it. The guide stays on the rod and the patch must be started into the bore without the use of the rod guide. This is a window of vulnerability when crown damage can occur, so extreme care is needed when starting the patch. Once the patch is a few inches down the bore, the muzzle rod guide can be slid down the rod and put in place on the muzzle.

Turn these rifles upside down in the cradle so that the solvent will not run down into the action parts. Put a rag in the action to catch the crud you push out of the barrel.

PATCHES, JAGS AND BRUSHES • Select the largest patch that fits in the bore with your jag. The patch should fit snug, but not so tight as to be difficult to push down the barrel, as a tight patch will wring the solvent off the patch. When I find a patch that fits well for a rifle that I shoot a lot, I buy a bunch of them. I prefer cotton, but buy whatever is on sale. To clean a rifle right, you will use a lot of patches and trying to extend their life by using them more than once is false economy, although I will admit to using both sides of the patch, particularly early in the cleaning process. I will run the patch down the bore, then flip it over so the other side contacts the bore and run it through again. But as I get closer to the goal of a clean rifle bore, the final patches are used only once and only on one side.

Brushes should be bronze for most cleaning chores. Most nylon brushes do not have the scrubbing ability and stainless steel can gall and ruin the barrel very quickly.

Although nylon brushes are handy when scrubbing with very aggressive copper-eating solvents, because these solvents will destroy a bronze brush quickly, but do not affect nylon. With any brush, I usually buy one size larger than my bore size. I make it a practice to never reverse a brush while it's in the bore. Some say it won't damage the bore; I am not willing to take that chance. I run the brush the full length of the barrel until it exits before reversing direction. Brass cores in the brushes are better than steel, as steel can damage the bore.

There are a lot of theories about jag design, some of them are practical and some border on esoteric. Mine is simple and pragmatic. The jag should fit the bore snugly with the patch you are using and it should hold the patch securely. I prefer brass and I don't trust stainless steel, although I'll admit that I use them quite often. I want a jag that is made of a material softer than my rifle bore so that it will not scratch or damage it. I am not sure that stainless steel is soft enough. When used correctly, it shouldn't contact the bore anyway, but why chance it? Plastic jags work, but are not very durable. Slotted patch holders are just about useless for cleaning the bore. However, an oversize one is useful for holding a big patch to wipe out the action, chamber and the bolt lug recesses.

You will also need a good action cleaning tool to wipe the crud out of the bolt recesses. Dewey has a good one, as does Midway USA. These are short rods with a device on the end to hold a cotton swab. The tool is used to turn the swab in the action to remove any solvent or crud from the bolt locking recesses.

SOLVENTS •

Solvents are the key to cleaning a rifle and it's there that we have made so much progress in the past couple of generations. Today's advanced chemistry is far better than my grandfather's generation had. I remember he told me that they used to put mercury into a barrel to remove metal fouling. Today we have chemicals that are much safer and more effective.

I would divide them into three categories. General use, aggressive copper removers and those that split the difference. The last category are the solvents that

Barnes CR-10 Bore Cleaning Solvent. This is a very aggressive copper removing cleaner.

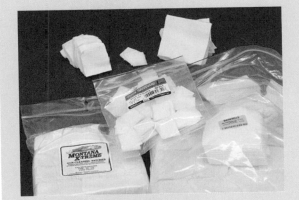

A selection of cleaning patches.

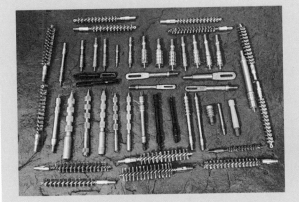

A selection of cleaning tips. A jag should fit the rod and rifle bore properly. Bronze brushes are best and should be a snug fit in the bore. Slotted patch holders are helpful for wiping out a wet bore or cleaning the chamber but are not good for bore cleaning.

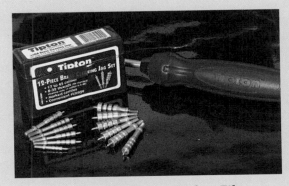

Tipton Jag Kit with Tipton Carbon Fiber cleaning rod.

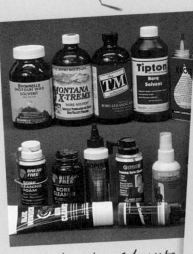

Cleaning Solvents

Hoppe's Elite System

Tipton cleaning products

combine general powder solvent cleaning abilities with more aggressive copper removal.

TECHNIQUE #1

TYPE "A" AGGRESSIVE CLEANING • Start cleaning the bore with a general bore solvent, making several passes through with a new wet patch each time. It's best to use each patch for only one pass before replacing it with a new solvent soaked patch, but I do sometimes use both sides of the patch at this stage of cleaning. Don't scrub, but instead push the patch straight through the bore. You may want to let the gun soak a few minutes between patches to allow the solvent to work.

Leaving the barrel wet with solvent, use a properly fitted brush dipped in and soaked with solvent to make several passes. Keep the brush wet with solvent, reapplying after every couple of passes. Don't dip the brush in the solvent bottle, as this will contaminate the remaining solvent. Instead, put some solvent in a long, thin container like a test tube and dip in that. Use the leftover solvent on the patches; do not put it back in the bottle. I keep a Dixie cup with solvent near me as I clean and I put several patches at a time in to soak.

Don't reverse the brush in the bore; instead, push it all the way out of the muzzle then pull it back through. Always use a bore guide or muzzle guide to keep the brush centered at all times, as the steel core of the brush can gall the barrel.

After use, always clean the solvent from your brush with a degreasing spray. This is to prevent abrasive debris from accumulating and also because some solvents will eat the bronze bristles.

Let the gun sit for a few minutes to allow the solvent to work, and then follow with one wet and several dry patches to remove all traces of solvent. Now pass a patch soaked with copper removing solvent through the bore. Be sure to read the instructions on the label. Most recommend that they not be left in the bore for more than 15 minutes. Let the bore soak for a few minutes and follow with another patch wet with copper solvent followed by a dry patch. Then repeat. The goal is to have no blue or green stains on your patches, indicating that there is no remaining metal fouling. Remember, though, that a brass jag can leave a "false" stain on the patch, although it's usually on the inside rather than the outside of the patch, so it's easy to distinguish from stains from bore fouling. When in doubt, use a plastic or stainless steel jag. When you have patches coming out with no trace of green or blue (it may take a while if the fouling is extensive), dry the bore with several clean patches.

Scrub the bore again with the general solvent, using

The progression of color on cleaning patches. Keep cleaning until the patches come out of the rifle with no blue or green stains.

patches and brushes. Then dry and repeat the copper solvent treatment. Sometimes, metal fouling can be trapped under layers of baked-on powder fouling that you must remove to allow the copper solvent to get at the metal fouling. Keep repeating this process until you have no sign of blue or green on any patches. If you let the solvent work for five minutes before you push a patch down the bore and the patch is the same color coming out as it was going in, your rifle is clean. If there are any stains on the patch, you still have work to do.

TECHNIQUE #2

THE "LAID-BACK APPROACH" • Because my workshop is close to my office, I use this technique quite often. I choose a solvent that is more aggressive than the general solvents on copper removal, but has a manufacturer's recommendation that it can be left for an extended time in the bore.

As before, I pass several patches that are wet with solvent through the bore. Then I scrub it with a wet brush, reapplying the solvent to the brush often so that the bore is well saturated.

Then I remove my rubber gloves, wash my hands and return to work. An hour or so later I run a few patches wet with solvent through the bore followed by a couple of dry patches. Then I repeat the process, using the brushes and patches. The crud that the solvent will loosen during this extended soaking is sometimes amazing. If the gun is not clean at the end of the day, I will let the solvent work overnight. A badly fouled bore may take a few days to clean, but in the end it's less work because I am giving the solvent more time to dissolve the crud.

TECHNIQUE #3

ELECTRONICS • If you clean a lot of guns, particularly guns with badly fouled bores, electronics can do the work for you. The Outers Foul Out Electronic cleaner is a device that uses an electric current to activate a reverse plating process. This removes the fouling from the bore and deposits it on a metal rod, speeding up the cleaning process a great deal. The system is not terribly expensive and anybody with several guns and an interest in shooting should have one.

First clean the bore with a general solvent and dry it with several patches. Then degrease the bore down

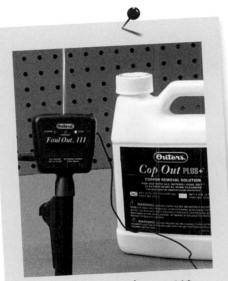

Outers Foul Out III

to bare metal, using patches impregnated with a good degreasing solution that dries without leaving a residue.

Plug the barrel at the breech with the rubber plug supplied with the Foul Out system and fill the bore with the proper solvent. There is one for lead removal and one for copper removal. Insert the metal rod with the rubber O-rings in place to isolate it from the barrel, and then hook up the Foul Out cleaner according to the instructions. After it has cycled through and is indicating "clean," dry the bore. Now clean with a general solvent again to scrub out baked-on powder fouling that might be hiding metal fouling underneath. Degrease and repeat with the Foul Out. Usually, one or two times is enough, but I once had a .338 Winchester that I cycled through thirteen times before the bore was clean. This renegade rifle was shooting three-inch plus groups and I was about to trade it, but after cleaning it started behaving again and I decided to let it stay in my gun room.

J-B NON-EMBEDDING BORE CLEANING COMPOUND •

Another method that is preferred by a lot of precision shooters is to use J-B Non-Embedding Bore Cleaning Compound, available from Brownells. This is a slightly abrasive cleaner that will help to remove tough deposits of fouling. Clean the gun with solvent and brushes following the steps listed above. Then dry the bore and run several patches that are wet with Kroil through the bore. Wet another tight fitting patch and smear it well with the J-B Compound. Do this on a jag or use a slightly undersize brush with the patch over top of it. Run this through the bore, scrubbing, using short strokes of three to four inches. Stroke back and forth about ten times before moving down a few inches and repeating until exiting the muzzle. Clean the bore with solvent and patches and repeat.

If the rifle has been used with moly coated bullets, this is the best way to clean the bore. Moly may coat the bore and is all but impossible to remove with conventional cleaning approaches. However, J-B Compound will remove the moly, although it may take a while.

J-B Bore Bright acts as a cleaner and a final polish. Finishing up with that product used the same way will help

J-B Non-Embedding Bore Cleaning Compound, J-B Bore Bright and Kroil shown with a patch wrapped around a brush coated with Bore Bright.

Despite what a lot of "gun guys" say, I have had good luck with WD-40 for short-term protection of firearms. This is particularly true on this Ruger's case-hardened frame where other "metal protection" products have failed.

to polish and condition the bore. Be careful when cleaning gas-operated semi-auto firearms, as the compound can creep into the gas ports and cause problems if it's not cleaned out before firing the gun.

FINISHING UP • Finally, after cleaning with any of the above techniques, dry the bore with several clean patches and apply a rust protector by running several saturated patches down the barrel. Wait a minute or two, then run one loose fitting dry patch through to remove the excess. This will leave just enough rust preventive to protect the bore. Be sure to run a tight fitting dry patch through the bore before shooting the rifle to wipe out any residual lubricant/protector. Do not let any lubricant accumulate in the chamber, as the brass needs to be able to grip the chamber walls when the gun is fired. Lightly wipe the chamber down with rust preventive, and then dry it with an oversize patch.

Before shooting, wipe the chamber with an oversize patch with a degreaser. If you are hunting with the rifle in foul weather, skip the degreasing in the chamber and wipe it out with dry patch, but leave a thin film of rust preventive. Then run a single dry patch through the barrel to remove any residual rust preventive. This will leave a very slight film of lubricant on the bore to ease the first bullet through.

Often, the first shot may be off from the group (usually high), so a fouling shot is not a bad idea before hunting or competing. With most guns, the bullet will still hit very close to the zero and it's probably not a big deal, particularly when hunting. However, some guns are different. I had one Remington Model 788 in .243 Winchester that would not even hit the target if there was any oil in the bore. It was one of the most accurate rifles I ever owned, except for that one little idiosyncrasy. When I was young and opportunities for deer were painfully

scarce, not knowing about it cost me a whitetail buck. I never hunted with that rifle again without firing a fouling shot. In fact, the lesson is so painful and ingrained that even today I rarely hunt with any firearm without firing a fouling shot.

Use an action cleaning tool to wipe out the bolt recesses. The action and/or bolt should be taken apart and cleaned every now and then. But, a quick-clean approach can be used by spraying with a good aerosol spray degreaser designed for use on gun parts. Work outdoors and with safety glasses or better yet, a face shield, rubber gloves and a respirator or painting mask. Hold the parts over a bucket to collect the run-off for proper disposal. Spray all the parts, letting the liquid run off so that it flushes the grease away. Work at stubborn deposits with an old toothbrush that is saturated with the degreaser. Direct the spray into all the little nooks and crannies until you have all the parts clean and free of any buildup. After the degreaser dries, the metal is chemically clean and is subject to rusting very quickly. Coat every surface with a combination protector/lubricant, making absolutely sure that the manufacturer guarantees it for use in extreme cold. If it doesn't say it works to at least −30 degrees, don't use it. The old standby is dry lubricant like graphite, which still works fine, except it provides little, if any, rust protection.

Also use the degreasing spray to clean the action of the rifle, including the bolt lug raceways. Do not attempt to take your trigger apart, but instead spray the trigger assembly from every possible angle and direct the spray into every hole and opening. Let the liquid flush away all the dirt and grease. After it dries, lightly spray a protector/lubricator, then shake out and wipe up any excess.

At least one premium trigger manufacturer recommends that the trigger be flushed with lighter fluid, the same stuff used to fill a Zippo lighter. Let it drain and

Dewey Action Cleaning Tool

dry. The lighter fluid will not only clean and degrease, but after drying it will leave just the right amount of lubricant in the trigger.

The outside metal of the gun should be sprayed with a good protector and then wiped clean, leaving a thin film. Clean the scope optics with lens cleaning paper and fluid available from any camera store. I prefer the Kodak soft brand of paper and avoid the stiff, hard kind that is often sold in camera stores. Use an optics brush to wipe away any dust or dirt. Then crumple up a lens cleaning paper into a loose ball. Put a couple of drops of fluid on the paper; never put the fluid directly on the lens. Then, gently wipe the glass in a circular motion. Crumple another paper and use it dry, to very gently wipe the lens dry. The coatings on the optics are delicate, so only use optical quality paper and fluid and be gentle.

If the stock is wood, I like to wet a shop cloth with a little linseed oil and wipe the stock down. This helps to hide any small scratches and the smell of linseed oil just goes great with rifles. A synthetic stock should be wiped free from any solvent. If it's dirty, clean it with a household spray cleaner. Use a shop towel and not paper towels, as they will leave lint behind.

The first step to gun repair is maintenance. This ensures that anything else you do will have the gun operating at peak performance.

I think that if Gramp had lived to see the super solvents and electronics of today, he might have had to change the dialogue when he showed that Mauser to a visitor.

A SIX-PACK OF CLEANING TIPS

1. Always clean a rifle as soon as possible after using it. The longer you leave the barrel dirty, the higher the potential for corrosion damaging the bore.

2. Use modern solvents that remove copper and powder fouling and keep cleaning until you have patches coming out without blue or green stains, indicating all fouling has been removed.

3. Always clean from the breech if possible, using a bore guide. If you must clean from the muzzle, use a rod guide to protect the crown from damage, and catch the crud coming out at the breech so it doesn't get into the action.

4. Before storing a rifle for any length of time, or after cleaning, always use a protectant on the bore and other exposed metal surfaces to prevent rust. If it's going to be stored for a long time, coat the metal with RIG grease.

5. Before firing, always wipe the bore clean with a patch to remove any excessive residual oil. But don't make it chemically clean by wetting the patch with a degreaser. Instead, use a dry patch so that a microscopic film of lubricant is left in the bore to protect it from the first bullet's passage.

6. Fire a fouling shot before hunting. Some rifles will shoot to a different point of aim with a clean bore than they do from a fouled bore. This is particularly true when there are traces of oil or other protectants in the bore.

Preparing Your Rifle for Extreme Weather Hunting

Rifles must be prepped to work under harsh conditions like this winter muskox hunt north of the Arctic Circle. Wind chills were nearly seventy below zero.

Although the wind was blowing very hard through this remote Alaska Peninsula river valley, the mountain I was looking at provided a clue to just how sheltered it really was here on the river. Near the top of the mountain a rain swollen stream ran over a cliff to form what should have been a waterfall. Instead, the wind was blowing the water back up the mountain and off the top like a geyser.

Later, when we exited the river and started across the unsheltered saltwater bay, we were hit with the full force of that wind and realized we were in trouble. The flat-bottomed jet boat was designed to run in shallow rivers, not wind-pounded seas. On the other hand, *The Queen Mary* might have had trouble in this water. The bay was a mass of foam and wind-whipped spray for as far as the eye could see, making the "Perfect Storm" seem like a few ripples.

For what felt like hours, we pounded on through this maelstrom with the water cascading over us in sheets with every wave we hit. It stopped being fun a long time before it occurred to me that we could die here. Finally, we admitted defeat and turned to the near shore. We made our way behind a finger of land that protected part of the bay enough to reach shore without smashing on the rocks. From there, we walked to a derelict cabin where we would spend a long, wet and cold night. Everything, including my custom Bansner rifle, was soaked with salt water, but there was nothing to be done to clean or dry any of it until we could get back to our camp. Clearly that would not happen on this night.

This was my third hunting trip to Alaska in as many years, and every one of them has been an endurance test for me and my rifles. It rains just about all the time and much of the hunting has been from tent camps where drying gear is but a wistful dream. It's a harsh environment to take a rifle into. But then, so are most places game is hunted.

In almost forty years of big game hunting, I have also used rifles in bitter cold, raging snowstorms, relentless sleet and blistering heat. I have hunted in the winter above the Arctic Circle where the wind chills were gusting to nearly seventy below zero Fahrenheit. We were living in a small tent with no floor other than a few caribou hides. It was so crowded that my rifle had to stay outside in the sled. At the other extreme, I hunted in the Zambezi River Valley of Zimbabwe in October when the temperatures were hitting more than 110 degrees Fahrenheit. Or another time hunting on the Yucatán peninsula in southern Mexico in May, when it was just as hot and a lot more humid.

Henry Ford was quoted as saying that the American buyer could have his car in any color they wanted, as long as it was black. That same variety of options applied for years to rifle stocks; a hunter could have any material he wanted as long as it was wood. The problem with wood in extreme weather is that it can absorb water and change dimensionally. We have all seen that when our screen door sticks during a humid spell in the summer. It sticks because the wood fibers have swollen from the water they absorbed. It's an annoyance when it happens to a door, but can be a disaster when it's a rifle stock. The metal to wood fit in a rifle is critical to how well a rifle functions. Bedding, which is the way the action and barrel mate to the wood, is important to accuracy and, in extreme examples, to function. The bedding may be perfect during a hot, dry summer day but a week of hunting in the rain will change the moisture content of the wood. This can lead to point of impact changes, accuracy problems and sometimes rifles that no longer work.

I love to read the work of the early gun writers and much of it is filled with tales of rifle stocks that caused problems after being exposed to harsh weather. In one story the rifle was unusable until they chopped the stock away with a hatchet! But today we rarely hear about this happening, for a couple of reasons. First is that most serious hunters who know they are going to be out and about in harsh weather use rifles with synthetic or laminated wood stocks. Both of these are resistant to absorbing water. Synthetic simply doesn't do it and the laminated wood is impregnated with a resin that seals the fibers.

Still, a lot of hunters use rifles with "plain ol' wood" stocks today and report few problems. The reason is simple enough: the coatings used for finishing the wood today are much better at repelling water than those used in the "olden days." Back then they used a lot of oil finishes

I do seem to recall one hunting trip in all those years when it wasn't cold, raining, snowing, sleeting, hot, windy or humid. We didn't see or shoot a damn thing. The truth is, hunting almost always exposes you and your gun to some of the harshest conditions possible.

While I have witnessed several, I have personally never had a weather related functional failure when the time came to shoot. I'll be the first to admit that some of that is luck, but a lot is because I think ahead. The key to keeping your rifle operating and/or keeping it from turning into a rusted, decrepit junker is in preparation. Preparing a gun for foul weather is a simple, but important, project for a hobby gunsmith.

The strategy in keeping a hunting rifle functioning and pretty is in recognizing the enemy. Weather-directed attacks generally come in two forms: temperature and moisture. Address these issues and you have most potential problems under control.

In repelling the ravages of moisture, the first step is in selecting the materials used for your rifle. Hunting rifles might be better approached with a pragmatic design rather than picking a gun for its aesthetics. Extreme hunting is really not the place for fine walnut and highly polished metal. These make for a wonderful looking rifle, but they rarely stay pretty for long. A smart hunter considers function over form in choosing a rifle.

Ruger M-77 MK II SS

WEATHER AND MOISTURE

Applying thinned polyurethane.

Sealing all exposed wood.

Applying paste wax.

that looked and smelled great, but didn't provide a barrier protection against moisture entering the wood. Today, we have high-tech finishes that seal the wood against moisture entering. However, the gunmakers cut corners in the places you can't see. Any wood stock should be removed from the rifle and sealed in all the hidden uncoated areas that many gunmakers skip.

Use a good grade of polyurethane and thin it according to the instructions on the can. Coat all the unfinished surfaces evenly with a thin coat. That includes the barrel channel, action and along the sides of the magazine well. Also remove the butt pad and grip cap and coat the end grain of the stock. The wood should absorb the thinned polyurethane. Allow it to dry and apply another coat. Continue until it is no longer absorbed. Finish with a single coat of uncut polyurethane in the areas that have a critical tolerance, such as where the action is bedded. The barrel channel and butt end where tolerances are less critical can get another coat or two. Make sure you have sealed every exposed wood surface. If water can't reach the wood, it can't be absorbed.

Or better yet, put the pretty wood stock in the closet until after hunting season and replace it with an aftermarket synthetic stock. Fit and glass bed it as detailed elsewhere in this book and you have a weatherproof, perfectly fitted rifle stock. After the hunting season is over, put the pretty wood back on the rifle.

The other problem that water can create is plain old-fashioned rust on any or all ferrous metal parts, including stainless steel. When the conditions are extreme and you do not always have the ability to properly care for your rifle, stainless steel has a bigger insurance policy in its greater resistance to rust and corrosion than does carbon steel, but stainless steel can rust. Both will stay rustproof if you can keep them protected with a barrier agent that keeps the water away from the metal, but that's not always possible. For hunters spending a lot of time in wet weather, one option is to have the metal permanently coated with a protecting agent. One very good option is DuraCoat, which is explained in another chapter. If you like the looks of your rifle, you can apply the clear DuraCoat which will maintain the appearance of the rifle, but provide a permanent protective barrier to the metal. Just remember that the bore and some internal and/or action parts are not coated, so they need other protective steps.

The concept with DuraCoat is basically the same as how oil protects your rifle, by creating a barrier between the water and the steel. The difference is that unlike oil or other chemicals, the coatings are permanent. You can change the color of the rifle, or put on a clear coat that only protects the gun, but either way adds material.

Spraying degreaser into a rifle trigger to clean and remove oil.

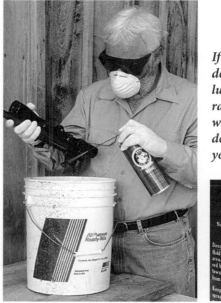

If the label doesn't say a lubricant is rated for cold weather use, do not use it on your rifle.

The other option is a chemical coating of some sort. The problem is oil or other coatings wear off rather quickly. Some of the new hightech waterproofing agents actually penetrate into the pores of the metal, which makes their protection last longer, but they, too, will wear off over time and with use.

The outside of a rifle can be covered with paste wax, which is said to last longer than oil or spray-on water barriers. This is particularly useful for areas of metal that are hidden by the stock, such as the underside of the receiver and barrel. These are always problem areas when using the rifle for extended periods in extreme weather. Applied protections often do not last for long, but a layer of paste wax will last through most hunting trips. However, it should not be used on any internal parts; instead, use a spray-on protector from a company that specializes in gun care products. Don't forget the chamber and bore of the rifle. Caution must be used here not to have a buildup or too thick a layer, as that can affect performance and perhaps even create a dangerous situation. Coat the surface with a rust protector, wait a few minutes and then wipe it off. In extreme weather, you should reapply daily. Even on backcountry hunts I take a small multi-section rod, a few patches and a small bottle of metal protector and lubricant. I try to tend to my rifle every evening. (Except, of course, those where I am stranded in the bush with no heat, no food and little shelter, as was the case in Alaska!)

Extreme cold presents another set of problems that must be dealt with in the shop before the hunting season. Cold can cause oil or grease in a firearm to gel up and prevent the gun from firing. I have seen congealed oil and grease inside a bolt stop the firing pin from moving or slow it down enough to cause misfires several times when the temperatures approached zero Fahrenheit. I have also seen a buildup of oil, grease and dirt make a trigger inoperable in cold weather.

Any rifle you will be using in cold weather should be completely degreased and relubricated with a product designed for use in extreme cold. Disassemble the bolt and/or action. If you have a parts cleaning tank, soak the parts well and use a brush to remove all dirt, oil or grease. Then dry with shop air and repeat.

When the gun is free from grease, gunk and dirt buildup, spray with a no-residue aerosol degreaser and let it run off to remove all traces of solvent. If you do not have a parts cleaning tank, use a good aerosol spray degreaser designed for use on gun parts. Work outdoors and with safety glasses, rubber gloves and a painting mask. Hold the parts over a bucket to collect the runoff

for proper disposal. Spray all the parts, letting the liquid run off so that it flushes the grease away. Work at stubborn deposits with an old toothbrush that is saturated with the degreaser. Direct the spray into all the little nooks and crannies until you have all the parts clean and free of any buildup. After they dry, the metal is chemically clean and it is subject to rusting very quickly, so immediately coat every surface with a combination protector/lubricant, making absolutely sure that the manufacturer guarantees it for use in extreme cold. If it doesn't say it works to at least −30 degrees, don't use it. The old standby is dry lubricant like graphite, which still works fine for lubrication, but provides little, if any, rust protection.

Also use the degreasing spray to clean the action of the rifle, including the bolt lug raceways. Do not attempt to take your trigger apart, but instead spray the trigger assembly from every possible angle and direct the spray into every hole and opening. Let the liquid flush away all the dirt and grease. After it dries, lightly spray a protector/lubricator, then shake out and wipe up any excess.

Finally, realizing that while these steps will help ensure that your rifle functions in extreme weather, resign yourself to the fact that a hunting rifle is going to show some use and is not going to look showroom pretty forever. You can keep it working, but the finish is going to carry the evidence of hard use. It's a badge of experience, show it with pride.

If you are going to hunt where the weather is harsh and unpredictable, prepare your rifle, but also bring a space blanket and a pocketful of granola bars. As I know all too well from experience, they may be what "gets you through the night."

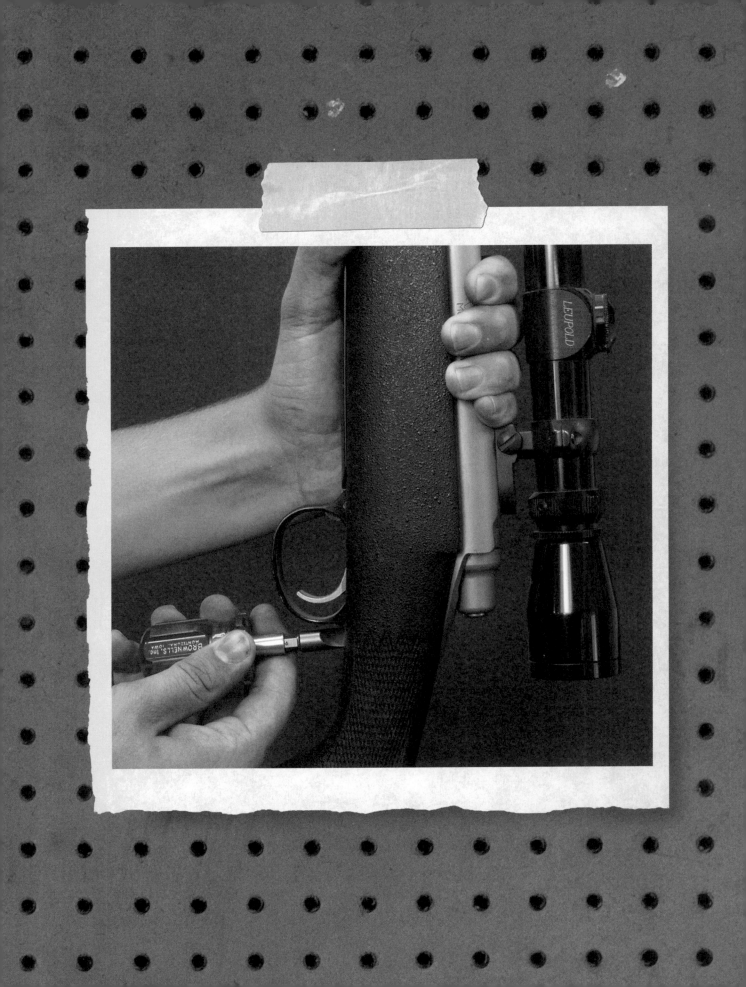

Enhancing Accuracy
Chapter 4

A common problem that a hobby gunsmith must deal with is poor rifle accuracy. Many of our projects are intended to increase the inherent accuracy of a rifle, but we are often called on to fix a gun that is suddenly not shooting as it should. These rifles gone rogue are both perplexing and aggravating, but a simple step-by-step approach can help eliminate the problem. Think of any rogue rifle as a puzzle to be solved by following a logical plan in a linear, step-by-step manner. First, keep it sensible. If it's not your rifle, take it out and shoot it. More often than not, accuracy problems are really shooter problems. Also, make sure you keep it all in perspective. Rifle design and cartridge selection will dictate the inherent accuracy of any rifle. It is unreasonable to expect that a lever action deer rifle will shoot as well as a bolt-action varmint rig. Nor should we expect a .30-30 Winchester to shoot as accurately as a 6mm PPC. Certain cartridges have a lot more inherent accuracy than others.

If you are dealing with a new rifle or one that you are working on for somebody else, experiment to determine what load the rifle likes best. If that doesn't correct the problem, try the following. Clean the bore down to bare metal and remove all fouling. Next, check all of the screws to be sure they are tight. Remove them one at a time and if any are loose, apply Loctite before replacing. Remove the stock to look inside and near the screw holes for cracks. If its' still not shooting accurately replace the scope.

If nothing changes, examine the bedding, particularly on a wood-stocked rifle where humidity can cause changes. Synthetic stocks can fail as well, especially the cheaper injection-molded types. You can sometimes detect bedding problems by holding the action at the junction of the metal and wood and alternately loosening and tightening the action screws. You should be able to feel unwanted movement that you can't see.

Another common bedding problem occurs when the stock contacts the barrel improperly. To check for adequate clearance with floating barrels, wrap a dollar bill around the barrel with the ends pointing up and slide it along between the barrel and the stock. It should pass easily for the length of the barrel, unless the rifle has a hard contact near the forend. Any drag or sticking indicates that the stock may be contacting the barrel and affecting accuracy. Removing material from the offending area will usually correct this problem. Bedding-induced accuracy problems can usually be easily corrected by glass- or pillar-bedding the action and floating the barrel.

Finally, if you still can't make it shoot and there are no obvious defects, consider a new barrel, the old one might be shot out or is just no good. Or maybe it's simply a rifle that needs to be traded.

But usually when you have done these things, the rifle will shoot much better and poor accuracy is no longer an excuse for missing, so you will need to find a new one.

The wind works for me.

Re-Crown a Rifle Muzzle

Eddie Stevenson checking zero in Argentina.

" **O**nly accurate rifles are interesting."

—Col. Townsend Whelen

I can't say I agree with the good Colonel on this because I have had some poor shooting rifles that were damn interesting. But I will concede that accurate rifles are a lot less aggravating.

If you have accuracy problems with a gun and load that has always shot well and has suddenly gone sour, my advice is to take these steps. First, clean the bore until all copper fouling is removed. This can take an unbelievable amount of time and work to get it right. But in about half the cases, it will fix the accuracy problem. When somebody brings a rifle to my shop that's not shooting well, the first thing I do is clean the bore. Most of them will argue with me and say, "I already cleaned the gun and you are wasting your time." I wonder why they brought the gun to me in the first place if they already know more than I do about the problem. But, I don't argue. I just clean the gun and if it's shooting accurately again, I don't even tell them what I did. I just let them think I am a miracle worker.

Next, check that all screws are tight and that the stock has not cracked or warped. Still not shooting? Replace the scope. If it's still not back to its former accuracy potential, re-crown the barrel.

The crown is the point in the muzzle that is at the end of the barrel. It's the last place that the rifle has any physical influence on the bullet and it is critical that it be perfect. The crown must be perfectly square with the bore, perfectly round and free from any defects. Even the slightest imperfection can impact the bullet as it exits the barrel and have an adverse affect on accuracy. One of the major rifle makers in the country told me that when a rifle comes in for repair with a poor accuracy complaint and no obvious defect is found, the first thing they do is re-crown the muzzle. In a surprising number of cases that corrects the problem.

I have seen a lot of poor crowns right from the factory.

These tools are used to reface the end of the barrel and to recut the crown. Left to right: 45-degree muzzle crown cutter, brass muzzle crowning lap, 90-degree muzzle facing cutter and brass pilot. Lapping compound and cutting oil.

I have one .45-70 rifle that had a big ding in the crown when I received the rifle. It would only shoot into about three inches at 100 yards. I re-crowned the barrel and now it groups at half that. A lot more rifle crowns have become damaged in the field. It only takes a moment of inattention to set the muzzle down on a jagged rock and the damage is done. But, the best way I know to ruin a rifle crown is by riding in the truck with the muzzle of the rifle down on the floorboard. The collected dirt and sand on the floor is abrasive and it grinds away at the delicate edges of the crown. If you must have the gun pointing down in a vehicle, at least protect the muzzle with something to keep it out of the dirt.

The simplest way to correct minor crown damage is with an inexpensive Brownells Brass Muzzle Crowning Lap. This is a tapered "cone" of brass with a stem to allow it to be inserted into a drill. Another style they offer is a large brass rod with the end rounded. Some old-timers used a large round head brass machine screw, and the Brownells tool is basically a commercial version of that. The idea is to "lap" the final edge of the bore until it is completely concentric and at a perfect 90-degree angle to the bore, smooth and free from any imperfections. The tapered brass lapping tool will ride in the bore and is self-centering. By slightly wobbling the tool as you work and by reversing the direction of rotation any minor imbalances or imperfections are compensated for and the crown will be true to the axis of the bore.

Before starting, plug the bore of the rifle with a tight fitting cloth patch and leave it about three or four inches down from the muzzle. Put the lapping tool in a variable speed ⅜-inch drill, coat it well with 600 grit lapping compound and insert it into the bore until it contacts the muzzle. Start the drill and rotate the lapping tool at slow-to-moderate speed while slightly wobbling the drill. After ten seconds or so, reverse the direction of rotation and continue to wobble the drill. It's better to work slow and check the results often. So, stop and wipe the compound off the muzzle and check your progress after ten seconds of rotation in each direction. There will be a bright ring on the muzzle from the lapping compound wearing away the metal. When it's complete, it should be completely around the bore and extend to the bottom of each of the rifling grooves and to the top of the lands. The best way to inspect it is with a magnifying glass or

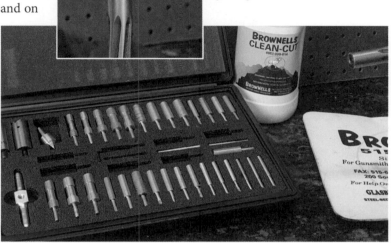

Brownells Brass Muzzle Crowning Lap on rifle barrel.

Brownells Chamfering & Facing Combo Set with pilots and cutters for crowning and facing barrels.

with a magnifying headset like those used by jewelers. If the ring is still not complete, put some more lapping compound on the tool and continue.

Keep working and checking until you have a clearly defined ring all around the muzzle, all the way to the inside edge and all the way to the bottom of the rifling lands. When that is complete, you are done. It's that simple.

If you want a more professional and contemporary looking job, consider using Brownells Muzzle Crowning Cutter with the appropriate pilot to cut a new crown. *See sidebar on page 100.* Brownells' also offers a cutter to square up the muzzle called the Muzzle Facing Tool, which squares the muzzle to the bore. If you have cut off the barrel this will also face off the barrel square with the bore, which is necessary before crowning. On an existing rifle, it's usually not necessary to reface the muzzle, but it makes for a more finished look. Use the muzzle facing cutter first and remember to use plenty of cutting oil with any cutter. Insert the pilot in the bore and turn the cutter until you have achieved the desired result. The cutter can be turned by hand or with a hand held drill. Use a very light touch with the cutter. If you use too much pressure, the blades can chatter, and once that happens it's very hard to correct when turning the cutter by hand. That's because the cutter will follow the contours of the surface

CORRECTING CROWN DAMAGE

1. Caliper measuring a pilot. It's critical that the pilot fit the bore of the barrel when cutting a new crown or facing the barrel.

2. Brownells Muzzle Crowning Cutter with paper pilot attached.

3. Shows the Brownells Muzzle Facing Tool in use. This tool cuts the face of the barrel square with the bore.

4. This rifle muzzle has been faced off with the Brownells Muzzle Facing Tool and then re-crowned with a 45-degree cutter.

created by the chatter and will simply keep repeating the same cuts and deepening the waves created by the chatter. To correct this problem, use the stop that Brownells sells which fits on the cutter. This stop will not allow the cutter blades to drop down into the valleys created by the chatter. This ensures a constant contact with the cutter that will hit only the high points and so will correct the "waves" created by the cutter chatter.

Next, put the pilot on the crown cutter and cut an 11-degree crown. (Actually it's 79 degrees, but it's commonly called 11-degree. That's because 90 degrees, minus 11 degrees is 79 degrees.) This is a very popular type of muzzle crown and is said by some to enhance accuracy. If you prefer, Brownells also has a 45-degree cutter that can be used for a deeper angled crown and one that can be made deeper in the barrel so that it is better protected from field damage. Finally, finish with a brass lapping tool to just break the edge.

Just remember that the metal will be bare after cutting. You can leave it like that or re-blue or finish it with a coating. Either way, it must be protected from rust.

Push the plug out of the barrel from rear to front. Then wipe the bore with a few solvent-soaked patches to clean the residual lapping compound. Always work from the rear or action end of the gun and push the patches out of the muzzle so that the gunk is not pushed into the action. Finish with a dry patch.

The Experience of Glass Bedding a Rifle Stock

This stock has the action and first few inches of the barrel bedded.

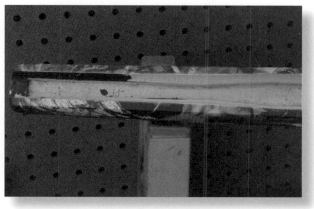

"Experientia docet" (Experience teaches) — Cornelius Tacitus

Wise words from one of the world's greatest histor-ians. But, no less a social commentator, Oscar Wilde said, "Experience is the name everyone gives to their mistakes."

It is no secret that glass bedding a rifle stock can often do wonders for the accuracy. If you believe all you read on the subject, it's also an example of a home gunsmith project that anybody with a few basic tools and at least a rudimentary ability to manipulate them can complete with wonderful results.

Don't believe everything you read.

In the early days of synthetic hunting rifle stocks, I decided I needed one. When my order arrived, what was in the box might have passed for a rifle stock, but barely.

It was a crude lay-up that lacked everything from a butt pad to holes for the action screws. I spent days sanding, drilling, shaping and filing. Then I mixed up about two pounds of bedding compound and filled the stock to the brim before bolting everything into place.

I am first to admit that I am not good with "sticky substances." So when all that excess bedding compound squirted out, I should have asked for help or at least not panicked. But I did neither. I was so focused on cleaning up the gun that by the time I noticed the big glob on the floor, I had already walked in it several times. In my many trips to the kitchen for more paper towels, I had a nice, even layer of bedding compound making a defined path on the carpeted cellar stairs and throughout the house. The stuff seemed to breed and reproduce and like the 1958 Steve McQueen movie *The Blob*, I thought it would soon

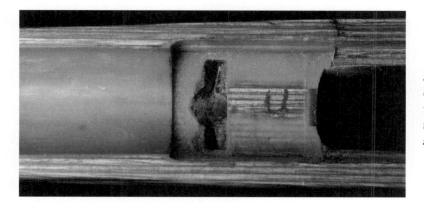

Note the support area left on the stock before bedding. This makes contact with the action, while the bedding fills in the areas that are cut away to the same level.

Materials and tools used for glass bedding.

Laminated stock ready for bedding work.

fill the world. What wasn't on the carpet or the kitchen's vinyl floor was on my shirt or in my hair.

None of it was "water soluble."

The directions recommended using vinegar to clean up, great if you have some on hand. I did not. In rushing to the store to buy vinegar, I didn't notice that I had bedding compound all over my pants, which transferred nicely to my truck seat. All the vinegar really did anyway was smear the compound around more and give everything a funky smell.

One way or the other, all messes clean up eventually and most marriages survive them. The next day I was ready to remove the barreled action from the stock. I had "bedded" the entire gun in one operation, pushing the action deep into the stock, and compound had squirted into all the holes and filled every void. After several hours of trying to separate the parts, I finally read the directions that came with the bedding kit, which mention all these things. Mostly stuff about not doing them.

Hours later, I found a gunsmithing book that suggested chopping the stock off the action with an ax, but before I went to the shed to get my hatchet I decided to give it one last shot. Back then I was young, and working every day in a telephone company line crew. I was as strong as I'll ever be in my life and I put all I had into the effort. With the gun on the bench and one knee on the stock, I yanked first on the barrel, and then on the wooden dowel in the action, alternating back and forth

Hand chisels and scraper.

until suddenly everything popped free! I fell backward off the stool I was standing on (with one foot) and the barreled action crashed beside me on the cement floor, breaking the trigger assembly off.

I have glass bedded dozens of rifles in the years since. And while there were damn few mistakes I didn't make on that first one, these years of experience have allowed me to correct that, and I think I have a complete collection now. So if you will allow me to teach you with my "experiences," I will make some suggestions on how to glass bed your rifle with a minimum of pain and aggravation.

First, read the directions. Like most guys, I wait until I am in trouble before taking this step. That's why I get in trouble. Next, make sure you have everything you need to complete the job on hand before you start. That includes materials to clean up any messes. Finally, go slow, pay attention to details and take it one step at a time. Every time I try to hurry or cut corners I get into trouble.

These instructions are for wood or wood laminate stocks, but they apply to most of the better synthetic stocks as well. The exception being inexpensive injection molded synthetic stocks. Bedding compound will stick to wood, metal, paper, concrete, carpet, hair, skin, glass and every known substance in the modern universe, except an injection molded rifle stock. I don't know who the genius was that came up with the material for those stocks, but if my kitchen floor had been covered with it instead of that expensive Armstrong vinyl, I would have had a

BEDDING FOR WOOD AND WOOD LAMINATE

1. Using a hand grinder to cut away a thin layer of stock material in front of the magazine and in the recoil lug mortise.

3. When removing wood from the action area in preparation for glass bedding, be sure to leave a section for support.

2. Using a small chisel to cut away stock material and rough the surface to prepare for glass bedding.

4. Shows completed stock bedding. Note the numbers imprinted in compound which illustrates the "skin-tight" fit. Note that the bedding at top does not contact the barrel. On left is a laminated stock before bedding.

much happier wife all those years ago. If you are bedding an injection molded stock, there are other steps that will be covered later which must be used to ensure the bedding stays in place.

To get started, first remove the bolt, then the scope, if for nothing else to protect it from damage. Then remove the action screws and take the rifle apart. Slide the magazine follower spring out of the floor plate and place it and the magazine box in a safe place. Place the stock in a cradle or gun vise that will hold it while you work.

Using a hand chisel, scraper or a small electric hand grinder, remove a thin layer of wood everywhere under the action in front of the magazine and in the recoil lug mortise, except for two support sections. To create these, leave a small strip about ½ inch wide between the action screw and the recoil lug mortise. This is to support the action at the proper height until the bedding compound has hardened. Do the same where the recoil lug face contacts the stock in the recoil lug mortise on the load-bearing side. This prevents the action from moving back in the stock. What you are doing is supporting the action and the recoil lug, which keeps the action in exactly the position it was already in. But, by removing the material from everywhere except those two support locations, you

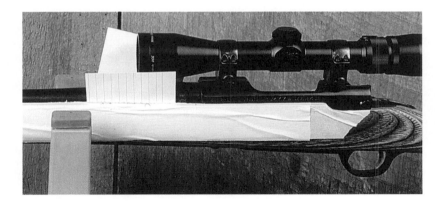

After preparation, the rifle is assembled and a cardboard index card is used to check for clearance between the barrel and the stock.

Masking tape on the stock to protect it from excess bedding compound.

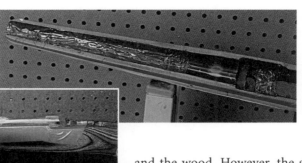

Bedding compound in the barrel channel for full-length bedding of the barrel.

have created a gap for the bedding compound to fill.

A master stock maker will spend hours smoking the action, trying the gun, and then scraping away the high points in the bedding as indicated by the black smudges. Then trying it again and scraping again, and again, and again, and again until there is a perfect match. But with glass bedding, the miracle of modern technology allows you to create the same or an even better fit in a fraction of the time. The idea is that the compound will mirror exactly the surface of the action. The match is so good that often in the completed job you can see the machining marks on the metal reflected in the bedding compound. That gives a complete contact with the load-bearing surfaces, which creates a solid and even match between the stock and the action. There will be no twisting, torque or uneven stresses placed on the action with a correctly bedded rifle. Instead, the stock and action mate in perfect harmony. The stock's job is to support the barrel and action and to allow the shooter to hold and aim the rifle. It should never induce any flexing or stress on the action and in a nutshell that is what you are trying to achieve here, equilibrium between the two parts of the gun.

Don't worry about keeping the areas you cut away in the stock neat or smooth. Actually, the rougher the surface, the more contact area for the bedding compound to mate with. The idea is to create a gap between the metal

and the wood. However, the small strips you leave in place ensures that the action sits in the same place as it did before you removed the wood. Because the bedding compound will match with them exactly, the supports left in place will transition to the compound seamlessly once the job is complete. Running your finger over the stock support to the compound will show no change in dimension if things are done correctly.

Once this is complete, put the gun back together (without the magazine "guts") and snug the screws, but not tight enough to crush the small supports you left. Wrap an index card, business card or similar piece of thin cardboard around the barrel and slide it between the barrel and stock to make sure there is clearance. For a tight fit, a dollar bill works very well. If the stock is contacting the barrel, mark the spot with a pencil on the top of the stock that corresponds to the tight area and after taking the rifle apart, remove the wood from the offending area. A barrel-bedding scraper makes this easier, but sandpaper and patience will work. Wrap the sandpaper around a large wooden dowel to help maintain the contours. But, the best way is to use a Barrel Bedding Tool available from Brownells. This is a series of round cutters mounted on a contoured rod with a handle at each end. The cutters maintain the round contours of the barrel channel while cutting with each stroke. They will not dig in or gouge, but take a nice even cut each time. These are available in several different diameters to match the barrel you are bedding. In terms of time saved and aggravation avoided, this is a "must have" for stock work and I have several in my shop.

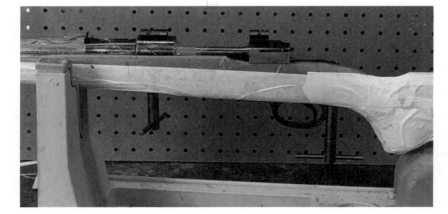

A rifle fitted with stock maker's hand screws during the bedding process. These T-screws are handy when doing work that requires assembling the stock and action often. Note that the stock is covered with masking tape to prevent any compound from sticking to it.

What happens under the barrel will not show, but remember that the inside edge of the barrel channel along the top of the stock will. So, go very carefully when working on this top edge of the barrel channel. Put the gun back together and check the clearance again. Repeat until the only places in front of the magazine making contact are the thin strips of wood you left to support the action and recoil lug. The action and barrel should sit

Brownells' bedding tape and .010-inch pipe wrap

high enough in the stock so that the centerline is above the top edge of the stock; this is particularly important with a round action like the Remington Model 700. The barrel should fit evenly in the barrel channel without big gaps, including underneath at the forend tip. You may want to make adjustments by removing more wood from the action support area to allow it to sit deeper or by placing a shim under the action to raise it higher. A strip of plastic or wood super-glued to the stock works fine for a shim. You can simply leave it in when bedding and surround it with compound so it won't show, except where it contacts the rifle.

Cover all the outside surfaces of the stock with masking tape. Overlap it into the barrel channel and use a sharp razor blade to trim it to the edge. I find it best to cover the entire stock with masking tape. Sooner or later you will have bedding compound on your fingers while handling the stock and the resulting "fingerprints" can be tough to remove without damaging the finish. Fill the magazine cutout and any other places you do not want bedding compound to flow into with clay.

Degrease the metal parts of the barreled action with a spray degreaser. Fill the magazine gap in the action with clay, as well as any screw holes or other places that should not have compound in them. On some actions, you can cover the magazine opening in the action with tape. Cover the recoil lug with two layers of masking tape, except on the load bearing rear face. This will create a gap around the recoil lug so that it does not contact the stock, except where it transfers the recoil.

I usually bed the first few inches of the barrel and float the rest. To do this, place two layers of 2-inch electrician's tape along the barrel. Or better yet, use Brownells .010-inch-thick pipe wrap tape. This 2-inch tape is the right thickness for a perfect floated barrel. It will also work in a single layer on the recoil lug. Masking tape will not work for floating the barrel, it is too absorbent and will stick to the compound. This makes it hard to remove and does not leave as nice a finished product. End the tape where you want the bedding to end and cut the end square. The tape will create a gap between the bedding and the barrel. Try putting the gun together to make sure the tape isn't hitting the barrel channel and preventing assembly. This is one of those things best discovered before you have the bedding compound in place. If the fit is too tight, switch to a single layer of tape, or open the barrel channel up a little more.

Now paint the entire barreled action with the release agent supplied with the bedding compound. Coat all the metal, tape and clay. Let it dry and repeat. Hold the gun

Rifle action and stock with clay filling the action and magazine opening to keep bedding compound out. Stock has masking tape to protect against overflow of bedding compound.

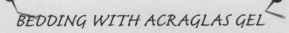

BEDDING WITH ACRAGLAS GEL

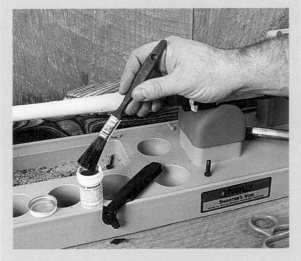

Painting release agent on barreled action before glass bedding. Note tape on barrel to create gap for floating barrel.

Acraglas Gel with dyes, thinner atomized metal and release.

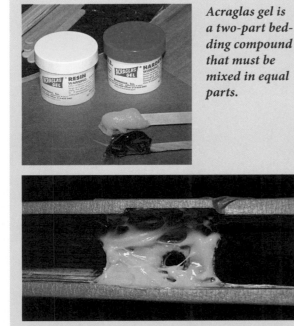

Acraglas gel is a two-part bedding compound that must be mixed in equal parts.

The recoil lug and the action area of the stock is filled with bedding compound.

under a light to make sure you have complete coverage. Let the release agent dry completely. Even though you will not be bedding the end section of the barrel, coat it anyway. You will handle it with compound on your fingers and if you don't, it will be very hard to remove the mess without damaging the bluing. (One tip—if you have "fingerprints" of compound on the metal that you are having trouble removing, try some Hoppe's #9 solvent. It will often remove stubborn spots of unwanted compound.) Don't forget to coat the action screws and inside the holes, as well as the trigger guard and bottom metal. Coat the tape along the top and down the sides of the stock. Be careful not to get release agent on the inside where you want the bedding compound to stick. Coat anything you do not want bedding compound to stick to. In my case I should probably coat my entire body, all my tools, my workbench, the shop walls and from past experience my wife's kitchen floor. But, I usually just coat the gun parts I don't want to stick and take my chances with the rest.

The best bedding compound I have used is Brownells Acraglas Gel. This two-part epoxy is mixed in equal parts. The package comes with brown and black dye which can be added to match the color of the stock. After mixing according to the instructions, use a flat "Popsicle" stick (I buy mine in big boxes at the local arts and craft store) to butter the compound on the stock around the recoil lug, action and the first few inches of the barrel channel. It's always best to bed one section of the gun at a time. For example, bed the forward action and recoil lug area in one step. If you are to bed the barrel or the rear of the action, do those in their own separate steps. Use a Q-Tip to make sure the hole for the action screw is clean of bedding compound. Put another Q-Tip into the screw hole in the action and guide the other end through the hole in the stock as you carefully place the barreled action into the stock. After the action is seated, pull the Q-Tip out through the bottom of the stock. This clears much of the passage for the stock screw. Use a few more Q-Tips to make sure the action screw hole is clean and free of compound. Then attach the bottom metal and replace the action screws. Snug them tight, but not too tight. You want the action fully seated, but not crushing the fibers in the stock where you left those small support sections.

Clean up the compound that oozes out. A Popsicle stick that has been cut to match the contours of the barrel works well. Then leave the gun alone overnight. Resist the temptation to "check" on it until the bedding compound has fully hardened. The next day, remove the action screws, turn the gun over and clamp it in the cradle.

Place a wooden dowel in the action and holding the stock down, alternate upward pressure on the dowel and the barrel. Keep rocking back and forth until the action comes free. If you have trouble, put the gun in the freezer for a few hours to contract the metal. Because the metal will contract at a faster rate than the compound, this will often break the adhesion. Or if, like me, you live in the north, putting the gun outside the shop if it's cold enough works too. Last winter I was bedding a stock and having trouble. It was 20 degrees below zero outside, which is a lot colder than my freezer. I just put the gun on the picnic table outside the shop. But I did it quickly.

If you still have trouble, Brownells sells a slide hammer tool that will "snap" the action free from the bedding compound. (Sure wish I had that on my first rifle!) It uses a rod in the action and the slide hammer is a weight that slides up a rod that is threaded at 90 degrees into the rod in the action. A stop at the end of this rod arrests the motion of the sliding hammer and transfers the energy to the shaft, and consequently to the action.

Once the action is free from the stock, use a small knife, dental pick or screwdriver to pick the tape out of the recoil lug mortise. The compound is still soft and will cut or file easily to clean up the areas where it does not belong. Usually, you will smooth the top of the stock with a small file to even the compound with the wood. Work carefully so that you do not damage the finish on the stock.

If there are gaps or missed spots, they really don't hurt anything unless they are excessive. But it looks better to fill them in and they can be filled by repeating the process. Just remember to clean the release agent off so the compound will stick. Use a cotton swab and lacquer thinner. If the release agent is water soluble, I usually put the stock in my laundry sink and scrub it under running water with a soft bristle brush. Then I let the stock dry for a couple of days. It's also a good idea to "rough up" the surface in the voids with a hand grinder to ensure a good surface for the new compound to adhere to.

To bed the barrel channel, simply keep the two layers of tape on the barrel, but recoat everything with release agent. Butter the barrel channel with bedding compound and put the rifle together. After the compound hardens, you can remove the barreled action and remove the tape. The gap left from the tape will give you a smooth and consistent gap between the barrel and the stock for a perfect free-floating barrel. This layer of compound will also provide a waterproof coating on the wood stock to prevent moisture from entering, and will add strength to the stock to resist warping.

If you are going to bed the rear of the action, repeat the process until you have completed everything. Often though, I find that bedding the action ahead of the magazine and floating the barrel is enough to make the gun shoot well and that bedding the rear of the action is not necessary. So my suggestion is to shoot the gun before deciding to bed any more of the action, unless you have an obvious fitting problem.

When all bedding is complete and the compound cured, remove all the clay, masking tape and release agent. Coat any exposed wood with a sealer. Wipe the metal down with a rust protector and put the gun back together, including the magazine parts and the scope. The action should fit tightly into the stock with no rocking or movement as you alternately tighten and loosen the screws. Finish with the screws snug but not tight. Check the barrel channel for clearance. If it's good, put the gun away for a week to let the

This stock has been glass bedded around the action. Accuracy was improved by this work. Glass bedding a stock is easy enough that anybody can do it, and it can make a dramatic difference in accuracy.

HOW TO GLASS BED A RIFLE STOCK

Masking tape on the stock to protect it from excess bedding compound.

Bedding compound in place for the action, recoil lug and the first few inches of the barrel.

Place a Q-Tip in the action screw hole before placing the barreled action in the stock. This prevents the bedding compound from entering the hole, and when you pull it out it clears the path for the screw.

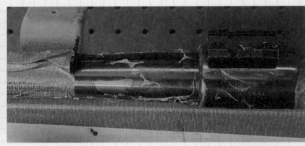

Shows the gun together during the bedding. Note the bedding compound along the edges. Note that the stock is covered with masking tape to prevent any compound from sticking to it.

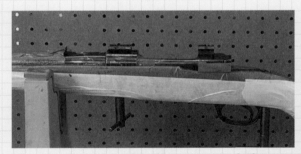

The assembled rifle with bedding compound. Shows the bedding compound oozing out around edges.

This rifle stock shows how the glass bedding job is a good fit on the action and recoil lug, but has gaps that need filling in the area under the barrel.

Illustrates how the slide hammer fits into the action. This tool from Brownells is used to separate a barreled action and stock after bedding.

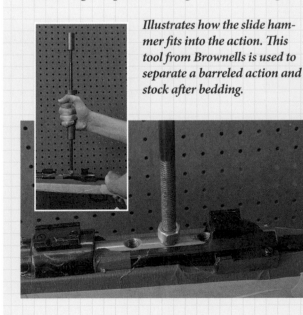

Using a file to clean up the overflow of bedding compound.

Shows completed stock bedding. Note the numbers imprinted in compound. This illustrates the "skin-tight" fit. Note area of bedding at top that is not contacting barrel.

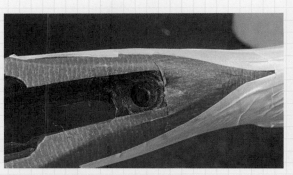

Bedding the tang area on the stock.

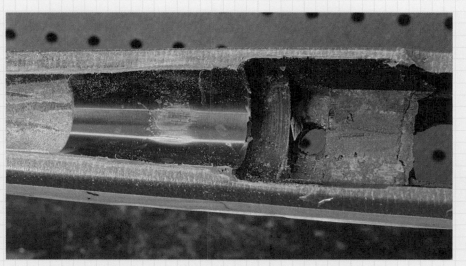

Illustrates the bedding compound after bedding. Note the sharp edge that ends the barrel bedding. This is created by using tape on the barrel.

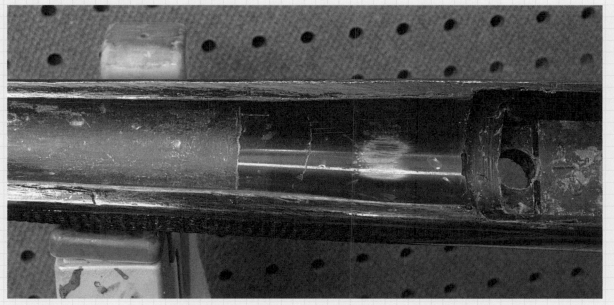

This stock has the action and first few inches of the barrel bedded. The barrel channel in the stock was also bedded using tape on the barrel as a spacer. This strengthens the stock and waterproofs the area that is bedded.

CORRECTING WARPING PROBLEMS IN A WOOD STOCK

One way to help correct that is to first remove enough wood so that the barrel is floated and there is enough clearance for bedding compound as well as the double layer of 2-inch electrician's tape or Brownells' .010-inch pipe wrap tape. This may result in a big gap between the barrel and the stock on both sides of the barrel, but that's unavoidable. It will later be filled in with bedding compound. But be advised, the line between the stock and the compound will show, so try to keep the lines straight.

Now use a hand grinder or a chisel to cut a channel in the bottom of the stock, deep enough to accept a ¼-inch steel rod with plenty of clearance above it. Cut a piece of ¼-inch threaded rod to the proper length, degrease it, put it in the bottom of the channel and make sure that you have at least ⅛-inch clearance between it and the bottom of the barrel channel. Tape off the stock, but leave the top of the sides along the barrel channel uncovered and free from release agent. Bed the barrel, using plenty of compound and making sure that you completely fill the channel and bury the rod in compound. Dye the compound to match the color of the stock as closely as possible, as it will be showing along the top of the barrel channel. Let the compound ooze out the top and then clean it off with a Popsicle stick, but leave it higher than the top edge of the stock. After it hardens and you remove the barreled action, you can file and sand the compound down even with the top of the stock. This will fill in the gap between the barrel and the stock. It will show, of course, but if you matched the color it won't be too noticeable and it will certainly look a lot better than a big air gap. It will probably be necessary to refinish the stock, as the top section will probably show some marks from filing and sanding the compound even with the stock. When doing this, use a stain to more closely match the compound color to make it less noticeable.

compound harden further. Then tighten the action screws and you are ready to head for the range. A lot of accuracy-affecting bedding problems occur when the forend of the stock warps, causing it to contact the barrel. This actually is the reason I ended up with one of the most accurate rifles I ever owned. I was on a deer hunt and the guide wanted my rifle very badly. We stopped for coffee at his house one night after the hunt and he started trying to trade me out of it. One of the items on the table was a Ruger M-77 heavy barreled varmint rifle in .220 Swift. I noticed that the barrel had a big gap on the left side of the stock while the right side had made hard contact with the barrel. I surmised that he was having trouble making it shoot and that he probably wanted to get rid of it. So, I worked that to my advantage and before the deal was done, he offered far more than my rifle was worth even without the Ruger in the mix. I am too honest to be a good trader and I pointed out to him that he was not getting a fair deal, but he wanted my rifle, so we traded.

When I got the Ruger home, my suspicions were confirmed. I took the gun apart and found several brass shims under the action. Shimming the action is a low-rent way to fix bedding problems and it told me that even though he denied it, he was aware of the gun's problems. I suddenly didn't feel so guilty about the trade. I opened up the barrel channel to float the barrel and glass bedded the action. The gun turned out to shoot quarter-inch, 100-yard groups. The downside is that I got stupid and traded it off a few years later for a gun that I don't really like.

My point is that the stock warping is a common problem and often even after you remove enough wood to fix the problem, it can continue to warp.

The rod imbedded in the compound provides structural strength and will help to keep the forend from warping again. Using threaded rod allows it to grip better in the compound than a smooth side rod, again adding strength. The compound covering the wood will help prevent water from entering the wood, which is what causes warping. As always, make sure to seal any exposed wood against moisture during the finishing process. It won't be the prettiest stock in your gun room, but it might be on your best shooting rifle.

WHAT IF IT STILL DOESN'T SHOOT?

Most rifles shoot well with the front of the action and first few inches of barrel glass bedded and the barrel floating. But some rifles simply prefer pressure on the barrel near the stock's forend tip.

If the rifle is still not shooting well after bedding, try a thin one-inch-wide shim between the barrel and the stock an inch or so back from the end of the forearm tip. Because the shim will become permanent, plastic is better than cardboard. Experiment with different thickness and placement until you find one that makes the gun shoot the way you want.

Mark the shim's location with a pencil. Take the gun apart and coat the barrel with release agent. On either side of the shim's location sand the barrel channel to bare wood, but leave a ½-inch strip that corresponds with the shim that is untouched. Trim the shim to a quarter inch wide and place it in the barrel channel perpendicular to the barrel. A drop of Super Glue will help keep it in place. Make sure that the barrel will center on the shim when the gun is assembled. Cover the shim well with Acraglas Gel and at least ½ inch out in each direction. Use enough bedding compound to ensure the shim is trapped and encapsulated. Reassemble the rifle. The shim will maintain the exact pressure on the barrel until the bedding compound has hardened. The next day, take the stock off the rifle and trim the compound to the 1-inch width of the original shim. (The ½-inch shim should be left in place.) Clean up the release agent, seal the bare wood and put the rifle back together.

If the pressure pad is too wide, it's easy to trim it to size with a hand chisel while the bedding compound is still soft. If you wait until the compound is completely set up, you can grind it to shape with a Dremel hand grinder.

This pad was installed in the forend to provide pressure on the barrel. This .280 AI shot much better after doing this.

STOCKMAKER'S HAND SCREWS

Any stock work will involve taking the gun apart and putting it back together several times. No matter how careful you are, it's easy to mark up the bottom metal or the screws with the screwdriver.

It's far simpler to use a set of stockmaker's hand screws. These have an extended "T" handle and are much faster than a screwdriver. Of course, Brownells sells them. So does Midway USA.

Pillar Bedding Your Rifle

Remington M-700 BDL SS DM in 7mm STW.
Zeiss Diavari 5-15 T* scope. Shows the stock after pillar bedding
and filling the barrel channel with Bondo.

Any mass-produced product, no matter how technically advanced, will have manufacturing tolerances that will dictate a variation in the dimensions of the parts. Rifles are not exempt from this, but it is inarguable that with the increasing use of computer controlled manufacturing machines, today's factory rifles have reduced those tolerances dramatically. Enough, it would seem, that the accuracy goals of a "tuned" rifle from a couple of generations ago are generally close to the minimum out-of-the-box standard today. However, while we may be getting closer, perfection is still elusive.

Dimension variations in bedding, which is the relationship between the metal and the stock of a rifle, particularly around the action, can be critical to the performance of a bolt-action rifle. Even a small variation in dimension can affect the accuracy if it is in a critical location. With the "drop-in" design of most factory-installed stocks, exact bedding is compromised for the sake of affordability and rapid manufacturing. In spite of that, today's rifles still shoot amazingly well. That said, as good as they are, almost any factory rifle will shoot better with improvements in the stock bedding.

Rebedding a rifle is usually the single most important change a shooter can make to improve accuracy. It's easily done in a home shop with a minimum of tools and by anybody handy enough to work a screwdriver without drawing blood.

So-called "glass bedding," when done properly, provides a bedding platform that is so tight to the action that often you can see machine marks from the metal mirrored in the bedding material. Properly done, glass bedding (actually, it's usually epoxy these days rather than fiberglass and resin) will provide a bedding foundation that not even the most skilled old-world craftsman could duplicate with wood to metal bedding. But there are a few problems with using just glass bedding on some stock, regardless if it is wood or synthetic.

One problem that is inherent with wood stocks is that wood will compress. When you glass bed the stock without pillar bedding, the action screws are putting constant pressure on the wood material of the stock. As the cells in the wood compress under that pressure, the tension of the action screws can change, affecting accuracy.

This is also true with some synthetic stocks, particularly the less expensive injection molded styles usually found on factory rifles. The plastic may not compress, but it can be malleable enough to move under pressure, causing the same end result.

I remember testing a rifle from a well-known gunmaker back in the 1980s when they were first offering synthetic stocks. The front action screw had a relatively small head and because it was a blind magazine style, the screw simply tensioned against the plastic stock. Every time I

checked the screw, I found it slightly loose. This puzzled me as I was using Loctite on the threads. Of course, each time the screw was loose, the groups would start to open up. However, it wasn't long before the head of the screw had imbedded itself more than a quarter inch into the stock, which was hard to ignore. It was actually tunneling into the stock, displacing material and, of course, never maintaining constant tension. Obviously, this rifle never shot as accurately as I thought it should. Within a very short time, that gun company started pillar bedding all its rifles, and those guns have a reputation for providing outstanding accuracy.

As they found out, pillar bedding is one answer to this problem. It is simply adding a "pillar" of metal or some other strong material to support the tension of the bedding screws. Most pillars are simply tubes of metal with a hole through the center for the screw to go through. The action sits on the top of the pillar, while the action screw tightens against the bottom of the pillar.

Sometimes nothing else supports the rifle's action except these two pillars. When bedded this way, the rest of the action simply floats slightly above the stock, making contact with the stock itself only at the recoil lug. Because the pillars are strong, noncompressible metal, the tension on the screws remains constant. Not only do the pillars provide excellent bedding support, but they are not affected by changes in dimensions caused by humidity.

Pillar bedding works best when done in conjunction with glass bedding of the action. For best results, you should not allow the pillars to be the sole support of the action. Instead, also glass bed the section of the action between the front of the magazine box and the recoil lug and the

rear tang area. Also, the recoil lug should be properly glass bedded so that there is clearance around all but the rear load-bearing surface. It's also a good idea with most rifles to bed the first two inches of the barrel, while free floating the rest. The section of the action between the rear tang and the front of the magazine box can be bedded, but it's usually better to free float it so that the action is supported front and rear, but floating in the center.

All this ensures that the action fits properly on the pillars and is especially important with round actions like the Remington Model 700 to ensure that it sits squarely in the stock. If the action only sits on the pillars, it can potentially roll slightly off center, but by bedding the action and recoil lug in conjunction with pillar bedding, the fit is so tight that the action can only fit in the stock one way.

My first stop was Brownells, where I ordered a pillar bedding kit which comes with a set of adjustable pillars, two tubes of pre-colored Acrabed bedding compound, release agent and assorted tools and gadgets needed for a pillar bedding project. It also includes detailed instructions.

You can order the kit with or without a $\frac{9}{16}$-inch wood drill to enlarge the action screw holes. It works fine if you are only going to do one or two stocks, but the Piloted Forstner Bit that they offer separately works much better as the pilot will follow the existing hole to keep the alignment of the drill in relation with the old action screw holes correct. If you are going to drill the stock with a hand-held drill, the piloted drill is a must.

The adjustable pillars are great. The length of the pillars is critical, as they need to support the action in the correct relationship to the stock. Rather than fooling with cutting them to length, you can simply screw the pieces in or out until you have the length that you need.

The toughest part may well be drilling the action screw holes larger to accept the pillars. The best way to do this is to use the piloted drill that has a pilot the size of the existing hole. The pilot follows the hole and keeps the drill exactly centered. This allows you to drill the holes even with a hand drill and keep things lined up properly. When drilling through an injection molded stock, a standard non-piloted drill has a tendency to grab the material and then set a course of its own. You never know where it might end up, but often it's not where you want it.

If this happens to you, don't panic. You can still salvage the job by simply drilling the holes even bigger and "floating" the pillars in bedding material. If you prepare everything and fill around the pillars with material at the same time you bed the action and put it all together, they will find their own "center" and when the material hardens, they should be placed properly. The only adjustment you may have to make is to relieve the pillar a little if the screw is hitting the inside. The best policy though is to drill the holes in alignment with the existing action screw holes, so always try for that goal.

When the job is complete, the action screw should never contact the pillar with the shank portion. The force of recoil must transmit to the stock only through the recoil lug and never through any of the action screws. To assure this, the screw only contacts the pillar on the head, never the shank.

If you are working with an injection molded stock, remember that the plastic used in these stocks is difficult to adhere to. Actually, that's an understatement, nothing except Alabama field mud will stick to the stuff and it's not stabile enough for bedding material. The answer is to drill anchor holes at various angles and make some undercuts to mechanically lock the bedding material to the stock. Make sure to do this inside the holes that will accept the pillars. After making all your cuts and roughing up the surfaces and just before you apply the bedding compound, make sure that the area to be bedded is chemically clean and free of oil by spraying with a degreaser that leaves no residue. In addition, after degreasing, but before bedding, I finish with a spray-on product I bought at the local auto supply store that is designed to aid adhesion of paint to plastic called Bulldog Adhesion Promoter, which seems to help.

Once you have the pillars correctly adjusted and fitted, coat them well with bedding compound or epoxy glue and put them in place. Screw the rifle together, make sure that everything is in correct alignment and wait for the glue to cure. Glass bedding the action and recoil lug should be done in a separate step after the pillars are correctly installed.

Once the pillars are in place, cut and gouge out the area of the stock that will be bedded to allow room for the bedding compound, leaving only a small support section behind the recoil lug to keep the action in the correct location front to back. The pillars will support the receiver. Do not go very deep or remove much material, just enough to ensure that the action contacts only the pillars and the small section of the stock material you left for the recoil lug to butt against.

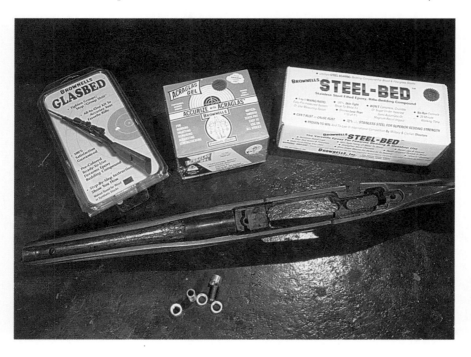

While this wood stock has been glass bedded without pillars, a variety of pillar kits are available on the market.

MARK BANSNER
Adamstown, Pennsylvania

I know of one custom gunsmith, Mark Bansner, who creates his pillars by first glass bedding the stock. Then he drills out the screw holes and fills them with glass bedding compound mixed with powdered metal (called Atomized metal by Brownells). He coats the screws, action and bottom metal with release agent and puts the gun back together. When the material has hardened, he takes the gun apart, cleans up the overflow and then drills the holes one size larger to ensure there is no contact with the screws and the pillars except at the screwhead.

This in effect creates a custom-sized pillar that is perfectly fitted. It's independent of the bedding and a lot tougher. Mark's guns enjoy a reputation for outstanding accuracy and durability. I know, I have three of them and they are all extremely accurate, tough and stable. I have hunted with them from Alaska to Zimbabwe and never had a problem. None of them are chambered in "sissy" cartridges. Two are wildcats I designed on the Remington Ultra Mag case, a .358 and a .416, and they are very hard recoiling cartridges that demand a lot out of the bedding.

All other areas should have clearance. The idea is to hold things in place until the bedding material has a chance to set up. If you are going to float the barrel, make sure that when the action is seated and the screws are snug, you can pass a business card between the barrel and stock along the length of the barrel without dragging.

The front, sides and bottom of the recoil lug should be covered with a layer of masking tape before the release agent is applied. But, do not cover the load-bearing surface of the recoil lug. That is the flat that is facing to the rear of the rifle. When removed, this tape creates a

slight gap around the recoil lug, ensuring that the only contact is on the rear load-bearing surface. The entire action and the first two inches of the barrel are usually bedded at this time. Apply a couple of layers of masking tape to the barrel ahead of where you wish to bed and one layer on the center section of the action, the part you wish to float. This will provide a few thousandths of clearance after it is removed. Put masking tape on the outside of the stock and along the top to protect those areas from the overflow of bedding compound. The best way is to put the tape on the top then trim the edges with a sharp razor blade. Tape up or remove the trigger assembly. Coat all the metal and any tape on the metal with a release agent. Mix the bedding agent according to the instructions and fill the areas to be bedded. Be generous and let the excess spill out. That ensures that all the gaps are filled. Put the rifle together and just snug the screws, but not too tight.

When the bedding agent has cured, remove the barreled action from the stock. (A little hint: After the bedding agent has cured, if you put the gun in the freezer for a couple of hours before you separate them, the metal will contract and make the job easier.)

If you are now going to glass bed the barrel channel, make sure there is plenty of clearance. Then cover the barrel with a layer of .010-inch pipe wrap tape available from Brownells. Then bed the length of the barrel. The tape serves as a spacer that, when removed, creates a perfect gap and leaves the barrel free floating.

This pillar bedding, along with glass bedding, is as solid a foundation as you can create for your rifle's action. It should be accurate, tough and permanent.

BROWNELLS' INSTRUCTIONS FOR PILLAR BEDDING •
Pillar bedding creates a uniform bedding surface and helps eliminate changes in guard screw tension, thus enhancing accuracy in many bolt-action rifles. Brownells Adjustable Pillar Bedding Sleeves are aluminum with steel sleeves threaded together to allow precise adjustment to fit individual rifles. Adjustable Pillar Bedding Sleeves eliminate the need to machine pillars to fit individual rifles. Rifles of the same make and model may have variations of over $\frac{1}{16}$ inch in distance from the underside of the action to the top of the trigger guard-floor plate unit. The main aluminum adjustment piece is reversible to easily adapt to either flat- or round-bottomed receivers.

NOTE: Brownells Adjustable Pillar Bedding Sleeves are not suitable for use on Mauser, Springfield, Ruger, or other rifles with the front guard screw directly threaded into the recoil lug or with very narrow rear tangs.

How to Use

We recommend that pillar bedding be done as a multiple step process, first installing and bedding the pillars and the area surrounding them, then the recoil lug area, and last, the trigger guard. Areas to be bedded normally are the rear ⅓ to ¼ of the action including the rear tang; the front area of the action from the front of the magazine box opening up to the barrel; and the breech end of the barrel to about the front of the chamber area, roughly 1½ inches to 2½ inches in front of the action.

Bedding Compounds

Brownells Adjustable Pillar Bedding Kits come with Acrabed, a brown, pre-colored bedding compound packed in squeeze tubes for easy measuring of its one-to-one proportions. When very heavy recoiling rifles are pillar bedded, we recommend the use of Brownells Steel Bed in the recoil lug areas, with Acrabed or Acraglas Gel used on the remainder of the job.

Drilling the Stock

The trigger guard screw holes in the stock must be opened up to allow use of the Pillar Bedding Sleeves. We recommend using a ⁹⁄₁₆-inch Forstner-type drill bit to cut the recesses in the stock for the Adjustable Pillar Bedding Sleeves. This type of drill bit is guided by its outer edge, and has little or no tendency to drift or to chip out wood from the hole being drilled. If a conventional wood drill is used,

always drill from the trigger guard (bottom) side of the stock toward the action side. Any chipping where the drill comes through will be covered by bedding compound. Use of the drill press or vertical milling machine for drilling the pillar sleeve holes will minimize problems with drilling and is highly recommended. If the original guard screw holes are not located correctly or are not at right angles to the bore line, now is the time to "adjust" the fit by setting up the stock so the sleeve holes will be "square" to the action. Re-inlet the action and trigger guard-floor plate unit if needed. Remember, the widest points of the barrel and action (the horizontal centerline) should be at or very slightly above the top level of the stock.

Fitting and Adjusting the Sleeves and Forend

Clamp the stock in a padded vise and place the barreled action and trigger guard-floor plate unit in it. Push the action back so the back face of the recoil lug is tight against its recess in the stock. Insert and tighten the guard screws to their normal tension. Inspect the forend area to be sure the barrel is free floated; there should be about .010-inch to .030-inch clearance (about one to two times the thickness of an average business card) for the full length of the barrel channel. Remove the barreled action and adjust the barrel channel with scrapers and sandpaper as needed. (Note: A stock with forend tip pressure against the barrel can be a source of point-of-impact changes from either humidity on

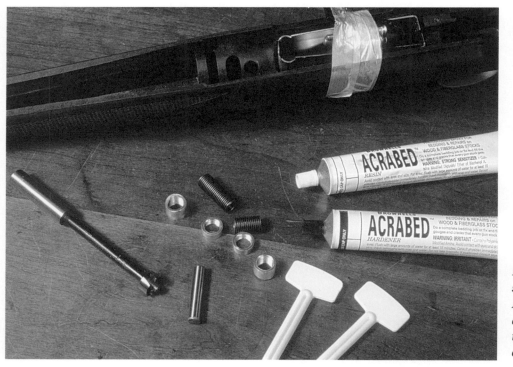

Remington synthetic stock, Brownells Acrabed, pillars and pilot drill. Note the removable pilot on the drill.

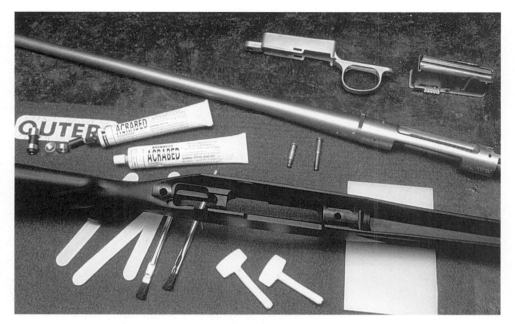

Disassembled Remington M-700 BDL SS DM with materials and tools for pillar bedding.

a wooden stock or sling pressure movement of the forend on a wood or synthetic stock.) Remember, when checking and adjusting your inletting, the widest points on the barrel and receiver should be at or above the top line of the stock. This will help prevent "mechanical locking" of the barreled action into the stock when using bedding compound. After the forend and inletting have been checked and adjusted, clamp the barrel in your padded bench vise ahead of the forend top area, with the underside of the action facing upward. If your action uses a separate magazine box, set it into the action. Set the stock onto the barreled action. Place the Adjustable Sleeves into their holes in the stock. If your action is round-bottomed, set the radiused end of the thick outer sleeves against the action. If it is flat-bottomed, like the Winchester M-70, set the flat sides against the action. Turn the slotted steel inner sleeves in or out until they are just below flush with the bottom of the inletting for the trigger guard. Adjust the narrow aluminum outer sleeves in or out until they are flush with the bottom of the inletting. Set the trigger guard-floor plate unit into its inletting and inspect to see if its outer surface is flush with the underside of the stock. Remove the guard and turn the narrow aluminum outer sections of the sleeves in or out until the fit is proper. The magazine box should have about $1/64$-inch to $1/32$-inch vertical clearance between the trigger guard-floor plate unit and the inside of the action. After adjusting the sleeves, carefully remove them from the stock and set them aside. A drop of epoxy, Loctite, fingernail polish, or Super Glue on the inside section, where the aluminum outer sleeve portions join the steel inside sleeve, will hold the sleeve assembly at its proper length while handling.

Metal Preparation for Bedding

Make certain the barreled action and trigger guard are clean and free from dirt, oil and any debris from stock work. Either remove the trigger assembly from the receiver or use Brownells Bedding Tape to completely cover it so no bedding compound can get into the mechanism. (Make sure it will still fit into its inletting in the stock if it is masked off rather than removed.) Use modeling clay and tape to fill or cover any grooves, slots, or rough areas that bedding compound could flow into and "lock" the action to the stock. Check the recoil lug to ensure that it is narrower at the bottom than where it meets the action and that there are no machining marks on its rear face that could cause a mechanical lock of the barrel to the stock. To provide proper clearance for future disassembly and reassembly, we recommend putting two layers of Brownells Vinyl Bedding Tape on the sides, front and bottom of the recoil lug. DO NOT put any tape on the rear vertical face of the recoil lug! Thoroughly coat all parts with a high quality release agent, such as Brownells Acra-Release or Brownells Release Ageny, carefully, following the instructions supplied with the release agent for application. Note: The exterior portions of the sleeves should not be coated with release agent, as they will be permanently bedded into the stock. Be absolutely certain that any portion of the barreled action, magazine box, guard screws or trigger guard assembly that may come in contact with the bedding compound is well covered with release agent. This will help avoid the possibility of damage during the initial disassembly following bedding. Be sure to use release agent on the guard screws (or Stockmaker's Hand Screws, if they are to be used for the bedding process). Coat all surfaces with the release agent. Use a cotton swab to coat the inside of the sleeves with release agent.

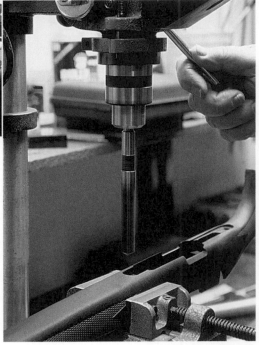

John R. Kascenska prepares to drill action screw holes larger to accept pillar bedding.

Below: Preparing to drill synthetic stock for pillar bedding.

Final Wood Preparation and Bedding of the Pillars

If pillar bedding is being done on a finished stock, make sure the stock finish is thoroughly cured before bedding. We strongly urge you to "mask off" the exterior of the stock with fresh, high quality masking tape to protect the exterior from any accidental contact with the bedding compound. Note: Incompletely cured stock finish may "pull off" from the stock when masking tape is removed. Old or poor quality masking tape can leave residues on the surface, which may harm the finish. The wood surrounding the front Pillar Bedding Sleeve should be removed on the action side of the inletting to a depth of about ⅛-inch. For round-bottomed receivers, such as the Remington 700, this should extend up about ½ inch to ⅝ inch on either side of the stock centerline. For flat-bottomed actions, such as the Winchester Model 70, cut wood away to within ¹⁄₁₆ inch of each side of the action's side walls. This "cutaway" area should extend from the front of the magazine box opening in the stock to the rear of the recoil lug inletting in the stock. DO NOT remove any wood from the vertical face behind the recoil lug beyond this ⅛-inch-deep area at this time; it will be done later. Wood must also be removed surrounding the rear pillar location. With actions that sit above the wood line at the rear, such as the Remington 700, set the action into the stock and lightly mark around the rear tang, using a pencil. Remove the action, and scribe a line about ¹⁄₁₆ inch inside the penciled line. This is your outer limit around the rear pillar when deepening the inletting by the recommended ⅛ inch. On actions where the rear tang is inletted into the stock, mark the stock about ¹⁄₃₂ inch inside of the inletting, and remove wood around the pillar's hole to about ⅛-inch depth to the marked line.

You may have to make "dams" of modeling clay in the stock to prevent bedding compound from running out of the pillar cuts. Be sure to "dam" or mask off areas where bolt release or safety components are located, to allow free movement. Mix up enough Acraglas Gel or Steel Bed bedding compound to completely fill the areas in the stock surrounding the pillars where you have removed wood, plus about 25 percent extra as a "fudge factor." Follow our directions for proper mixing. Double-check that all of the metal parts are properly coated with release agent. Clamp the stock in a padded bench vise with the vise jaws clamped lightly but firmly on the forend, and the toe of the stock supported by your workbench. Coat the outside of the Pillar Bedding Sleeves with bedding compound and place them in their proper holes in the stock. Place the trigger guard into its inletting and hold it in place with masking tape. Put the bedding compound into the stock, working out any bubbles that may form. Try to avoid getting any bedding compound into the guard screw holes in the sleeves. If your action is round bottomed, double-check that the radiused ends of the thick aluminum portions of the sleeves are properly aligned. Place the action into the stock with the recoil lug held firmly against its recess. Install and tighten the guard screws or stockmaker's hand screws. Note: There is no need to overtighten these screws. Tighten them just enough to hold the parts in position with the centerline of the barrel at, or slightly above, the top of the forend. If a very heavy barrel is on the rifle being bedded, a small amount of modeling clay in the barrel channel or even one or two business cards under the barrel near the forend tip will help to support the barrel during this process. Following our instructions, allow the bedding compound to cure to "handling strength." When the bedding compound has cured to this "handling strength" point, remove the barreled action from the stock. Clean off all release agent for the barreled action AND from the bedding in the stock. If bedding compound has migrated into any areas where it is not needed, remove it along with the modeling clay used as dams when bedding the pillars.

Bedding the Recoil Lug and Barrel Breech
Proper bedding of the recoil lug is absolutely essential in a large caliber rifle to prevent recoil from splitting the stock. In any rifle, improper bedding of the recoil lug can cause inaccuracy. Before bedding the recoil lug, remove about ⅛ inch of wood from the area behind the lug, and about ¹⁄₁₆ inch on either side of it. Bedding the breech end of the barrel to the front of the chamber area (roughly 1½ inches to 2½ inches in front of the receiver) will help to support the barrel, and will usually aid in increasing accuracy. If the barrel is a heavy contour, a small amount of modeling clay in the barrel channel near the forend tip while the bedding compound is curing will help to support the weight. If any voids are visible in the portion of the bedding completed so far, now is the time to fill them. First, clean out and slightly roughen the voids with a small scraper or wood chisel. Using a cotton swab, clean out the voids with TCE or lacquer thinner. Allow to air dry until no trace of solvent or thinner odor is present in the void area. CAUTION: Both TCE and lacquer thinner can damage fresh bedding as well as stock finish if allowed to "pool" on it. Check the solvent or thinner maker's instructions for specific warnings relating to their use. Check the tape on the sides, front and bottom of the recoil lug to be sure that it is still intact, and replace if necessary. Following our instructions, recoat the barreled action, including the taped areas on the recoil lug, with release agent. Recoat the front guard screw with release agent. Mix enough bedding compound to replace the wood removed from the recoil lug areas, the barrel breech, and any voids to be filled, plus about 25% extra. Secure the stock horizontally in a padded bench vise with the action area facing upward. Put the bedding compound in the stock. It may be helpful to use a 10cc polypropylene syringe with bedding compound in it to fill any voids. Do not overfill the voids, as any excess bedding compound will cause high spots in the bedding job. NOTE: If you fill the corner between the front of the recoil lug and the barrel with bedding compound (placed directly onto the steel), you will eliminate most instances of bubbles or voids in the bedding at that area. Place the barreled action into the stock. Tighten the guard screws or stockmaker's hand screws just firmly enough to hold the barreled action in place. Be sure the action is fully down in its inletting and the horizontal centerline of the barrel is at, or very slightly above, the top of the forend.

Allow the bedding compound to cure to "handling

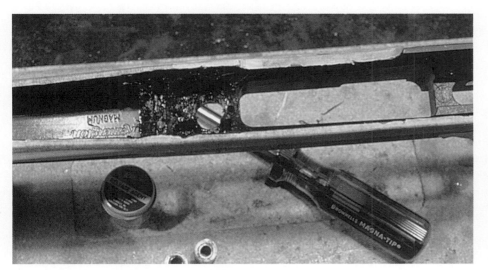

Shows the Remington M-700 BDL SS DM stock. Note that the area around the action has been roughed up and anchor holes have been drilled for bedding material. Hole for pillar is drilled and masking tape is applied.

strength" and remove the barreled action from the stock. Clean up any excess bedding compound. Use a good quality stock finish to seal the barrel channel and any areas in inletting where raw wood is exposed. This will help to minimize moisture transfer and possible stock warping through the forend.

Bedding the Trigger Guard-Floor Plate Unit

Many factory inletted rifles and some prefinished synthetic stocks allow the trigger guard's exterior surface to be below flush with the exterior of the stock. When the Adjustable Pillar Bedding Sleeves were adjusted to the stock and barreled action, this situation was corrected by setting the pillar's overall lengths. To "finish" this part of the job, and give proper support to the underside of

the trigger guard-floor plate unit, it must be bedded. Carefully scrape away any stock finish in the inletting where you will be adding bedding compound. Coat the trigger guard-floor plate unit, the guard screws and their holes in the receiver, and the inside of the pillar bedding sleeves with release agent. Mix an appropriate amount of bedding compound and put enough into the inletting to allow the trigger guard-floor plate unit to be properly supported when it is cured. Hold the barreled action in a padded bench vise by the barrel, ahead of the forend tip. Place the stock on the barreled action, and put the trigger guard-floor plate unit into the stock. Install and lightly tighten the guard screws, and allow the bedding compound to cure. When cured, remove the guard screws and the trigger guard-floor plate unit and clean up any excess bedding compound. Reassemble the rifle and make certain the floor plate (if it is hinged) is able to function easily through its normal range of movement, and that its latch is also free.

Pillar Bedding Blind Magazine Rifles

Rifles with blind magazines (no floor plate assembly), such as the Remington 700 ADL, can be successfully pillar bedded using Brownells Adjustable Pillar Bedding Sleeves. If the diameter of the escutcheon surrounding the head of the front guard screw is smaller than $\frac{9}{16}$ inch, you will not be able to use both aluminum adjusting rings. Carefully remove the escutcheon from the stock, and drill a ½-inch hole through the stock for the steel inner sleeve, drilling from the bottom of the stock toward the action side. Drilling from the inside of the stock, next drill a $\frac{9}{16}$-inch-diameter hole about ½ inch deep for the thick adjustment ring. (This method can be used on a stock

Above: Applying release agent to rifle metal.

Right: Remington M-700 BDL SS DM. Note the masking tape on stock and trigger. Also on all but the load-bearing rear surface of the recoil lug. Release agent has been applied to the metal and the tape on the gun.

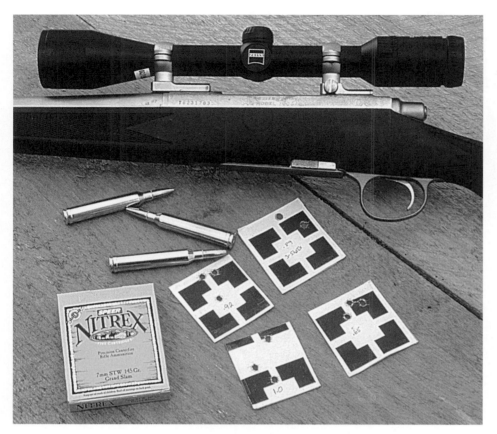

Remington M-700 BDL SS DM in 7mm STW. Zeiss Diavari 5-15 T* scope. With Nitrex 145-grain ammo. Shows the accuracy of the rifle after pillar bedding the stock and filling the barrel channel with Bondo.

with a trigger guard-floor plate unit that is narrower than ⁹⁄₁₆ inch at each end for the guard screws.)

Pillar Bedding Synthetic Stocks

Pillar bedding can benefit synthetic stocks by preventing distortion of the action area from overtightening of the guard screws. Bedding compounds will bond to most laid-up synthetic stocks, once any paint or release agents are removed from those areas to be bedded. Many injection-molded stocks are made of materials that will not chemically bond to bedding compounds. These stocks can still be bedded if a series of small (⅛-inch diameter), shallow "anchor" holes are drilled or ground into the surfaces to receive the bedding compound, with the holes going at different angles to each other. A Dremel or Foredom hand grinder using a ⅛-inch diameter ball end carbide cutter is ideal for this job. CAUTION: Do not drill these anchor holes through to the exterior of the stock! If your synthetic stock is hollow under the breech end of the barrel, a small wood block (one to two inches long) can be fitted to the recess at that point, as long as it is coated with bedding compound on all surfaces. This will help to support the weight of a heavy barrel and will usually aid in increasing accuracy.

Finish Notes

With any bedding compound, let the finished bedding job "cure" for three to ten days before shooting the rifle. Remember, the cooler your shop area is, the longer the bedding compound will need to cure. Make certain all excess bedding compound is removed from the inside of the stock inletting. Be ABSOLUTELY SURE that no bedding compound has "migrated" into the inside of the receiver through the guard screw holes or the cartridge feed ramp. Clean up all traces of release agent from both metal parts and the bedding compound, following the instructions for the release agent. Be sure to put a light coat of a good grade of gun oil on the steel parts to prevent rust.

Reassemble the firearm according to the manufacturer's instructions. Check for proper functioning using Action Proving Dummies. Make sure ALL SAFETY MECHANISMS are fully functional as designed and approved by the manufacturer. If these tests prove satisfactory, test-fire the firearm with live ammunition in a SAFE and APPROPRIATE manner. IMPORTANT! Start the live ammunition tests by first loading an Action Proving Dummy, then a live round, into the magazine. Only after several tests have been conducted in this manner should additional rounds be placed in.

Fixing Injection Molded Stock Problems

To fix the noisy, hollow butts of injection molded stocks, inject foam, or simply fill with packing material and crush it tight.

I have noticed that many of the rifles with injection molded synthetic stocks I have tested in recent years didn't seem to shoot as well as I thought they should. For the most part, they were acceptable, but never quite as accurate as I knew they should be. The problem seems to be even more pronounced in guns chambered for the bigger, more aggressive cartridges. I have always suspected that most of the trouble was with the much too flexible designs of these stocks. I wondered what it would take to correct the problem.

To be honest, I think the main reason that injection molded stocks are so unruly, particularly with bigger guns, is because of forend flexing. On my Remington Model 700 7mm STW I could move the forend back and forth easily and independently of the barrel and this was a gun that uses forend tip pressure on the barrel. If I could move the forend that easily with my hands, the forces of shooting would have an even more dramatic effect. No rifle will shoot well if the bedding is inconsistent, and with this rather fluid bedding situation on the forend tip I wasn't surprised this gun was not accurate. The best that gun would shoot was about three-inch groups with the factory stock, which is edging into "terrible" territory with a new bolt-action rifle. Particularly for a Remington Model 700,

which enjoys a much deserved reputation for excellent out-of-the-box accuracy.

Rather than spring for an expensive new stock, I thought it was a good candidate for pillar bedding and I decided to see what I could do with that misbehaving STW. But, my first attempts were disappointing. Even after pillar and glass bedding the stock, the rifle wasn't as accurate as I felt it should have been. I was pretty sure the problem was with that forend flexibility and I decided to float the barrel and remove any hard contact near the forend tip. But it still wasn't all that accurate. The stock was so flexible that my guess was that it was flexing and hitting the barrel as I fired the gun. The stock must be a lot more rigid than it was if good accuracy was going to be achieved.

The first step was prepping the barrel channel the same way as the action area for pillar bedding. I roughed up the surfaces with a hand grinder and drilled several anchor holes at different angles. I drilled the anchor holes any place there was enough material. Then I used a hand grinder tool with a cutter blade to undercut a lip the entire length of the barrel channel just under the top of the stock, and on both sides. This acts like a mechanical anchor to lock the bedding to the stock in the event the compound will not adhere to the stock material. I covered the barrel with

two layers of two-inch electrician's tape (this was before I discovered the .010-inch tape from Brownells) and coated the tape with car wax to act as a release agent. I sprayed the stock with Outers Crud Cutter degreaser and let it dry. Then I sprayed Bulldog Adhesion Promoter agent to help the bedding material bond with the stock. I bought this at an auto parts store and it's designed to aid paint in sticking to plastic body parts. I reasoned that it would probably help things stick to the injection molded stock as well. I can't say for sure that it made a difference, but every time I have used it, the bedding compound has stayed put. Several times when I did not use the adhesion agent, the compound became loose in the gun, so the evidence would support that it works as claimed.

Next, I filled the stock with fiber-enhanced auto body filler, available at any auto parts store. This two-part filler is lighter than glass bedding and it's relatively strong. While I don't believe it's strong enough to bed load-bearing surfaces such as the action and recoil lug, it will work fine

for this non-load-bearing bedding job.

After filling the barrel channel with the auto body filler, I assembled the gun quickly as the filler sets up very fast. When the filler hardened, I removed the barrel and action from the stock and removed the tape. The gap from the tape creates an almost perfect floated barrel. With a little spot sanding on the high spots, a business card would pass between the stock and the barrel with no drag. A quick coat of flat black spray paint finished the job. Remember to tape off the rest of the stock, including the bedded area around the action before painting. The stock is much stiffer now, particularly along the barrel channel. This also added some weight, which was welcome in this hard recoiling rifle. Before doing this work I could move the forend back and forth independently of the barrel with my hands, but after this treatment the stock was solid.

The proof, however, is shown at the target. I headed for the shooting range with the completed rifle where I tested four different factory loads; firing four, three-shot groups with each at 100 yards. The average of all sixteen groups was 1.12 inches. The best average was with now-defunct Speer Nitrex 145-grain ammo and measured only .85 inch. The best group I fired was also with Nitrex and measured a dainty .65 inch.

It looks to me like the problem is cured.

Auto body filler can be used to fill forend on an injection molded stock.

FIXING NOISEY SYNTHETIC STOCKS

Some injection molded synthetic rifle stocks, particularly the early ones, have hollow butts that are noisy when they hit any brush or scratch against anything. The hollow, empty space acts as a sound chamber and amplifies the sound and may have turned off a lot of hunters to "plastic" on their rifles. The best solution I have found is to fill the space with the spray foam sold at home improvement stores. This stuff expands and grows and gets all over everything, so tape off the stock with masking tape. Because the butt is so deep, do not try to complete the job all at once. Instead, fill the stock in several sessions. Spray in a couple of inches of foam and allow it to expand and cure for

a few hours, then repeat until the stock is full. You can use a sharp knife to trim the excess and then shape it to the opening in the back with a wide file or a Surform tool. Reinstall the butt plate or recoil pad, remove the tape and it's done.

Another approach that is cheaper, faster and easier, but not quite as good, is to fill the stock with those ubiquitous Styrofoam peanuts that are used in shipping. Remove the recoil pad and cram the stock full. Really work them in, crushing and crunching until you fill the space with as much foam as you can, then replace the recoil pad.

Either method only adds a few ounces, but it quiets that hollow sound so common to these stocks.

"Pimp My Rifle"
Chapter 5

Some of the most popular television shows these days deal with makeovers. Whether it's a house, car, or person, we are fascinated by creating something new and better from the worn and familiar. So, why not do a "total makeover" on a rifle?

It's a great concept and it's an excellent hobby gunsmith project to fix up an old gun. We all have a beater gun or two around that needs "pimping," or if not what better excuse to buy another gun? It probably won't cost much and as long as the the action and the barrel are good, who cares what it looks like? If the bore is good and the mechanics function correctly, it's a candidate for "pimping."

I had planned to do this with my old Remington Model 760 pump action .30-06 Springfield. I bought it new in 1973 and it was my "deer rifle" for many years. The bluing is worn in several places and the stock is dented and scratched. It was a perfect candidate for this "makeover" treatment. So I ordered a synthetic stock, DuraCoat, for a new metal finish and a new scope and mount. But, sentimentality got the best of me.

Every ding and every dent on that gun had a memory associated with it. For example, the bluing is worn off the left side of the barrel in an oval patch. I recall how it happened because it was the day I got lost deep in the Green Mountains of Vermont in a raging blizzard and missed a chance at a buck I had pursued for years.

I found his tracks early that morning and followed them all day. By late afternoon, the wind was blowing snow and sleet into my face and I had to squint through my eyelashes to see where I was going. I pounded up an icy hill with my gun in my right hand which was protected by a brand-new glove. As I topped the ridge I spotted the buck and a young apprentice running for cover.

The protégé had an impressive rack, but it seemed tiny compared to the one on the other buck. This buck was finally mine. I had spent hours shooting at moving targets with that rifle and there was no way I could miss. I raised my gun and sighted through the scope. The driving snow turned my view into an opaque white wall. I lowered the gun and they were still out there, visible to the naked eye. I raised the gun and once more was blind, I dropped it and they were gone.

Hours later I staggered into camp. I was hungry, cold, angry and discouraged. As I put my rifle in the gun rack I noticed that a spot of bluing on the barrel that had been worn away by the new abrasive leather of my glove-clad thumb. I was pretty upset then, but now it reminds me of that day, which was one of the best in a long line of hunting days. I never did get that buck, but I think about him every time I see that worn spot on my 760.

Total Rifle Makeover

126

The finished version of our Winchester Ranger Model 94 rifle makeover.

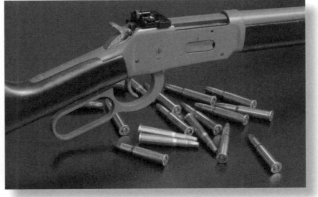

With my aborted "project" gun safely ensconced back in the vault, I set out to buy another Remington pump rifle. The problem is I couldn't find one at a reasonable price. I guess I am partly to blame for that. I have written two books about tracking deer with the legendary Benoit family, *Big Bucks the Benoit Way* and *Benoit Bucks,* and both have been successful. The Benoits shoot an amazing number of big whitetail bucks and they do it with Remington pump action rifles. That has made these guns very popular here in the Northeast and a used one, even a beater, commands a premium price.

I was running up against a deadline for this book and decided that an alternative might be the way to go. While traveling on business, I stopped at a gun shop about two hours from my home to see what they had kicking around. I found a Winchester Model 94 Ranger in .30-30 Winchester on the shelf and wearing a price tag of only $150. I have an interest in lever actions lately, partly because they are what I started hunting with forty years ago and partly because of all the Cowboy Action Shooting I am doing. So, I bought the old beater and decided to use it for this "Pimp My Rifle" project.

There was also an older Savage Model 99 lever action in .300 Savage right beside it. That gun begged and whimpered until I agreed to take it home as well.

I usually stop at this gun shop when I am passing by and I think they have some kind of magnetic field on the door that alters your brain activity with subliminal messages, because every time I stop in there I buy two guns. The last time was only a couple of months earlier and I left with a Remington Model 14 pump action rifle in .30 Remington and an old-style Ruger M-77 bolt action in 7X57 Mauser. Whatever that gun shop is doing, it borders on marketing genius.

I cleaned the bore on the .30-30 and it looked like it was in good shape. Next, I loaded a few cartridges and made sure it would shoot. It was hard to check the accuracy because the front sight was damaged and looked like a confused beaver had chewed the top off of it. It didn't matter because I had planned to replace it with a fiber-optic sight but until I did, the best I could do was make sure the gun would shoot and that it had minute of backstop accuracy.

The hardwood stock was stained to look like walnut, but like a country cousin no amount of makeup could hide its plainness. The finish was worn and chipped and there were a few dents here and there. The bluing on the metal was worn and the receiver was pitted with rust. But the part that shoots, all seemed to be in good shape. It appeared to be a good candidate for the project, so it was anointed worthy.

My son Nathan was helping me on this and he took the stock and forend off the gun while I gathered up some tools. The next step was to take the rest of the gun completely apart. That included using a punch to drive the rear sight out of the dovetail. The front sight on a Ranger Model 94 is also dovetailed into the barrel, as opposed to most Model 94 rifles that have a ramp on the barrel with the sight on the ramp. So, I also drove the front sight out of the dovetail. Because the front sight was damaged and useless and I had plans to trash the rear sight, I used a steel punch. If I had wanted to save them, I would have used a brass or nylon punch. I ordered a new fiber-optic front sight and an FP-94 SE rear peep sight from Williams.

The action was caked with grease and gunk, so all the metal parts went into the solvent tank to soak for a while. While they were soaking, I sanded the wood to rough up the finish and I

Note the front sight damage.

Note the rust on receiver around the loading gate.

Note the dent of the plain wood forearm.

filled the dents with automotive body filler. My idea was to paint the plain wood stock black so it would look like synthetic, so it didn't matter that the body filler was a pink color.

In a project like this, the stock has the most options available. (They are the only "stock options" I understand. I tried the others and they seem to just be a great way to get rid of money.) In this circumstance I am painting the stock, which is the simplest and fastest way to the end result. Another option would be to replace the stock as I had planned to do with the Remington 760. In that case I had a synthetic stock, but there are also laminated wood stocks and, of course, you can always upgrade to a finer grade of walnut. There are many aftermarket synthetic stocks available for most rifles, far too many to list. I will note that I have had very good luck with High Tech Specialties, Bell & Carlson and McMillan

Fiberglass Stocks: Boyds Gunstock Industries has a good selection of laminate wood and wood stocks. I have used a lot of their rifle stocks over the years and can highly recommend them for quality, fit and finish. If you are feeling really frisky, consider a high grade walnut stock blank and make your own stock. You will notice that project is conspicuously absent from this book, as is anything on checkering. I have tried them both and like Clint Eastwood said in one of his best movies, "A man ought to recognize his limitations."

Perhaps the best alternative is to simply refinish the wood on the gun. This is an easy project these days with the many kits available. Simply strip the old finish and sand the stock until it's smooth. If you want to stain the stock, do so at this time. It's best to try a little of the stain first in a place that will not show, such as the barrel channel or under the butt pad. After staining, use a stock filler to fill the grain and pores and follow with a few coats

Degreasing parts of the Model 94.

of final finish. Remember to follow the instructions with the final finish. Most will recommend light sanding or using steel wool between coats. I have had good luck with Birchwood Casey products for refinishing and am now trying some wood finishing products from LCW, the makers of DuraCoat. I don't have a lot of experience with them at this time, but I like what I see so far.

But my goal was to do the project fast and easy and get a unique look for this Model 94. Flat black paint was my secret weapon. I gave the stock two coats of flat black primer and followed with four coats of high quality flat black spray paint. That should have been the end of it.

I hate going through life clumsy and this was another reminder that I am stuck with that affliction forever. I had the stock and forend hanging on wires from a handcart (like you would use to move a refrigerator) parked in front of the shop so they could air dry. At the end of the day I was wheeling the cart back inside when the stock fell off the wire and landed on the crushed stone in front

of my shop. I couldn't stop myself in time and I stepped on the stock. The paint was still soft and it was ruined. I tried to sand out the bad spots, but it just wasn't working. Part of that was because I got in a hurry and tried to do it that night when the paint wasn't completely set. The paint balled up under the sandpaper and made a mess out of everything. So I put it on the bench, locked the shop and headed to the house for a drink to drown my sorrows.

The next morning I used paint stripper to clean the stock down to bare wood. Then I sanded it with several decreasing grits of sandpaper until it looked ready for some paint. I hung it back on the same wire, but this time I twisted the wire back on itself. Two coats of primer and four coats of paint later, it looked pretty good.

To add a "touch of class" to the "Pimp Rifle," we decided to jewel the hammer, the trigger, the locking bolt and the link. The link is the big block at the bottom of a Model 94 rifle that the lever passes through. It moves as the gun is opened and drops down. This piece fills the bottom of the action and is an excellent candidate for jeweling.

The hammer looks great, as does the locking bolt. The hammer you can see, but the bolt you will need to take my word on. The Williams receiver sight that we installed covers it up. If I had realized that in the beginning, I would not have wasted the time involved in jeweling the locking bolt. (Actually, I just polished the part while Nathan did the actual jeweling on the bolt.) The trigger is another thing altogether. It's a casting and the metal didn't polish up or take the jeweling as well as I had hoped it would. I suppose I could have worked at it for a while to reshape it with a file and add a higher polish. But, I simply cold blued the part instead. I wasn't satisfied with that result and finally decided to give it a coating of DuraCoat. The link, though, looks great.

stripping the old finish off a stock.

Painting the stock.

Any carbon steel part can be jeweled. Jeweling is also called Engine Turning and Damascening. It is the process of polishing small swirls into the surface of the metal. This is usually done in an overlapping "fish-scale" pattern. It adds a nice touch to any rifle and is very easy to do. It also holds oil better than non-jeweled metal to prevent rust. Jeweling is sometimes done inside a gun to reduce friction, but in this circumstance we are using it for cosmetics only.

The key to a good jeweling job is in the preparation. The part must be polished before starting. I polished the hammer sides and the top of the locking bolt on flat bench stones, starting with fine India and finishing with a hard Arkansas. The key is to just remove any machine marks and polish the surface without removing any more metal than is absolutely necessary. Check the progress often and as soon as the entire surface shows the same sheen, move to the next finer abrasive. I finished with a buffing wheel with red jeweler's rouge buffing compound. One tip while buffing with a wheel is to watch the angle and where on the part you are buffing; if the buffing wheel catches the front edge of the part, it will snap it from your hands and fling it against whatever is behind the buffing wheel. This can put holes in the wall, damage the part and cause harm to you or any bystander. Do not let the wheel get close to the top edge of any part. Polish to just past the halfway point, then reverse the part and polish from the bottom up until they meet.

The link was not perfectly flat, so I couldn't polish it on a stone. It was also very rough and needed more than a simple polishing. I had a lot of machining marks that had to be removed, as did the old bluing. So I clamped it in a soft-jawed vise and used a fine, single cut file to draw file the surface.

Draw filing is a technique to use a file in a way that gives a better finish. It's often used to create the final surface on a part and to remove any machining marks. One good example is an octagon barrel. While the mass-produced barrels are done with CNC machines, the old craftsmen and those still practicing their trade used draw filing to make the flats. A craftsman would pride himself on a perfect flat on the barrel, one that is straight and free from ripples. The best file for this is a Brownells draw file, but any new, single cut file will work for draw filing.

The file is often called a "poor man's milling machine" and if that's so, then draw filing is the finishing cutter. With regular filing, the file is pushed longitudinally across a piece of metal. With draw filing, you use a single cut file and operate it like a draw knife in woodworking. That is, you hold both ends and pull it toward you across the work. In other words, draw filing is basically to hold the

Jeweled link on Winchester Model 94 Ranger.

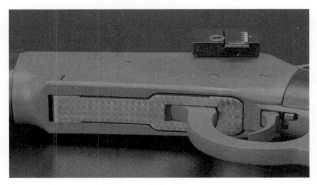

Buffing and polishing wheel.

file at a 90-degree angle to the part and to pull both ends to drag it along the part. Because the file's teeth are at 45 degrees, you have to be careful not to let the file drift to the side while making a cut. The angled teeth will try to force the file to the side and you need to hold it against that so the teeth cut, rather than ride to the side. I find it's helpful to grasp the file on both sides and push the knuckles of my index fingers against the sides of the part. This keeps the file from shifting to the side and keeps the teeth cutting. Again, use only a single cut file, and

Draw filing

the abrasive slurry on the part and lightly touch it with the spinning brush to form a swirl on the polished surface of the metal. The brushes work well on any flat surface and are the best option if you are doing curved surfaces like a rifle bolt, as they will follow the contours.

The other method, and frankly the one that worked a lot better for me, was to use Cratex rubber rods impregnated with abrasive. While you can simply chuck a rod in your drill press, they are fragile and break easily. The best way is to hold the rod in a "Damascening Tool" sold by Brownells. This has a brass rod that will hold the rather delicate abrasive rods, but is small enough to allow working around bolt handles and other obstructions.

It is not necessary to use any abrasive compound with the Cratex rod, simply apply the spinning abrasive rod to the polished surface of the part. Keep the end of the rod trimmed with a file so it stays sharp and square. This by far gave me the best results. I suspect that the brush has a longer learning curve as I know they can provide excellent results, but the Cratex rods turned in a good job the first time out of the chute. This is, of course, on

remember, files only work in one direction, so don't back up. Keep the file clean, as any chips embedded in the teeth of the file will cause damage to the surface. Keep a nice steady pull without excessive down force, and you can make a surprisingly flat and polished surface with very little effort and a minimum of cleanup work.

After draw filing the link, I polished it with a wheel and an abrasive polish, then I cleaned the wheel and added jeweler's rouge and gave it a final polish.

Before jeweling, all the polished parts must be free from oil, grease or buffing wax. I used degreasing spray and a large, clean, cotton cleaning patch to scrub them. Then I sprayed again with degreaser, letting it run off and air dry.

I have heard for years that a pencil with a rubber eraser makes a good jeweling tool. Simply clamp it in the drill press, smear some abrasive lapping compound on the metal and go to town. The first time I tried this it ended with an empty pencil box and one very frustrated hobby gunsmith. In that case I ended up abandoning the project and using a different finish on the part. This time I got a little smarter and ordered the tools the pros used from Brownells.

They basically offer two different tools. One is a small brush with metal bristles. This is held in the drill press, or better yet in the spring-loaded brush holder that Brownells offers. This holder helps to regulate the pressure used and gives a better result. The bristles tend to spread, so there are some small O-rings included in their kit that slip over the brush and help hold the bristles in place. The O-ring tended to migrate up the brush, but I found that I could hold it in place with my index fingernail, letting it slide along the oiled surface and that would keep it from slipping up the brush.

Mix a small amount of 120-grit Silicon Carbide Abrasive with a few drops of Do-Drill oil to form slurry. (They are also included in the kit from Brownells.) Spread

TOOLS FOR JEWELING

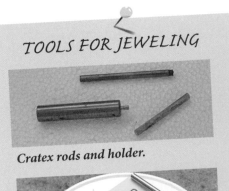

Cratex rods and holder.

Shown with Winchester 94 hammer.

Shown with Winchester 94 link.

Jeweling the link on a Model 94.

flat surfaces as they cannot follow contours as well as the brushes.

The most important thing is to have a way to keep your lines straight and the swirls indexed at the correct spacing. The pros use a milling machine, but you can get just as good results with a drill press. You will need an indexing table or vise on your drill press. Clamp the piece in soft or rubber jaws to prevent marring. Plan out the pattern on the piece. Some pieces may have a long narrow section, such as the hammer spur. This requires that the pattern follow the shape of the piece. For the best results, you will want to use that same line for the rest of the piece. There may be gaps, but simply skip past the gaps to keep the same lines throughout the entire piece.

The indexing vise should be clamped to the drill press table. Set the piece up so the tool is centered at the end nearest to you. Run the piece all the way to the other end to make sure that you have everything lined up properly and that the piece is still centered with the jeweling tool at the opposite end. Make any necessary corrections to ensure that everything is square, and then lock down the drill press table. Run the indexing vise back to the edge closest to you and start with the tool about halfway on the edge and centered on the piece. (Or you can start at one side edge rather than the center, depending on the results you are looking for.) Turn on the drill press at a relatively high speed and lightly touch the tool to the metal and let it run for a few seconds. Now index so that the next swirl will overlap the first by ⅓ to ½. On my indexing vise, that is one

complete revolution of the handle for the 3/16-inch Cratex rods. Form the next swirl. Watch to see how much pressure and time it will take to give you the result you desire. Stop the drill press and wipe the piece with degreaser and a cotton patch, but do not remove it from the vise or move the vise. Check the swirls with a strong light. If you have the result you want, move on. If you do not, reapply the rod to the same spot again. The swirl will be subtle so don't get upset if it's not as defined as you expected. Remember, you are going for a total finished effect and the whole is much more dramatic than any single mark. One or two swirls will not be impressive, but when you are finished and are able to hold the piece and turn it back and forth so that it catches the light on the entire jeweled surface, things change and the effect can be startling.

Once you know how much pressure and time is needed, index the vise and make the next swirl. Continue until you run off the end of the piece being jeweled. Do not make the next line in the opposite direction as all lines should be made in one direction. Run the indexing vise all the way back to the end of the piece closest to you again. Now index left or right to give the same amount of overlap. Make the next line of swirls, overlapping the first line and each other. Continue with this pattern until you are to the edge of the piece. Now return to the center and do it on the other side of the piece until that is covered with jeweling. Or if you started on one edge, continue until you have jeweled everything to the opposite edge.

Once you are done and satisfied, remove the piece from the vise, degrease it again and then coat it with a rust preventive.

This is fine for flat parts like those we did on this Model 94 "Pimp Gun." But for a round part like a bolt, you will need to add another tool. A jig to hold the bolt and to index it around the center. In this case, you will clamp the jig in your indexing vise and keep the tool centered. Run the line down the length of the bolt, and then return to the start. Turn the bolt in the indexing jig for each new line. B-Square makes a bolt jig that is marketed by Brownells.

The rest of the metal parts were retrieved

Jeweling a rifle bolt, using the B-Square fixture and an indexing vise.

APPLYING DURACOAT FINISH

1. Final degreasing in preparation for DuraCoat. This tank contains TruStrip degreaser from DuraCoat.

2. Measuring and mixing DuraCoat.

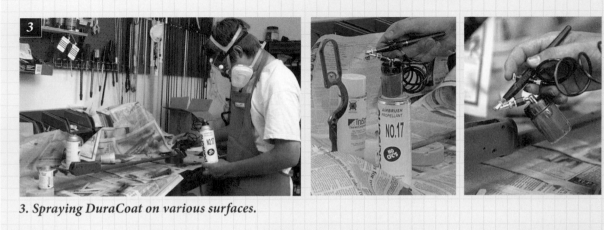

3. Spraying DuraCoat on various surfaces.

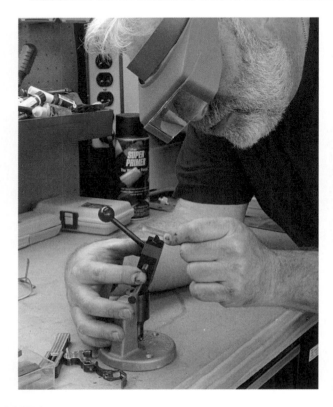

Using a hard Arkansas stone to polish the trigger sear.

from the solvent tank. The internal parts were sprayed with a degreaser to remove the solvent and then coated with Break Free CLP to keep them from rusting. All the parts that will be visible externally, including all the screws, the hammer, trigger and bolt were again degreased with Trustrip degreaser and cleaning fluid from DuraCoat. This is available in bulk for use in a tank or in an inexpensive spray can. I used emery cloth to buff the blued surfaces to rough them up and to remove any rust. The gun had a scope on it at one time that had been removed and the mount screw holes were empty. The two rear holes would be used for the peep sight, but the front two holes needed plugs. Brownells offers a set of plug screws that includes every conceivable size and shape, so I selected two 6-48 plug screws that were short enough to go in the holes until they were flush with the top, but not bottom out. I installed them with a little Loctite to keep them in place. I lined the slots up with the bore for a more "finished" look. Then I degreased everything again with TruStrip.

While I had everything apart, I polished the trigger sear with a hard Arkansas stone to smooth up the trigger pull a bit. I also very lightly polished the trigger notch.

DuraCoat is a modern gun coating that is unique because it can air dry. Most of the gun coatings on the market require an oven to cure, which is tough for a hobby gunsmith to handle. Most kitchen ovens are too small and a commercial oven is very expensive. DuraCoat eliminates this problem. An oven speeds the process up, but the coating can air dry with equally good results.

While I have a spray gun and compressor to apply DuraCoat, I wanted to try their $49.99 DuraCoat EZ Finishing kit as this is what most hobby gunsmiths will use to start out with. The kit comes with an airbrush sprayer with all the hoses and couplings, a nine-ounce can of airbrush propellant with a valve, a color bottle with cap, four ounces of DuraCoat in any stock color, one ounce of DuraCoat Hardener, two ounces of DuraCoat Reducer, a 16-ounce aerosol can of TruStrip and an instructional DVD. This kit is designed for the hobby gunsmith who isn't looking for a big investment in spray guns and air compressors and it has enough material to coat two to four firearms. The airbrush is powered by a can of propellant rather than an air compressor. If you want to do more, simply buy more compressed air and more DuraCoat, the airbrush will work for many guns if you take care of it.

One thing that is not included, but might be needed in a project like this is Durafil. This is a filler product that is sprayed on first to fill in any gouges or rust pits that might be too deep for DuraCoat to cover. The pitting on the receiver on my Model 94 was mild, so I took a chance that the DuraCoat would cover it and did not use the Durafil. However, if I had deeper pitting or gouges to fill, I would order a can of Durafil and start with that as a base coat to fill these spots.

DuraCoat is offered in a wide selection of colors and given the theme of "Pimp My Rifle" I had considered something like Electric Lavender. I am secure enough in my manhood to use a rifle like that, but I just couldn't do it. In the end, this is a hunting rifle and I wanted something more to that theme than a parade gun for Gay Pride Day. I settled on a color called SOCOM which is designed for "tactical" use on rifles for police or military. But, this low-key, nonreflective gray with a slight hint of green was a perfect color for a hunting gun as well. There are 55 stock DuraCoat colors, seven electric colors and clear. So undoubtedly there is a color to suit any taste.

Bryce Towsley proves he is secure enough in his manhood to use a lavender rifle.

It was a simple matter to follow the directions to set up the airbrush and to mix the DuraCoat. I spent a minute adjusting the air pressure and the volume of DuraCoat by spraying at a piece of newspaper until I had the spray pattern just right. It's best to apply DuraCoat in very thin layers, so I adjusted for a fine spray. Then I coated the barreled action, the magazine tube, the bolt, the heads of all the screws, the trigger and all other exposed parts with DuraCoat. The jeweling on the hammer and the link was masked off with blue, painter's masking tape and the other surfaces on these pieces were coated. One thing to remember is that any screw that shows on both sides of the rifle must be coated on both ends. Do you wonder why I know that? I coated only the heads on those screws. Of course, I discovered that mistake after cleaning up the spray gun and putting it away. I had to mix up more DuraCoat, spray the end of the screws, then dump out the excess and clean the airbrush again. It's a lesson I will remember.

A rear sling swivel installed on the Winchester Ranger Model 94.

Inset: This front swivel would not stay in place until it was coated with rosin.

I also coated the barrel band and the forend band. Because I had planned to replace the rear sight with the Williams peep sight, I had a plug to fit in the dovetail for the rear sight. I made sure to degrease it and coat it with DuraCoat as well.

All the parts were left undisturbed to air dry overnight and I gave it a full 24 hours before putting the gun together. It took a little filing and fitting to make the Williams front sight fit in the dovetail. But with a 60°-Standard Slot file from Brownells this was easy. This file is a true parallel, 3-square file with only one side cutting and the other two sides safe. The file can be used to widen dovetail slots in gun barrels without danger of deepening the slot or damaging the edge not being worked on, because only one side cuts. As a true parallel file, you have absolute control over the angle of the dovetail, which is impossible with tapered triangle files. It should be in every gunsmith's shop.

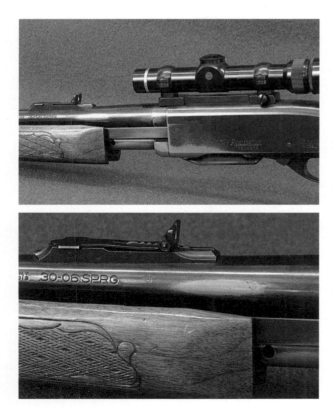

I used it to adjust both the too-tight dovetail slot in the gun barrel and the corresponding dovetail on the sight. Once the sight was in place, I degreased it and put some cold blue on the shiny spots that were showing. After the color was right, I hit it with a little oil to stop the bluing action.

Another good piece of advice is to pay attention to how the parts fit together when you take the gun apart. In the excitement of starting a new project, it's easy to just start taking things apart, thinking you've got it covered. But then later you will find yourself staring at a piece and wondering what the hell it is and where it goes. It has been a while since I had a Model 94 fully apart and that happened to me here. The exploded view book told me where the "cartridge guide left hand" and the "cartridge guide right hand" went, but it was a damn liar. Nothing would fit no matter what I tried. I even sent my son Nathan to the gun vault to gather up some more Winchester Model 94 rifles so that I could peer into their bowels and cipher their mysteries. I knew I had everything right, but it wasn't working. Then out of desperation, I tried reversing them and putting everything in backwards, and they fit. Ok, so maybe it wasn't backwards after all, maybe it was right.

That accomplished, I was off to the next challenge, which was getting all the parts and springs back in the trigger and hammer assembly. The key is to be patient, keep trying and never, never force anything. Parts are made to fit and if they do not, it's you—not the parts—causing the problem. I have a buddy who has a bad habit of trying to make things fit the way he wants them to rather than how they are designed to fit. If he is having trouble, the first thing he does is start modifying the parts. He will grind, file, drill and sand, but, of course, in the end, nothing ever fits quite right. He will curse the manufacturer and claim it's shoddy workmanship and a decline in the American work ethic, but in the end he has things all screwed up. The better approach is to work slow and think more than you act. It all fit together nicely when you took it apart, so it should all fit back together again when you put the pieces back. If it does not, the problem is very likely with you and what you are

Two examples of oval patches where the bluing has worn off of this Remington 760, due to abrasive leather gloves.

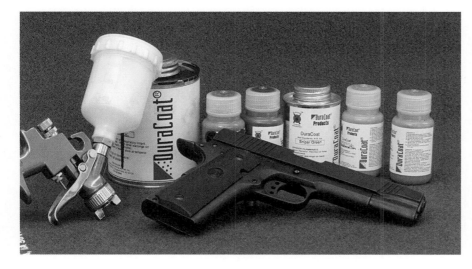

project like this one can be completed in a day.

I still have my eyes open for a Remington pump action rifle for the next "makeover" project. I am planning to cut the barrel down to 20 inches, swap out the stock and coat it with a dark green DuraCoat called Sniper Green. I'll fix up the trigger and add a 1.5-5 Leupold Vari X III scope, which I'll also DuraCoat. It will be the ultimate whitetail hunting "woods" rifle, and will be unique in this world. I already have an imported 1911 pistol in .45 ACP which I bought new with a project in mind. I will strip the gun, add new sights, an ambidextrous safety and a flared magazine well. I'll tune up the trigger, tighten the slide bushing and then coat the slide and frame in contrasting DuraCoat colors. I am thinking of OD Green for the slide and flat black for the frame, but I have not entirely ruled out the Electric Lavender option. No matter what color it ends up, it will be an inexpensive IPSC competition gun as well as a cool carry gun. Then after that, I am planning on a . . . .

Well, I guess you can say this project was addicting. It was an inexpensive and fun way to add some "custom" guns to my collection. I made some mistakes, but that's how you learn. I can see that perhaps this could turn into a television series; I think I'll call it "Pimp My Piece."

Anybody know a good agent?

doing and not with any inherent defect in the parts.

Nathan added a set of Michael's of Oregon sling swivels, using the methods detailed elsewhere in this book. The front was a clamp that went on the magazine tube and it would not grip tight enough. It would turn and slip with only a little pressure. So I had him take it off and put a little powdered rosin on the piece. That solved the problem and it now grips like they are welded.

Once the gun was put back together and tested for function, I let it set for a week so that all the DuraCoat and the paint had a chance to harden.

This rifle now looks dramatically different. It went from a scratched, dented and rusted, decrepit-looking rifle to what one recent teenage visitor to my shop proclaimed as "way cool!"

The total work time was about 12 hours. But, that included fixing the mistakes (like stepping on the stock) and figuring out how to do a lot of the work and shooting some photos. With some more experience, I think a

An Excuse for a New Rifle

Chapter 6

Turning fifty is destined to be a love/hate thing for me and I have no doubt it will be a traumatic event in my life. The "love" part stems from the fact that I wasn't sure I would make it that far. Much of my family doesn't and I inherited the problems that cause a lot of them to check out early. It looks, though, like I will beat the odds and for that I am grateful.

On the other hand, my fiftieth birthday represents a passing through the gate into an age class that none of us really wants to venture into. It's one of those milestones in life that causes us to run head-on into our mortality. It's a rude message pointing out that a lot more of my life is behind me than ahead. Turning fifty is a reminder that my days in the field and nights around the campfire are diminishing, that what makes life worth living is no longer a well-stocked supply room, but is instead a dwindling and horded cache.

This birthday is traumatic, depressing and unavoidable, so I did what any panicked midlife-crisis-kind-of-guy would do, I booked a safari in Africa. I leave on my birthday.

Of course, I needed a new dangerous game rifle (any excuse, right?) But, rather than another "store-bought" gun, I decided to build it myself. Ownership of a custom rifle is pretty appealing to most shooters and hunters, but the idea of paying for one is not. Well-executed custom rifles built specifically for hunting are for the most part works of pragmatic art, but some of them cost as much as a good used car.

I am a blue-collar guy with a rich man's appetite and that means I have to pick and choose. The safari got the bucks, but the rifle got my attention. I figured if I couldn't afford a new custom rifle, I could build it myself. The truth is, after paying for the safari, there wasn't much money left for new guns and this looked like a solution to the age-old problem of feeding the need for another hunting rifle.

Build Your Own Custom Rifle

Applying a DuraCoat finish to a rifle barrel and action.

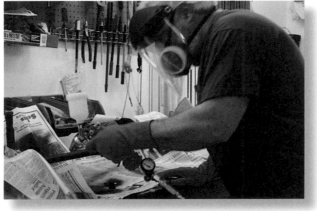

Building a rifle would seem on the surface to be an impossible task for the uninitiated. When first starting out on the journey, the feeling will likely be that it might be easier to design and build a new space shuttle. But by the time you are shooting the rifle at the range, you will have reached an understanding that this really is not all that complicated or difficult. You will also experience a feeling of immense satisfaction. It is very cool to pick up a rifle and say, "I built this." It's also OK to gloat a little when you show it to your hunting buddies. At least it better be, because I have done a bunch of it.

I wanted to approach this like an advanced "hobby" gunsmith. Something that a reasonably well-equipped shop can do, but without the need for a lathe or milling machine. As this project progressed, it became clear that building a rifle like this is easy and fun. It required a few new tools, but tools are like guns, you can never have too many. This first rifle inspired me to build several more and most of the tools find continued use in those projects, so the cost is continually spread out. It has also opened the door to several aspects of gun work that I might not have otherwise have explored; for example, metal coating finishes and fitting a new barrel on an existing action. This approach to building a rifle gives you a "custom rifle"

finished product at off the shelf pricing and it's one of the best projects a hobby gunsmith can tackle.

What follows is the step-by-step journey of building the rifle. Most of this will apply to any bolt action rifle. For example, my next gun is already in the works and it's going to be a .358 Winchester on a Remington short action Model 700 rifle. The Remington will require some different tools than the Mauser. For example, the action wrench will be different as will the bolt lapping tools. But, other than a few specialty tools, the process is the same. The only real difference in building that .358 Winchester and this .458 Winchester is the feeding system. The Remington is a push feed action and the Mauser is a controlled round feed action. Other than the steps directly related to the extractor and feeding, there is very little difference in building the two rifles.

Any building starts with the foundation, and the foundation of a rifle is the action. If there is a more famous, or more revered, rifle action among hunters than the Mauser 98, it has escaped my notice. The controlled round feeding is respected in hunting fields around the world and is considered a must for dangerous game rifles.

Controlled round feeding is a bolt action design where the cartridge rises up from the magazine and is captured

This Cape buffalo was taken in Zimbabwe by the author using the .458 Winchester rifle he built on the Charles Daly Mauser action rifle, as described in this chapter.

by the extractor on the rifle bolt as it is guided into the chamber. Because the bolt has the cartridge firmly in its grasp, the possibility of a jam is reduced. If the shooter short strokes the action, depending on how far the bolt is cycled back, the cartridge stays with the bolt and is either ejected and thrown clear, or is held in position to feed into the chamber. It's as close to a foolproof system as we have for bolt action rifles. While other systems, such as push feed rifles, have their merits, the controlled round feed system is considered the best available for a dangerous game rifle where a jam can get you stomped, bitten, gored, clawed and leaking body fluids.

The Mauser 98 is considered one of the best controlled round feeding designs ever made and it's the inspiration for many of our modern-day rifle actions. It's also the basis for a lot of dangerous game bolt action rifles, including mine.

Another problem with rifle actions these days is it's very hard to find one to build a rifle with. Most rifle makers do not sell actions because of some perceived "liability" issue. That means that you must buy a complete rifle and then remove and throw most of the parts in the trash. This, of course, is wasteful and foolish.

However, Charles Daly is now importing Mauser actions in several lengths and

sizes. I selected a magazine length of 3.375 inch. My rifle is in .458 Winchester Magnum and the SAAMI cartridge overall length is 3.340 inch, so there is plenty of room. I also selected the bolt face diameter of .532 inch, which matches with most belted magnums. These actions are offered "in the white" which means that they are not finished or blued. They are available in chrome-nickel steel or stainless steel.

The first step is to completely disassemble the action. Then degrease everything. Be careful with the small parts and put them in a safe place so they won't get lost. It might be a while before you are ready to use them again, so don't just leave them on the bench. Instead, put them in a container that you can find. Remember that chemically clean steel will rust very fast, so spray some rust inhibitor or oil on all the parts. Make sure that you have an exploded parts diagram so that you can put everything back together. It's easy to forget where the parts fit by the time you are ready to put it all back together.

LAPPING THE BOLT • For the best accuracy in any rifle, the bolt locking lugs must seat evenly and completely in the receiver. Also, by having all lugs bear evenly, the back-thrust stresses placed on the bolt during firing are distributed uniformly; no one lug is subjected to undue pressure. This can aid not only in accuracy and dependability, but will also help prevent premature wear on the action. Finally, if the lugs are lapped with a fine abrasive, the bolt will close with that slick, smooth feeling of quality that is common to custom rifles.

The Brownells Bolt Lapping Fixture helps to maintain

A Brownells Bolt Lapping Tool and lapping compound were used to lap this Mauser bolt.

BROWNELLS BOLT LAPPING TOOL & LAPPING COMPOUND

1. After applying lapping abrasive on the bearing surface of the bolt lug recesses, screw the bolt lapping fixture into the receiver threads.
2. Install the bolt and push it into the locked position.

3. Lift the bolt to about 45° (not far enough to allow the lugs to move out of the lug recesses) and close it to the locking position repeatedly for about 50 times.

4. Check the degree of lug contact by examining the amount of polish on the bolt lug faces.

constant, even pressure on the bolt while the locking lugs are being lapped to match the receiver recesses. This is simply a tool that threads into the front of the action where the barrel fits, and has a spring-loaded plunger that will apply pressure to the bolt face.

Disassemble the bolt, removing the extractor, firing pin and spring. The extractor collar can be left on, although you should probably remove it to allow coating or polishing later. Degrease all the parts.

Next, a light coating of Dykem or layout blue should be applied to the rear surface of the locking lugs on the bolt as well as the corresponding surfaces of the receiver locking lug recesses or seats. A felt-tip marker also works well here, simply coat all of the contact surfaces on the bolt lugs and receiver.

Install the Bolt Lapping Fixture by screwing it into the receiver threads where the barrel would fit. Apply only moderate pressure to the "T" handle of the Bolt Lapping Fixture to fully seat it against the inner collar of the receiver.

Now, install the bolt and move it into the locked position. It should close hard against the spring pressure from the Bolt Lapping Fixture. Lift the bolt handle approximately 45 degrees and then return it to the locked, or "down," position several times. Remove both the bolt and the Bolt Lapping Fixture. The rear of the locking lugs on the bolt and the locking lug recesses or seats in the receiver can then be examined carefully to determine the extent of contact that is being achieved. This is indicated by the area where the Dykem or felt-pen markings are worn off, showing contact. Anything less than 90 percent contact is unsatisfactory.

Remove the Bolt Lapping Fixture and place a small amount of silicon carbide lapping abrasive (600 or 800 grit) on the bearing surface of the bolt lug recesses in the receiver. Do not allow any abrasive between the plunger and the face of the bolt. The lapping compound should be applied before the Bolt Lapping Fixture is installed through the front of the forward receiver ring. Apply just enough abrasive compound to cover the lug seating area; a small amount will go a long way.

Reinstall the Bolt Lapping Fixture. Put the bolt into the action, pushing it as far forward as possible when closing, to keep the compound from being squeegeed off when you close the bolt. Lift the bolt about 45 degrees and push it down again, repeat about fifty times. Do not raise the bolt far enough to allow the lugs to move out of the lug recesses. If this occurs, you can lap metal off the sloped lead-in surfaces of the lug seat and other areas that should not be tampered with. Remove the bolt and check for the amount of contact on the lug face. This will be evident by the polished surface on the lugs after you wipe the lapping compound away. It's unlikely that you can achieve 100 percent contact without removing too much metal, so don't set your goals that high, but try for at least 90 to 95 percent. If you are not there yet, put a little more lapping compound on the lugs and go back to work until you hit your goal.

Make sure to clean out every bit of lapping compound from the bolt and action after you finish. It has a way of working into nooks and crevices, so be diligent. This is not something you want left in the gun, as it can cause damage. A parts cleaning tank is probably best, but you can use spray degreaser as well. Finish with shop air and a close inspection.

After completion, apply layout blue or a felt-tip marker to the lugs and lug recesses; reinstall the bolt and the Bolt Lapping Fixture and seat the bolt a few times. Remove the Bolt Lapping Fixture and bolt, and again carefully check to see if you have less than 95 percent on either lug. If so, reapply the lapping compound, reinstall the Bolt Lapping Fixture and repeat the lapping procedure. Once you are finished and the lapping compound is cleaned out of the action, celebrate a little, because you have just completed your first "gunsmithing" operation on this rifle!

It's important that bolt lapping be done before installing the barrel and setting the headspace. Lapping the lugs removes metal and this can have an effect on headspace. So if you decide to do it to any other rifle, make sure that you check the headspacing before shooting the rifle again. If lapping has taken the headspace out of tolerance, it will need to be corrected, which will require some lathe work. But, by lapping the lugs on the rifle before installing the barrel and setting the correct headspacing, we eliminate that potential problem.

POLISHING THE ACTION RACEWAYS •
The "glass smooth" actions seen on most custom rifles are a result of a lot of polishing to smooth up the contact surfaces of the moving parts. It's a simple fact that the action of metal moving against metal flows most smoothly when both surfaces are polished. This basic tenant is key to custom gun work. Anytime there are two metal surfaces sliding against each other, if you polish the contact surfaces they will slide easier and make the gun feel smoother.

So, the next step is to polish the bolt raceways for a smoother working of the action. The action raceways are the "bed" on the action where the bolt's lugs ride as the action is being worked. If the surfaces are rough from machining, it will make the action work hard and feel sticky and rough. If they are polished, the bolt will work

BROWNELLS RECEIVER WAY POLISHER

1. Wrap abrasive paper around the head of the tool. Apply a small amount of kerosene or stoning oil to the raceway surfaces. 2. Insert the receiver way polisher into the rear of the action so that the tip rides on the bolt raceways.
3. Keep downward pressure on the tool move and it back and forth to polish the surfaces.

Using a hard Arkansas stone to polish the feed ramp.

Polishing the feed ramp on the Mauser action.

with that slick feeling that makes a custom gun so desirable. In this case I am building a dangerous game rifle and I want the action to work as slick and smoothly as possible. This gun may be called upon to stop a charge from a big and angry critter bent on my destruction and I want each cartridge to chamber as fast and as smoothly as possible.

The first step is to disassemble and degrease the action, but in this case we have already done that. Any trace of grease or oil should be removed, so if you have put an anti-rust preventive on the metal, clean it off with a spray degreaser. Now coat the surfaces to be polished with machinist's layout fluid (Dykem) or color them with a felt-tip marker.

Once again, my tool for this job is from Brownells. It is called the Receiver Way Polisher. It's a heavy bar with a flat at the end with a split in the center. To use it, simply cut a piece of 220 or 330-grit abrasive paper to 1.5 x 2.5 inches. One end is tucked in the slot, the paper wrapped around the tool and the other end tucked in the same slot, then the set screw is tightened to hold it in place. The tool is inserted in the rear of the action and rides on the bolt raceways. Apply a small amount of kerosene or stoning oil and then add elbow grease to polish the surfaces. Keep polishing until you have a uniform, smooth surface. Keep some downward pressure on the tool by using your "off" hand to push on the top of the toolhead as you move it back and forth with your other hand gripping the knurled handle. Take care that it is contacting both raceways evenly.

Stop often and check your progress. You will see the machinist's layout fluid is polished off from the high points and it should give you an idea of where you are in the process. The goal is to remove as little metal as possible while still creating a smooth surface. It may be possible to have the entire surface polished mirror smooth, but with a really rough action that might require too much material removal. However, if you have removed all the peaks, and now have them at a uniform height and well polished, a few valleys will not be a problem. The bolt will ride on the polished and uniform high spots and pass over any low spots. That's not to say that just polishing a few high points is enough. You need to have the majority of the raceway at a uniform polished height. So, shoot for at least 80 percent of the area polished.

There is no point in polishing the raceways and then running a rough bolt over them. However, the bolt is usually much smoother to start, so it's less work. The bolt body can be polished with a cloth wheel and buffing compound. Polish the bottom of the lugs, the surfaces that ride on the action raceways with a hand-held Dremel grinder with a small polishing wheel and buffing compound. Be very careful not to remove any metal from the back of the lugs where they contact the action or from any other surface or edge, other than the bottom of the lugs where they ride on the raceway and polish them only sparingly.

POLISHING THE FEED RAMP • The feed ramp is the angled "ramp" just under the barrel that helps to guide the cartridge from the magazine into the chamber. This ramp will pick up the nose of the bullet and slide it up to the back of the chamber. It should be smooth and polished for the best feeding. I used round and half-round stones with plenty of oil. Then I finished with a cloth wheel in a hand grinder and buffing compound for a final polish.

INSTALLING A BARREL • If the action is the foundation of a good rifle, then the barrel is the heart. The quality of both the barrel and the installation is critical to how well your gun will shoot. A custom gunsmith will buy a barrel blank and then turn the contour on the outside, cut the threads and shoulder, crown the muzzle and ream the chamber. This takes a lot of time, a lot of skill and a good lathe. This is specialty machining that takes years of training to learn. It also requires thousands of dollars of tools and equipment. While it makes sense for a custom gun builder who is making several guns a year, it's beyond the reach of most hobby gunsmiths.

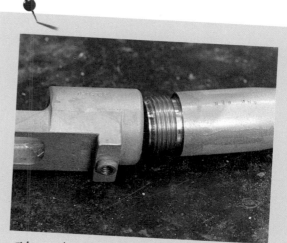

Threads of Mauser action & barrel

But that doesn't mean you can't put a barrel on your rifle. Actually, it's easy to install a new barrel, even without a lathe. Simply purchase a "short-chambered" barrel. These are essentially finished barrels. They have the final contour on the outside, the threads and shoulder are all cut and the chamber is reamed, all but the finishing. The barrel on my .458 Winchester came from Midway USA. It is the Adams & Bennett Series 3, in .458 Winchester Magnum. It has an F44 Contour, a 1 in 14-inch twist and is 24 inches long. The barrel is chrome moly steel and in the "white."

Short chambered means that the chamber is not reamed to its full length and is left about .050 inch short. That allows you to set the chamber for the exact headspacing needed for your action. Doing that will require finish reaming to the correct depth. That sounds a bit intimidating, but if you pay attention to what you are doing, work slowly and think before you act, it's not all that difficult.

In addition to a chamber reamer and a wrench to turn it, you will need a set of "go" and "no-go" gauges to check headspace. These are gauges that look a little bit like a cartridge and are designed so that one is slightly longer than the other. To use these gauges on a controlled feed action like the Mauser, slide the rim in behind the extractor like a cartridge and close the bolt. If the extractor is not on the bolt, simply place the gauge in the chamber and close the bolt. If the bolt can close on the "go" gauge, it indicates that the chamber is long enough to accept a cartridge. The "no-go" gauge is slightly longer and the bolt should not close when that gauge is in the chamber. If the bolt does close, that indicates that the chamber is too long and has what is commonly called "excessive headspace." In this circumstance it means you have cut the chamber too deep. If you make a mistake reaming the chamber and go too deep, the barrel must be turned on a lathe and a small amount removed from the end to shorten the chamber enough to start over. Those of us hobby guys without a lathe should take all precautions possible to avoid that. However, if you do go too far with the reamer, it's not

"Go" and "no-go" gauges

a total disaster. It just means you need to take the barrel to a machine shop and have them turn a little metal off the shoulder and an equal amount off the back of the barrel. If the barrel is stamped with lettering so that it must index to exactly the same place when tightened, you need to remove the length of one thread from the rear threaded portion and the same amount from the shoulder. That is so that the lettering will line up properly when the barrel is reinstalled. However, with a blank barrel with no lettering you can remove a small amount of metal, just enough to put the chamber back into a "short" condition.

There are a couple of ways to go at cutting the chamber. The first is to install the barrel in the action and then ream a little. Clean the chamber and try the "go" gauge. If the bolt doesn't close, remove the gauge, put the reamer back in and ream a little more. Then clean and try the gauge again. This approach is acceptable if you are more patient than Job himself, because it's going to take a while. It also opens the door to a lot of opportunities for mistakes or damage to the reamer, simply because you are putting the reamer in and taking it out so many times.

However, this approach was my plan until I called my buddy and master gunsmith Mark Bansner. He explained how the pros do this job.

Doing it the way Mark explained will require a depth micrometer. It must be a micrometer, as a dial caliper is not accurate enough for this kind of work. Make sure that the bolt does not have the firing pin or spring installed. Place the bolt in the action and close it fully. Measure the distance from the end of the action to front of the bolt face. Write the number down. If it's your first time using a depth micrometer, it will be confusing as you are reading it backwards from a conventional micrometer. Now measure the distance from the shoulder on the barrel to the end of the barrel threads. Subtract that barrel thread shank length from the receiver to bolt face measurement and write down the number. Make absolutely sure that the chamber in the barrel is clean and then place a chamber "go" gauge in the chamber. Measure the distance from the back of the gauge to the back of the barrel. Subtract that number from the first number and the difference is how much you need to lengthen the chamber. The two numbers should match before installing the barrel. Actually, Mark likes to add in .003 inch of "crush factor" when installing a new barrel. So the number should be .003 inch less than equal before installing the barrel. That makes the chamber .003 inch too deep, but when the barrel is tightened to the receiver, the threads "crush" and make up the difference.

The chamber reamer has a ⅜-inch square to drive it and can be turned with a large tap wrench. Always turn only in the direction that the reamer cuts. Never back up any reamer or cutter, as that can chip the cutting surface and ruin the reamer.

I didn't trust myself enough to go all the way, so I stopped a few thousandths of an inch short and installed the barrel. Then I inserted the reamer and turned it a little, cleaned the chamber and tried the "go" gauge. Then repeated the process. Reaching through the action to turn the reamer proved to be a challenge. I finally used a long ⅜-inch drive socket wrench extension. I reversed it so that the female end would fit over the reamer and clamped a pair of vise grips on the male end to turn it. After I completed this rifle, I did a little research and found out that it would have been far better to use the Clymer 12-inch rifle extension or the Clymer Rifle T-Handle. I already ordered both from Brownells' for the next job.

Headspacing is correct when the bolt will close on the "go" gauge, but will not close on the "no-go" gauge. A lot of shooters like a "minimum headspace" chamber. That is one that is on the tight side of the tolerance, which is to say a chamber where the bolt will barely close on a

"go" gauge. This will usually result in better accuracy from factory loads and will be easier to handload, although it can cause some ammo to chamber hard. However, I took a slightly different approach on this rifle. Because this is a dangerous game rifle, reliability is more important than accuracy. I need to know that when I close the bolt, the gun will chamber the ammo and will fire, every single time. My life can depend on this rifle working and I think that's more important than shaving another quarter-minute off the group size. (On the other hand, I will set the headspacing on the .358 Winchester I am building next to a tighter tolerance. I will be shooting primarily handloads and whitetails are not hard to stop when they charge. Just take their Visa Card away.) I wanted the chamber in my .458 Winchester Magnum to be large enough to accept any ammo and under any conditions, but still tight enough to ensure accuracy and reliability. Mark suggested that I adjust it so that the bolt will close about halfway on the "no-go" gauge which puts it closer to the upper end of the tolerance, so that's what I did.

I should have listened to him on cutting the chamber as well. After I had it exactly correct, I made a witness mark on the barrel and action so I could tighten them back to exactly the same location and removed the barrel. I checked the measurements again with the depth micrometer. The chamber that I had fitted perfectly with the "turn and try" method measured exactly what Mark had told me it would. If I had trusted myself enough to cut the chamber fully before installing the barrel, I could have saved a lot of work. On the other hand, there is no room for error and my way was a little safer for a first-timer.

The way I did it can save you money. Depth micrometers are a bit pricy and the "hybrid" method I used could work with a dial caliper. Simply cut the chamber to within .010 inch, then install the barrel and use the "turn and try" method until you have the headspace correct. Using a dial caliper to get close allows you to do a lot of the cutting with the barrel out of the action where it's easier and faster. It also saves you the price of a depth micrometer.

Be very certain that you have all the chips out of the chamber and that it is perfectly clean before you insert the "go" or "no-go" gauge. Anything at all in the chamber can affect the readings.

You will need a barrel vise and an action wrench to install the barrel to the action. My vise is the Wheeler Barrel Vise from Midway USA. The vise is shipped with three sets of oak blocks. Two of them will clamp on just about any size barrel, one has a one-inch hole and the other has a ¾-inch hole. The third set is uncut so you can custom fit them to your barrel if necessary. They should be clamped on the barrel close to the receiver where the barrel

REAMING THE CHAMBER

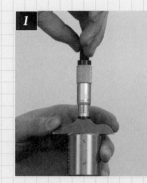

1. Using a depth micrometer to measure from the front of the action to the bolt face.

2. Measuring the length of the barrel shank.

3. Inserting the "go" gauge into the chamber to check for the head-spacing.

4. Measuring from the back of the "go" gauge to the face of the barrel.

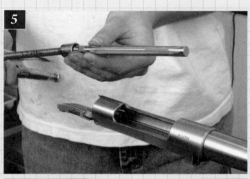

5. Reaming the chamber on a .458 Winchester barrel. Note the barrel in the action and the socket wrench extension with vise grips to turn it.

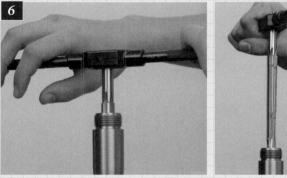

6. Reaming the chamber with a Clymer T-handle.

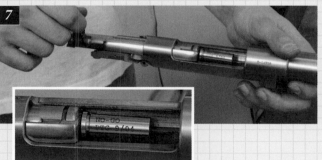

7. Inserting the "go" gauge into the chamber to check for the headspacing. Inset shows detail.

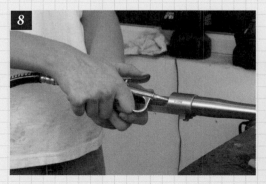

8. Cleaning the chips from the chamber with shop air before inserting the "go" gauge into the chamber to check for the headspacing.

9. A completed chamber for the .458 Winchester, which is a belted case.

Tightening a Mauser barrel in a Wheeler Barrel Vise. The wooden vise blocks are fitted with lead shims to prevent slippage.

Inset: Note cardboard on the action wrench to keep from marring the top of the action.

is large enough to accommodate the chamber. I soon found that no matter how tight I clamped the vise, the barrel would turn in the wooden blocks. I tightened the vise so much that I destroyed two sets of blocks, but still the barrel would slip and turn before I could get enough torque to seat the barrel correctly to the action.

So, I did some more research. Midway USA sells lead shims that help the grip which should work fine. But, on Bansner's advice I ordered some ground rosin from Brownells. This comes in a one-pound can that will probably be enough to last a lifetime. I sprinkled a little on the wooden blocks and the problem was solved. I suspect that this stuff might help with scopes slipping in the rings on hard recoiling rifles and handguns as well, and I plan to find out.

You will also need an action wrench to tighten the action against the barrel. Again, I turned to Midway USA for their Wheeler Engineering Action Wrench. These are specific to the rifle's action, so I ordered the Mauser style which fits most actions that are flat on the bottom. The other style is for round receivers like the Remington 700. One tip that Bansner passed on is to place some cardboard on the top of the action where the wrench contacts it to prevent marring.

How much to tighten the barrel is a little bit of a mystery. The Brownells tech department told me that there isn't any real number as far as the torque needed to install a barrel. They said that generally the barrel is tightened enough to account for about a .002-inch crush factor. A rule of thumb is to hand tighten the barrel and then turn it about 10 degrees more. Reid Coffield from Midway USA said that generally a large ring Mauser is tightened to 65 to 75 foot-pounds of torque. Which would be great information if I had a torque wrench that would fit on the action. But, of course, I do not and am not aware of any on the market. However, they both gave me useful information that helped to make an informed judgment. I have tightened enough threaded things over my lifetime to have an instinctive knowledge of how tight the barrel should be based on their information. I tightened the barrel and action until it was snug. Then I pulled up on the wrench until I was lifting my bench off the floor. I think that the wrench moved about 10 degrees and that I was probably applying about 75 foot-pounds of torque. I know that the barrel is tight in the action and is torqued to an amount that is compatible with this size and type of thread.

Is that too ambiguous? I suppose it is, but sometimes things are best done by the seat of your pants and this may well be one of those times. Simply put, tighten the barrel in the action until it's tight enough, but not too tight.

After installing the barrel, if you have not finished chambering the gun, do so. If you have the chambering complete, check with the "go" and "no-go" gauges to make sure headspacing is correct. Once the headspacing is correct, make a witness mark on the barrel and the action so they can be returned to the same location. You can do this with a center punch or a small chisel to make a mark on both the barrel and the action exactly opposite of each other. Don't use a felt marker as that will be sandblasted away or covered up when doing the finish on the gun. If you remove the barrel and reinstalling it, tighten until the two marks are lined up and the headspacing will be correct again.

Now is a good time to mark the cartridge designation

Wheeler Barrel Vise and action wrench from Midway USA being used to tighten a barrel in a Mauser action.

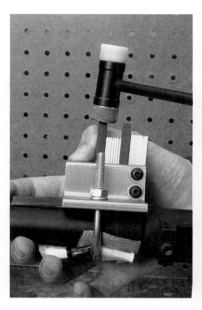

Stamping the numbers on the barrel, using Wheeler Engineering stamps and a B-Square guide sold by Brownells.

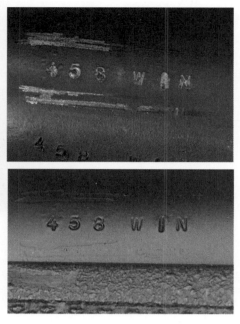

Illustrating mistakes made while stamping the gun.

Below: Shows markings on barrel after touching up the scratches with DuraCoat. Note that the scratches still show.

on the barrel. This is done with a set of stamp punches and a guide. I made the mistake of doing it after finishing and the guide clamp scratched the gun, so I had to touch up the DuraCoat. It's better to do it before sandblasting or coating the gun. That way any slight marks left by the guide will be blasted away and covered. My stamps are from Wheeler Engineering and sold by Midway USA. They are ¹⁄₁₆ inch and come in a complete kit. My guide is made by B-Square and sold by Brownells and is specific to the ¹⁄₁₆-inch-size stamps. Be sure to work out the spacing and layout before stamping the barrel. I used a piece of scrap cold rolled rod to check everything out and it took several tries before I got it exactly right. (Actually the truth be known, I tried to stamp the barrel without the guide. I used a piece of tape as a guide and hand held the stamps. The result was embarrassing. The good thing is I screwed it up in another way, too, and marked it too low on the barrel so the stock covered it up.) That's when I ordered the guide.

Once the spacing is worked out, clamp the guide on the barrel and stamp the barrel. It takes a little practice to know how hard to strike the stamps. For example, the "I" stamp makes a much deeper imprint with the same striking power than say the "8" or "W." Obviously, that's because there is less area to imprint. At least it's obvious now. I wish I had thought of that before marking the barrel. I hit them all with equal force with the hammer, but the "I" is deeper and more pronounced than the larger numbers. This is one more reason to practice before stamping your rifle, because like diamonds, the stamp marks are pretty much forever.

Now take the barrel back off the action for sandblasting.

If you try to sandblast while the two are still assembled, some blasting media will work into the joint and thread, which will cause problems. So the barrel and action are disassembled for degreasing and sandblasting and then reassembled for coating.

METAL FINISH • Metal finishing is not as complicated as you might think. In days past, you would have had to have bluing tanks and all the toxic chemicals that entails. While bluing is still an excellent way to finish a rifle, the hobby gunsmith has some new options. Also, bluing will not work on stainless steel and so these new options are a better, perhaps only, choice with that metal if you want a finish other than the natural steel.

These days you can easily apply a finish that not only looks good, but will protect the metal from rust in a way that bluing cannot. Bluing is a form of rust and offers no protection. The protection must be applied in the form of a barrier to water, such as oil. However, the coating finishes are in effect a barrier themselves that insulate the metal from moisture and the air. This prevents rust and oxidization. Many coatings are easy to apply and the prep work is much easier than the polishing required for a good bluing job.

There is several coating-type metal finishes on the market, but most require oven drying. A rifle's barrel and action is too long to fit in the kitchen oven, so that means buying a very expensive shop oven or making one, which is also expensive and time consuming. At least one coating though, DuraCoat, can air dry. DuraCoat is available in a wide variety of colors, including seven "electric" neon colors and 55 stock colors. They also offer it in clear to cover a stainless steel gun when you want to retain the

To prepare it for sandblasting, this action has clay packed into the holes and ports. Tape is placed over other components to block the sandblasting in these places.

natural look or to cover bluing to prevent rust. In keeping with the all-black "pragmatic hunting gun" theme of my rifle, I chose flat black.

This stuff is tough enough that some military special forces use it on their guns. I talked with my buddy Randy Luth who owns DPMS, one of the premier makers of AR type rifles, and he says he has had outstanding luck with DuraCoat on his guns. It is so easy to apply that I got it pretty much right on the first try and I am not good with sticky substances or anything resembling painting. Believe me, if I can do this anybody can.

Because I could see that this was headed for a lot more "project" guns, I got the relatively inexpensive gravity feed spray gun that is powered by my shop air compressor. This is offered by Lauer Custom Weaponry, the company that makes DuraCoat. They have a complete line of products for coating firearms with several different options besides DuraCoat. They also have a complete line of tools and accessories. But if you are just building one or two rifles, for $49.99 you can buy the DuraCoat EZ Finishing kit that comes with an airbrush sprayer, propellant, hoses and all the materials.

All the metal must be degreased with a solvent that dries without residue. This can be done with aerosol spray cans of degreasing agent. But if you take this approach, be sure to degrease the gun before you assemble the barrel and action and then again just before coating. If you do not, oil in the threads can "weep" out of the joint between the action and the barrel and cause the DuraCoat not to stick. It's better in every circumstance and necessary if the barrel and action are together, to have a tank of solvent. I used TruStrip Solvent available from Lauer Custom Weaponry, and one of their solution tanks. This tank is long enough to put the entire barreled action in with room left over. I scrubbed the gun with a small brush and then let it soak for half an hour before removing it and letting it air dry. After that, I handled the gun only while wearing gloves. I use latex gloves and wash them to remove the powder. However, Midway has cotton inspection gloves that would be a better choice.

Tape is wrapped over the barrel threads to protect them during the sandblasting process.

A clay plug in the muzzle prevents sand from damaging the bore and rifling.

Sandblasting the Mauser action to prepare the surface to accept the DuraCoat finish.

While DuraCoat can be applied over just about any clean surface, it's best to sandblast the metal parts to be coated so that the DuraCoat has plenty of area to adhere to. The rough surface from sandblasting actually increases surface area for the DuraCoat to grip and gives it "tooth." Tape off anything you don't want sandblasted with several layers of masking tape. Plug any holes with modeling clay. I fitted a tapered wooden dowel into the muzzle of the barrel to plug that and also to act as a support to suspend the barrel for spraying.

I used the gravity feed LCW Speedblaster sandblaster sold by LCW. Most shops use a blasting cabinet so that the blasting sand can be recovered. But for a one-time job, I considered $5.00 worth of sand a consumable item and did the blasting outside, catching what sand I could in a cutoff plastic 55-gallon barrel. Blast with 120 Grit Aluminum Oxide Media. The operating range of this sandblaster is 60 psi to 125 psi of air pressure. I ran it with about 100 psi and had good results. Keep the sandblaster moving all the time and watch the metal so that you have an even sheen to the finish. Be sure to wear thick leather gloves, long sleeves, a respirator, face shield and goggles. I know from painful

experience that this stuff will sandblast the skin off your hands in a split second. The manufacturer recommends that you wear a rubber rain coat for protection from the flying sand. It would be easier to clean up as well, as the sand imbeds in your clothing.

After completing sandblasting so that all the metal has an even texture, remove all the tape and clay and reassemble the barrel and action. Don't forget to sandblast all the small parts that you are planning to coat. That includes the bottom metal, scope mounts, action screws and even the bolt. If you decide to coat the bolt, make sure to tape off the lugs as you do not want to sandblast or coat them. Small parts like the extractor retaining ring can be blasted and coated.

I coated the bolt on my gun, but I am not sure I would take this approach again. It's already showing wear marks in places, which is to be expected. I think that just the bare metal or perhaps a jeweled bolt would work better, at least on a Mauser type action where the extractor moves on the bolt and can mark up the coating. Also, I coated the polished raceways on the action, but the bolt tended to stick when running on straight DuraCoat. So, I used the raceway polishing tool to polish the raceways out again. The DuraCoat filled some of the valleys and now I think the action is even slicker than before. But, in the future I will tape the raceways off to prevent coating them.

THE STOCK • It's probably a good idea at this point to fit the stock rather than risk marring the metal finish later. I used a Bell & Carlson Carbelite Classic stock in basic black, which I ordered from Midway USA. Because there are so many variations on the Mauser and because mine was a relatively heavy barrel contour, fitting the stock took the most time of anything in this project. I had to open the barrel channel up considerably. With a lot of synthetic stocks that would not have been possible as it would have resulted in structural weakness. However, I called Junior Dunn at Bell & Carlson and he told me that as long as I kept the aluminum skeleton intact and well supported in the stock, I would be fine. To open the barrel channel I used a Barrel Bedding Tool from Brownells. This is a series of round cutters mounted on a contoured rod with a handle at each end. The cutters maintain the round contours of the barrel channel while cutting with each stroke. They will not dig in or gouge, but take a nice even cut each time. These are available in several different diameters to match the barrel you are bedding. It's a "must-have" for stock work and I have several in my shop.

Brownells' Barrel Bedding Tool is used to scrape away material and open the barrel channel in a rifle stock.

Painting Brownells' release agent on a rifle action in preparation for glass bedding the action into a rifle stock.

It took a lot of cutting and trying to finally make the barrel and action fit in the stock. I could have ordered the Varmint/Tactical-style stock from Bell & Carlson, which has a larger barrel channel, but I like the classic styling of the Carbelite Classic on a big game hunting rifle.

The Charles Daly has the safety on the trigger rather than on the bolt like a lot of Mausers. The safety lever sticks off to the side and it took a lot more cutting and fitting of the stock to clear the safety. I had to remove some metal from the internal aluminum block for the safety to clear. I used a Dremel hand grinder with a cutting tool to do that, working slowly and carefully to make sure I got an exact fit with just a minimum amount of clearance. I didn't want to remove any more metal than necessary on a hard recoiling rifle like this one. I also had to modify and cut down the top of the stock to allow clearance for the safety.

Once I had everything fitted together, I bedded the action and barrel channel using Brownells Acraglas. I bedded the action and first three inches of the barrel fully, except around the recoil lug where only the rear, load-bearing surface has contact. The barrel is free floated other than the first three inches in front of the action. The exact procedure for bedding a rifle stock is covered in another chapter of this book. The only thing I would do different next time is to add some Brownells Atomized metal to the bedding compound for more strength in such a hard recoiling rifle. The tungsten will add weight and strength or the stainless steel for a little less weight.

APPLYING DURACOAT FINISH

1. Wooden dowel used to plug the muzzle on the barrel while applying DuraCoat finish. This dowel also supported the barrel.

2. DuraCoat is applied to the small parts individually.

3. DuraCoat is applied to the action screws.

4. DuraCoat is applied to the bottom metal and magazine box.

APPLYING THE METAL FINISH • LCW says

that for the best possible finish, the gun can be Parkerized before applying the DuraCoat. Parkerizing has been used for years on military guns and it provides a durable, no-shine finish to protect the metal which by itself is a very good option for serious hunting gun. The Parkerizing will absorb oil and protect the metal. I have a Remington 7600 pump action rifle in .35 Whelen that I had Parkerized back in the 1980s. It has been on a lot of whitetail hunts and still looks as good as it ever did.

Parkerizing is easy to apply and does not require a lot of polishing time like bluing. In fact, it works best over a blasted surface. What I have is Zinc Phosphate Parkerizing Solution from DuraCoat Products. To use it, simply mix according to instructions, which is four parts water to one part solution. This is put in a tank which is then heated to 170-185 degrees Fahrenheit. A heated bluing tank works perfectly and runs off propane. The heated solution is conditioned by immersing a pad of coarse steel wool in the solution for 30 minutes. Then simply put the prepared gun in the tank for five to fifteen minutes. This will produce a traditional gray Parkerized surface on the metal. Follow by immersion in LCW post Treatment Solution, which is water displacing oil, or by applying DuraCoat. A gallon of solution will last for many Parkerizing sessions and is an economical gun finish option as well as a base for DuraCoat.

LCW suggests that DuraCoat can be applied over the Parkerized surface for the very best adhesion. However, I elected to use another option they offer and skip Parkerizing and apply the DuraCoat directly over the sandblasted metal.

After again degreasing the barrel and action, I used the wooden dowel in the muzzle and another inserted in the action to suspend the gun above my newspaper-covered bench. After adjusting the spray gun for the proper flow (which took a bit of fooling with air pressure) I "spray painted" the barrel and outside of the action with microscopic coating of DuraCoat.

Then I did each of the other parts I wanted covered one at a time. When everything was coated and dried, I put the gun together.

Applying DuraCoat is covered more completely in another chapter in this book.

TRIGGER & FEEDING • The trigger on the

Charles Daly Mauser is adjustable, so I set it at 3.5 pounds, which is fine for a dangerous game rifle. I had some feeding problems, which are not fine on a dangerous game rifle. The first two cartridges out of the magazine would feed without problems, but the third cartridge

Adjusting the trigger on a .458 Winchester Mauser. Wrenches are from Brownells.

would often twist with the bullet pointing off to the left. This would jam the nose of the bullet against the left edge of the barrel at the chamber. This is, of course, completely unacceptable in any rifle, but particularly so in a dangerous game gun. There were actually two problems at work here. The fact that it was always the last cartridge in the magazine indicated that there was probably a problem with the magazine follower. The other two cartridges are feeding off the top of another cartridge, but the third and last cartridge is feeding off the top of the follower. I tried several different followers before discovering that a plastic follower out of a new Model 70 Winchester

Shows the replacement follower from a Winchester Model 70 rifle installed in custom Mauser.

Mauser action controlled round feed.

Classic Stainless rifle would feed better. That helped the problem by about 50 percent, which told me I was on the right track. I then ordered a steel follower designed for a Model 70 belted magnum. The Winchester follower has a lip in the bottom rear that makes it much thicker. This prevented loading three cartridges in the magazine. I ground that off and thinned the front of the follower as well, which allowed the follower to go low enough to load three cartridges in the magazine and barely have enough room to compress them so the bolt can be closed without feeding the top cartridge.

The new follower helped even more, but the gun still would on occasion jam the last shot. This was particularly true with blunt nose ammo. The big, blunt Winchester 510-grain factory load has a lot of exposed lead in the tip and was the worst offender. But the Federal 500-grain Trophy Bonded Sledgehammer Solid with its flat nose didn't feed very well either. Pointed bullets like the Federal Trophy Bonded Bearclaw ammo worked fine.

I made up some dummy cartridges with no powder and inert primers. By watching the cartridge as it fed out

of the magazine, I realized that it was not coming all the way up behind the extractor. The worst offender was the last cartridge in the magazine, as that's when the magazine spring has the least amount of power.

I took the extractor off the bolt. To do this, clamp the extractor retaining ring in a soft-jawed vise. This holds the bolt and compresses the ring. Then use a screwdriver to pry the front of the extractor up while tapping the back of the extractor with a plastic hammer. This will force the extractor forward where it will come free from the retaining ring.

My extractor had a burr along the bottom which I carefully stoned off. Then I polished the entire extractor using a Dremel tool with a felt polishing wheel and polishing compound. Before reinstalling the extractor, I flexed it backwards by holding both ends and pushing in the middle. This slightly bent the extractor and caused it to have a little less spring tension against the cartridge that was trying to feed up behind it.

I polished the front bevel or leading edge on the extractor so that it will slip over a chambered cartridge. This allows single loading or topping off a full magazine with a fourth cartridge in the barrel. Many Mausers will not allow loading this way, as the extractor will not slip past the cartridge rim and they must be fed from the magazine. However, this limits the capacity to what the magazine will hold. By polishing the front of the extractor and lightening the spring tension, my gun would easily single feed by placing a cartridge in the chamber and closing the bolt.

The extractor is reinstalled on the bolt by carefully lining it up with the retaining ring and tapping the front with a plastic hammer. It may be necessary to slightly lift up on the front of the extractor to allow it to slide over the front of the bolt.

The gun fed better, but the cartridges were still not feeding all the way into the bolt behind the extractor. In watching this action, I could see that the shape of the extractor was part of the problem, as the bottom protruded too far out and the cartridge had a hard time moving up past that point. So, I removed the extractor again and very carefully removed a little metal with a hand grinder. I only took off a few thousandths of an inch, then shaped and polished the leading edge again. I polished the entire lip of the extractor and I used the

Shows new and modified Winchester follower with Brownells' 10 percent stronger spring beside original follower and spring.

Dremel tool to polish the bolt face. After that, the gun fed almost perfectly. Just to be sure, I ordered an extra power magazine spring from Brownells. This spring has 10 percent more power than the standard Mauser spring and provides more push to the cartridge as it slides up behind the extractor. I added the spring and it seems to do a better job. Now, the rifle is feeding perfectly.

SIGHTING OPTIONS • The Charles Daly Mauser action is already drilled and tapped for scope mounting. I mounted a Kahles 1.1–4X24, 30mm scope in Warne mounts using the procedures detailed elsewhere in the book. I selected this scope for the low end magnification, which is almost zero. For an experienced shooter, a scope is faster and more accurate than any iron sights, but on a dangerous game rifle too much magnification can be a problem. When you have a buffalo charging and he is close, a scope with too much magnification might result in not being able to identify what part of the buffalo you are shooting at. On the Kahles, 1.1X is virtually zero

magnification. The upper end of 4X allows me to crank up the scope for range work or for the occasional longer shot. This scope is a 30mm tube, so it's bright in poor light and has lots of adjustment latitude.

Warne rings and bases are made like tanks; they are virtually indestructible and I think they might survive a direct missile strike. They are a little heavy, but weight is your friend with a big gun like this. Warne rings are quick release so I also have another Kahles 1.1-4 X24 scope, this one with a lighted reticle, mounted in rings and zeroed for the gun. This will serve as a backup in case of problems. Kahles scopes are tough, but "stuff happens" so a backup is a good idea. I have seen scopes smashed when the hunter fell down a mountain, or dropped the gun on some big rocks, and I have seen several that were run over by trucks. For a big expensive trip like an African safari, I try to leave as little as possible to chance. The lighted reticle may also be useful for low light hunting situations such as leopard hunting or perhaps the gloomy weather of Alaskan bear hunting.

A SIMPLER APPROACH

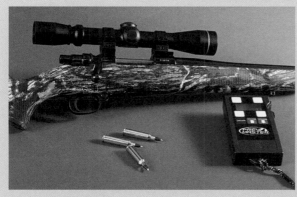

Custom .22-250 Remington built on a Charles Daly Mini-Mauser action. Built by Bryce and Nathan Towsley. Owned by Nathan Towsley. Leupold Compact 2-7 scope.

The most daunting part of building a rifle is fitting the barrel and cutting the chamber. If you are not comfortable with this big of a project to start, consider a simpler approach to a "custom" gun. Charles Daly also sells barreled actions. These are offered in stainless steel, polished blue or matte blue. They have the barrel already installed on them and the headspacing is set. All they really need is a stock and a scope. Or, if you like, you can refinish the metal with DuraCoat for better rust protection and a different color option.

Bell & Carlson offers synthetic stocks and Boyds has laminated wood stocks to fit all the models, including the Mini-Mauser.

Nathan and I both ordered barreled "Mini-Mauser" actions. His is in .22-250 and mine is in 7.62X39. We fitted a Bell & Carlson Carbelite synthetic stock to Nathan's gun and installed a Leupold Vari-X II 3-9 Ultralight scope. Mine is in a Boyds Ross Thumbhole laminated wood stock and is fitted with a Leupold 2.5-8 Vari-X III scope. They look and feel like two very different rifles, but the only practical difference is the stock.

These were simpler projects, as all we had to do was fit the stocks and glass bed them and then mount the scopes.

The rifles are small, lightweight, compact and accurate. We built them with coyote calling in mind, but my 7.62X39 is also a good rifle to loan to a recoil-shy kid during our annual youth deer hunt.

If your choice runs more to a full size rifle, Charles Daly offers all their actions barreled and ready to stock in most popular calibers from .22 Hornet to .458 Winchester.

The gun is a hefty 9 ¾ recoil-reducing pounds with the scope mounted. Add four cartridges and a sling and it's over ten pounds. Heavy enough to soak up some recoil, but still light enough to carry all day.

After a few shots to zero the scope, I began to shoot some groups to test ammo. My first three-shot group was my best and it measured .8 inch with Winchester 510-grain soft nose ammo. That was a lucky group and the rest of the groups with that ammo measured an average of 1.25 inches. Federal 500-grain Trophy Bonded and 400-grain Trophy Bonded shot just over one inch. The Federal Trophy Bonded Sledgehammer 500-grain solids went into 1.5 inches. Obviously, I was delighted with this accuracy. Mark Bansner had told me that most .458 Winchester rifles are excellent shooters and he was as usual—right.

But, this is not a gun made for shooting off the bench. So after testing the ammo and zeroing the scope, I switched to shooting from hunting positions. I am shooting it quite a bit to prepare for this safari. I practice primarily shooting off hand and fast, because that safari is for two of the most dangerous game animals on the planet: elephant and buffalo. I know it's going to be exciting and I expect that taking them with a gun I built myself will raise the needle on the satisfaction and thrill meter to new levels.

My son and I have been practicing a drill we call "charging firewood." We have some chunks of firewood that were cut from a tree that fell on our range during a storm. We stand them up randomly at about 40 yards. We start with the gun loaded with three cartridges in the magazine, the bolt closed on an empty chamber. Using a timer, at the buzzer we see how fast we can hit all three. I can get the first one in about two seconds and all three in five seconds. This is where all that polishing earns its keep, as the action is slick and smooth. It's great practice to learn fast and accurate shooting with this big gun. Recoil recovery is important and this teaches us how to roll with the recoil as we work the action and bring the gun back on target. On top of that, it's great fun! The big slugs really make the chips fly when they hit the firewood!

I built this rifle in a big cartridge because of the upcoming safari; but if you build one, it doesn't have to be such a cannon. The same techniques I used here will work with any rifle chambering. While you may not have an interest in hunting dangerous game on The Dark Continent, just imagine how it will feel to drop the hammer on a big whitetail with a custom rifle that you built in your home shop. The money you saved on the rifle will more than cover the taxidermy bill!

Custom .458 Winchester on a Charles Daly Mauser action. Built by Bryce and Nathan Towsley. Kahles 1.1-4 scope, Warne mounts.

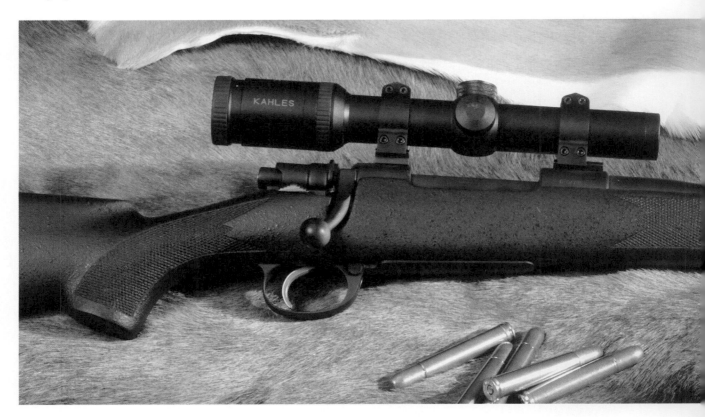

TOOLS FOR THE PROJECT

This is a list of the tools that I acquired specifically for this project. I already had things like gunsmithing screwdrivers, an air compressor, workbench, vise, etc.

    Most of these tools can be used for years; so, the actual costs are spread out over numerous projects.

Bolt Lapping Tool*	Brownells	$49.97
Receiver Way Polisher*	Brownells	$39.97
PTG Solid Pilot Chamber Finish Reamer	Midway USA	$106.99
Forster Headspace "Go" Gauge Belted Magnums (.535" Base)	Midway USA	$18.19
Forster Headspace "No-Go" Gauge Belted Magnums (.535" Base)	Midway USA	$18.19
Starrett Depth Micrometer*	Brownells	$207.87
Wheeler Engineering Action Wrench #1 Mauser Flat-Bottomed Receiver	Midway USA	$39.99
Wheeler Engineering Barrel Vise with three Wood Bushings	Midway USA	$46.49
B-Square Steel Stamp Guide*	Brownells	$35.95
Wheeler Engineering Steel Letter and Number Barrel Stamp Set ¹⁄₁₆"*	Midway USA	$42.99
LCW Speed Blaster, gravity feed media/sandblaster	LCW	$87.00

* Indicates optional tool.

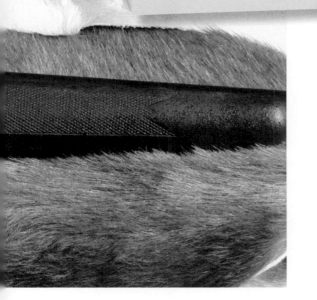

NECESSARY PARTS

This is a list of the parts that I acquired specifically for this project.

Mauser Action		
Adams & Bennett Barrel	Charles Daly	$359.00
DuraCoat EZ Finishing Kit	Midway USA	$104.99
Bell & Carlson Carbelite Classic Stock	LCW	$49.99
RIFLE TOTAL	Midway USA	$152.99
		$666.97
Warne Rings & Bases		
Kahles 1.1-4 scope	Brownells	$73.99
	Midway USA	$849.00

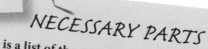

Index

A

Accuracy enhancement
  bore cleaning, 81-91
  causes of accuracy problems, 97
  fixing injection molded stock
    problems, 122-123
  glass bedding a rifle stock,
    101-111
  pillar bedding a rifle stock,
    112-121
  re-crowning a rifle muzzle,
    98-100
Acrabed, 116
Acraglas Gel, 13, 56-57, 106, 150
Action raceways, 141-142
Adjustable Pillar Bedding Sleeves,
  115-116, 120
Air compressors, 20
Allen head screws, stripped, 44-46
Allen wrenches, 44
Aluminum oxide stones, 20
Aluminum rod alignment, 70
Aprons, 30-31
Arkansas stone, 19-20, 132, 142
Auto body filler, 123

B

B-Square, 16, 131
B-Square screwdriver set, 44
Bansner, Mark, 35, 115, 144, 146
Barnes, 83, 87, 97
Barrel Bedding Tool, 104, 149
Barrel breech bedding, 119-120
Barrel installation, 143-147
Barreled actions, 153
Barrell cutting, 76-79
Bedding
  glass, 101-111
  pillar, 112-121
Bedding tape, 105, 117
Bell & Carlson, 149, 153
Belt and disk sander, 21
Bench, 12-13
Bench blocks, 29
Bench pads, 27
Bench vises, 14
Birchwood Casey, 50

Blasting cabinets, 149
Blind magazine rifles
  pillar bedding, 120-121
Bluing, 147
Bolt lapping, 139-141
Bolt Lapping Tool, 139
Bolt raceways, 141-142
Bore cleaning, 81-91
Bore guides, 86
Bore polishing, 52-53
Bore Tech Patch Guide, 82, 86
Boyd's, 153
Brass Muzzle Crowning Lap,
  98-99
Bronze brushes, 86-87
Brooks, Coni, 97
Brownells
  Adjustable Pillar Bedding
    Sleeves, 115-116
  Barrel Bedding Tool, 104, 149
  Bolt Lapping Tool, 139-140
  Brass Muzzle Crowning Lap,
    98-99
  chamber flex hone, 52-53
  Damascening Tools, 130
  files, 17
  Muzzle Facing/Chamfering Tool,
    78-79, 99
  Muzzle Radius Cutter, 78-79
  pillar bedding instructions,
    115-121
  polishing tools, 26
  Pull & Drop Gauge, 37
  Receiver Way Polisher, 141-142
  rosin, 45, 71
  Scope Shim Kit, 74
  screwdrivers, 15-17
  stockmaker handscrews, 111
  stone files, 19
Buffing and polishing wheel, 129
Building a rifle, 138-155

C

Cabinets, 14
Carpenter, Russ, 3
Cartridge feeding, 151-153
CDI Torque Products, 69, 70

Ceramic stones, 19, 20
Chamber flex hone, 52-53
Chamber polishing, 52-53
Chamber reamers, 144-145
Chapman, 15, 16
Charles Daly Mauser action rifle,
  137-155
Chisels, 27, 28
Cleaning patches, 86-87
Cleaning rifles, 81-91
Cleaning rods, 84-85
Clymer Rifle T-Handle, 144-145
Coating finishes, 147
Coffield, Reid, 146
Cold weather, rifle preparation,
  92-95
Comb height, 40-42
Cordless drill, 22
CR-10 Bore Cleaning Solvent, 87
Cratex, 26, 130
Crown damage, 100
Crush factor, 144, 146
Custom rifles, 137-155
Cutting chambers, 143-144

D

Damascening tools, 130
Decker, 26-27
Degreaser, 95, 132
Degreasing parts, 128, 148
Dental picks, 27
Depth micrometers, 144-145
Dewey action cleaning tool, 91
DPMS, 148
Draw filing, 130
Dremel tools, 25-26
Drill bits, 22-23
Drill presses, 21-22
Drills, 22
Drive grip, 67
Dunn, Junior, 149
DuraCoat, 94, 132-135, 147-151
Dwyer, Sean, 48
Dykem Layout fluid, 71, 75

E

Electronic cleaners, 89

Engagement surfaces, smoothing, 64-65
Engine turning and damascening, 129
Excessive headspace, 143
Extractor polishing, 152
Extreme weather hunting, rifle preparation, 92-95
Eye and ear protection, 23-24

F
Face shields, 23-24
Factory triggers, 48-51
Federal Trophy Bonded cartridges, 152, 154
Feed ramp polishing, 142
Feeding, 151-153
File cards, 19
Files, 17-19
Follower modification, 152
Forester Products, 14
Foul Out III, 89
.458 Winchester Magnum, 137-155

G
Glass bedding, 101-111
Gloves, 31
"Go" and "no go" gauges, 143-145
Grinders, 25-26
Gun safety, 32-33
Gun vises, 26
Gunsmith shop. *See Work shop*

H
Hacksaws, 28
Hammers, 25
Hand grinders, 25-26
Handheld cordless drill, 22
Headspace, 143-145
Hoppe's Elite System, 88

I
Indexing vise, 131
India stone, 19, 20, 28
Injection molded stock problems, 122-123

J
J-B Non-Embedding Bore Cleaning Compound, 89-90
Jags, 86-87
Jewelling, 128-131

K
Kahles scope, 153-154
Kascenska, John R., 113, 118
Kroil, 90

L
Laminated wood rifle stocks bedding for, 103, 110
Lapping the bolt, 139-141
Latex gloves, 31
Lauer Custom Weaponry, 148
LCW, 149, 151
Level-Level-Level, 74
Lighting, 12
Loctite, 30, 68, 71
Luth, Randy, 148
Lyman, 15, 16, 58

M
Maintenance
  bore cleaning, 81-91
  preparing rifles for extreme weather hunting, 92-95
Marble, 58-59
Marlin tang sight, 58-59
Mauser action rifle, 137-155
Measuring tools, 28
Metal finishing, 147-149, 151
Michael's of Oregon, 54, 57
Micrometer adjustable torque screwdriver, 70
Micrometers, 144-145
Midway USA, 15-16, 144, 146-147
Miles & Gilbert, 38-39
Mini-Mauser actions, 153
Moisture sealing, 94
Muzzle facing/chamfering tool, 78-79, 99
Muzzle radius cutter, 78-79
Muzzles
  re-crowning, 98-100

N
Norton, 19-20, 28

O
Outers Foul Out III, 89

P
Pachmayr, 16
Parkerizing, 151
Parts cabinets, 13-14
Parts cleaning tank, 26

Paste wax, 95
Patch Hog, 84
Pegboard storage, 14
Pillar bedding, 112-121
Pipe wrap, 105
Polishing action raceways, 141-142
Polishing tools, 26
Polyurethane, 94
Pull & drop gauge, 37
Punches, 24-25

R
Re-crowning a rifle muzzle, 98-100
Reaming chambers, 144-145
Receiver way polisher, 141-142
Recoil lug bedding, 119-120
Recoil pad installation, 36-39
Refinishing shotgun stocks, 42-43
Remington 7600 Carbine pump, 66
Remington M-700 BDL SS DM, 112, 117, 119-121
Remington Model 760 .30-06 Springfield, 125
Reticle leveler, 72-73
Rifle makeover project, 126-135
Rifle muzzles, re-crowning, 98-100
Rifle stocks
  fixing injection molded stock problems, 122-123
  glass bedding, 101-111
  pillar bedding, 112-121
Ring lapping kits, 72
Rod guides, 85-86
Rosin, 45, 71
Ruger triggers
  repairing, 60-65

S
Safety. *See Gun safety*
Safety goggles, 23-24
Sandblasting, 147-149
Sanders, 21
Sanding jigs, 38-39
Sandpaper, 30
Savage Snail Trap Range System, 32-33
Scope base alignment, 68-69
Scope mounting, 66-75, 153
Scope shims, 74-75
Screw kits, 30

Screw pitch gauge, 28-29
Screwdrivers, 15-17
Shelving, 14
Shop materials, 30-31
Shop rags, 30
Shop tools. *See specific tool by name*
Shotgun stocks. *See Stocks*
Sighting, 153-154
Silicon carbide stones, 20
Sinclair International, 69, 70
Slide hammer, 107
Sling swivel stud installation, 54-57, 134-135
Slip stone, 28
Socket sets, 27
Solvents, 87-88, 148
Speedblaster sandblaster, 148-149
Spyderco, 19, 20
Stamp punches, 147
Stevenson, Eddie, 98
Stock modification, 40-43
Stockmaker handscrews, 111
Stocks
    cutting, 37
    fitting, 149-150
    fixing injection molded stock problems, 122-123
    glass bedding, 101-111
    modifying, 40-43
    painting, 128
    pillar bedding, 112-121
    stripping finish, 128
Stones, 19-20
Stop Collar System, 78-79
Storage areas, 13-14
Stripped allen head screws, 44-46
Stripping finish, 128
Stud installation, 54-57
Surform tools, 18
Swiv-O-Ling vise, 14
Synthetic stocks
    bedding for, 110
    pillar bedding, 121

T
Table saws, 23
Tang-mounted peep sight, 58-59
Tap & die sets, 29
Timney Triggers, 48-51
Tipton, 26, 88
Tipton Jag Kit, 87
Toolboxes, 14
Tools. *See specific tool by name*

Torque wrenches, 69, 70-71
Towsley, Bryce, 23, 32, 37, 71, 75, 93, 133, 138-139
Towsley, Nathan, 22, 27, 40-41, 49
Trash cans, 31
Trigger guard-floor plate bedding, 120
Triggers
    adjusting, 151-153
    design, 47-48
    factory, 48-51
    installing, 48-51
    repairing a Ruger trigger, 60-65
Triple Shock bullets, 83
Trophy Bonded cartridges, 152, 154
TruStrip Solvent, 148

V
Vinyl gloves, 31
Vises, 14, 144, 146
VLC X-Bullets, 83

W
Warne mounts, 153-154
Water stones, 20, 28
WD 40, 90
Weather issues
    preparing rifles for extreme weather hunting, 92-95
Wheeler Barrel Vise, 144, 146
Wheeler Engineering, 74, 146-147
Winchester Ranger Model 94 rifle, 126-135
Wood carving chisels, 27, 28
Wood rifle stocks
    bedding for, 103, 110
Work shop
    air compressor, 20
    aprons, 30-31
    belt and disk sander, 21
    bench, 12-13
    bench blocks, 29
    bench pads, 27
    dental picks, 27
    Dremel tool, 25-26
    drill bits, 22-23
    drill press, 21-22
    eye and ear protection, 23-24
    files, 17-19
    gloves, 31
    grinders, 25-26
    gun vise, 26

hacksaw, 28
hammers, 25
hand grinder, 25-26
handheld cordless drill, 22
latex gloves, 31
lighting, 12
loctite, 30
measuring tools, 28
paper towels, 30
parts cleaning tank, 26
punches, 24-25
rags, 30
sandpaper, 30
screw kits, 30
screw pitch gauge, 28-29
screwdrivers, 15-17
shop materials, 30-31
socket sets, 27
space requirements, 11
stones, 19-20
storage, 13-14
table saw, 23
tap & die sets, 29
trash cans, 31
vinyl gloves, 31
vise, 14
wood carving chisels, 27, 28
wrenches, 27
Wrenches, 27

Z
Zinc Phosphate Parkerizing Solution, 151